TRAINING AND DEVELOPMENT

CONCEPTS AND PRACTICES

TRAINING AND DEVELOPMENT

CONCEPTS AND PRACTICES

Emerging Developments, Challenges and Strategies in HRD

S.K. BHATIA
Director
Human Resource Management Foundation, New Delhi
and
Senior Faculty,
Business Management Institutes

Formerly :
- Director (Personnel), Oil India Ltd.
- Director (Pers. and PR), Mekaster Group Co's.
- Add. General Manager (Pers. and Admn.) Bharat Heavy Electricals India Ltd.

Foreword by

DR. ABAD AHMAD
Former Pro-Vice Chancellor and Professor of Management
University of Delhi, Delhi

DEEP & DEEP PUBLICATIONS PVT. LTD.
F-159, Rajouri Garden, New Delhi - 110 027

TRAINING AND DEVELOPMENT
Concept and Practices

First Published : 2007
Reprinted : 2009
Reprinted : 2013
Reprinted : 2017

ISBN 978-81-7629-660-0
(PAPERBACK EDITION)

Typeset by S.S. COMPOSERS
3190, Mohindra Park, Shakur Basti, Delhi - 110 034

Printed in India at MAYUR ENTERPRISES
WZ Plot No. 3, Gujjar Market, Tihar Village, New Delhi - 110 018.

Published by DEEP & DEEP PUBLICATIONS PVT. LTD.
F-159, Rajouri Garden, New Delhi - 110 027
Phones : 25435369, 25440916
E-mails : ddpubs@gmail.com • ddpbooks@yahoo.co.in
Showroom :
2/13, Ansari Road, Daryaganj, New Delhi - 110 002 • Telefax : 23245122

Contents

UNIT III

ORGANISATION DEVELOPMENT INTERVENTIONS

UNIT IV

EXECUTIVE DEVELOPMENT—PERSPECTIVES

UNIT V

EMERGING DEVELOPMENTS IN TRAINING

UNIT VIII

TRAINING INSTRUMENTS/TESTS

UNIT IX

MISCELLANEOUS

Foreword

It gives me great pleasure to write a foreword to this text titled "Training and Development", which will find its way into trainers' kits and for students of Human Resource Development.

Training programmes are directed toward maintaining and improving current job performance, while development programmes seek to develop competencies for future roles. Training is required for all employees including workers, supervisors and managers, as they need to be enhance their abilities to perform their duties effectively, to grow as persons, and acquire maturity of thought and action. Training and Development constitute an ongoing process in any organization.

Carefully planned and conducted training and development efforts help employees to achieve goals through higher levels of skills and competencies. Further, training develops individuals and teams to meet the changing needs of the organization. Training is an investment in human resources with a promise of better returns in future. It results in greater stability, flexibility and capacity for growth in an organization. Future needs of employees and organisations are met through development programmes.

In the new millennium, the knowledge revolution has brought tremendous changes in information technology. The training inputs cannot remain constant because of the dynamic pace of change. Obsolescence will occur fast as there will be constant gap between the job requirements and the individual's capabilities. As such there is need of greater emphasis on acquainting the trainers and HRD professionals with the emerging approaches and concepts. A large number of organizations today are incurring more expenditure on training and development than they did earlier. With the growing concern and awareness for results of training and development efforts, evaluation of training has become important to determine the effectiveness of such programmes.

In order to make training and development efforts and practices effective, action may have to taken on the following aspects:

(i) Evolving a carefully thought training policy based on a well conceived and articulated overall HRD philosophy.

(ii) Systematic training and development plan and process involving several steps: (a) determining organization objectives and strategies, (b) assessment of training needs, (c) establishing training goals, (d) devising training programmes, (e) implementation of the programmes, and (f) evaluation of the training results.

(iii) Management to commit itself to allocate major resources and adequate time to training.

(iv) Ensure that training contributes to competitiveness of the organization.

(v) Training and retraining to be done at all levels on a continuous and ongoing basis.

(vi) Ensure that there is proper linkage among organizational, operational and individual training needs.

(vii) Create a system to evaluate the effectiveness of training.

(viii) Create a supportive and positive HRD climate in the organisation through enlightened and forward looking management practices.

(ix) To extend the frontiers of knowledge, understanding of the management concepts and philosophy that enable organizations to become effective and sustain their competitiveness.

It is true that all development is basically self-development, and it must be generated from within by the person himself/herself. However, carefully thought and skillfully conducted training programmes and development efforts can make a significant difference by enabling the members of organization at all levels to grow and achieve higher levels of competence, and enhance organizational capability and effectiveness.

The coverage of the book is very comprehensive, and I am sure it will serve as a concise guide to a wide range of areas that are relevant in the field of training. The book has been written keeping in view the needs of practitioners, and will be helpful in improving training effectiveness.

I have no doubt that this book will be very helpful to students, teachers, and practicing managers. My congratulations to Mr. S.K. Bhatia on his thoughtful endeavour and contribution to the field of Training and Development.

Delhi

DR. ABAD AHMAD
Former Pro-Vice Chancellor and
Professor of Management,
University of Delhi, Delhi

Preface

India is fast changing and shining—the feel good factor is awakening Indians to take its rightful place in the new world order. India, the invincible, is aiming towards superpower on all fields. If rate of development is to further accelerate, the quality of management has to keep pace with this progress. This calls for emphasis on training and development of the human resources in all sectors—i.e., corporate business, services, industry, health services, education, agriculture, entertainment, NGO and many more.

Training and development activity both in terms of quantity and quality will need to be augmented. Training and management education is a growing industry today. Training process involves systematic professional approach, i.e. training needs diagnosis, setting objectives and plans for training, implementation and evaluation of its effectiveness.

In order to fulfil the needs of curriculum of increasing management students, trainees, and trainers, this text has been attempted for Indian conditions. This book titled "Training and Development: Concepts and Practices" is divided into nine units containing sixty chapters and annexures. Some unique features of this book are that it focuses on following critical aspects:

- Emerging perspectives and developments in training;
- Simulation and experimental methods which is the present need;
- Tests and training instruments;
- Training designs in specific fields;
- Process OD interventions;
- Online learning;
- Model for systematic approach to training; and
- HRD mechanisms.

This book will provide total and uptodate knowledge on the subject of training and development. Suggestions for improvement of the book would be welcomed by the author.

S.K. BHATIA

UNIT I

TRAINING AND DEVELOPMENT—PERSPECTIVE

CHAPTER

1

Training and Development: Concept

Importance of developing men can well be highlighted from the following Chinese saying: "If you wish to plan for a year sow seeds, if you wish to plan for ten years plant trees, if you wish to plan for a life-time develop men." Employee development is the process whereby people learn the skills, knowledge, attitudes and behaviours needed in order to perform their job effectively.

It may be relevant to mention that the growth rate of an organisation is likely to be limited more by its personnel than by any other factor. The ability to maintain and help good people is tied partially to proper payment, but is significantly influenced by the ability of a company to provide opportunities to each individual to develop fully, to utilise his abilities to the full, to find continuing job satisfaction and individual will to learn. As such no organisation can ignore the learning and development needs of its employees without seriously effecting their performance in a rapidly changing society, employee training and development are not only an activity that is desirable but also an activity that an organisation must commit resources to, if it is to maintain a viable and knowledgeable work force.

Ashutosh Pande states that, "Today most organisations operate in a business environment where uncertainty, risk and complexity in the external environment have become a fact of life. Pressures of international competition and market globalisation are forcing Indian organisations to match global standards. Whatever their structure or business strategy, organisations are realising that it is the performance of their human assets that can make a difference between success and failure. With increased emphasis on technology, quality and service we are moving away from a mechanised workforce to an intellectualised one and thus need competent and self-directed employees to assume responsibility as per the changing demands of the work situation.

Control-oriented organisations filled with barrier-laden bureaucracies, time consuming committees, and cumbersome approval processes are being scrapped in favour of the re-designed and re-engineered to increase flexibility and efficiency thereby empowering employees. More than consistency it is now innovation and constant improvement that holds the key. Such a dramatic change requires to accept new values, behave differently, learn new skills and competencies, and often take more risk. Such a transformation is possible only through an effective training and development programme.

Characteristics of an Effective Training System

Training is a systematic process of changing knowledge, skill, behaviour and/or motivation of employees to improve their performance on the job as per the goals and objectives of the organisation. Training should also facilitate introduction of newer technology, new work methods, innovations and all round enhancements of productivity and quality of products and services. An effective training system has two key characteristics: first, it is based on *systematic approach* to training need assessment system, and, second, it *utilises the training need information* in a cost-effective manner for improving performance on the job.

Transfer of new knowledge and skills depends on how the training is designed, delivered and, moreover, how the manager measures its effectiveness in real-work situations. According to Professor Baldwin, professor, Indiana University Business School, even in a developed country like the USA "Not more than 10 percent of training expenditure actually results in transfer to the job."

Inter-linkages

Training is one of the most significant constituents of HR, and is closely linked to other HR activities such as manpower planning, performance appraisal, career planning and staffing decisions. For example, skill shortage for an expanding plant can either be filled through recruitment or through re-training and re-deploying existing man-power. Similarly, performance appraisal information may be used for identifying the gaps between expected performance and actual performance. Providing the appropriate type of training to an employee will then narrow these gaps.

Training function can be applied both as a reactive, problem-solving approach as well as a forward looking and proactive approach to deal with future problems or opportunities. (Ashutosh Pande, *Training and Management*, Oct. 2003: 23).

Thus employees at all levels, e.g. workers, supervisors, executives, managers need to be developed to perform their duties effectively and also to grow in actions. Training and development constitutes an ongoing process in any organisation. The need for training and development is determined by the employee's deficiency as under:

Standard Performance (expected) – Actual Performance = Training and Development need

Training and development activities are main mechanisms through which individual's goals and aspirations can be integrated with organisational goals and requirements. Such an integration can be achieved only when training and development efforts are linked with the organisational requirements and are carried out in a systematic manner throughout the organisation.

Nature of Training and Development

To begin with we shall discuss few terms such as training, education, learning, development, management development. There are three terms, training, education and development frequently used. In all 'training' there is some education, and in all education there is some training, and two processes cannot be separated from 'development'.

Training

Training is an act of *increasing knowledge, skill* and *attitude* of an employee for improving his performance on the job (see Fig. 1.1).

Training is concerned with imparting specific skill for doing particular job. For example, a clerk on typing. It is task-oriented activity. It is for job-related purpose and short-term.

Education

Education is concerned with increasing general knowledge and understanding of an employee's total environment. A course on human relations is education.

Learning

Learning is a broad one which includes both training and education. Learning is *observable modification* of behaviour as a result of some experience.

FIG. 1.1

Knowledge, Skills and Attitude

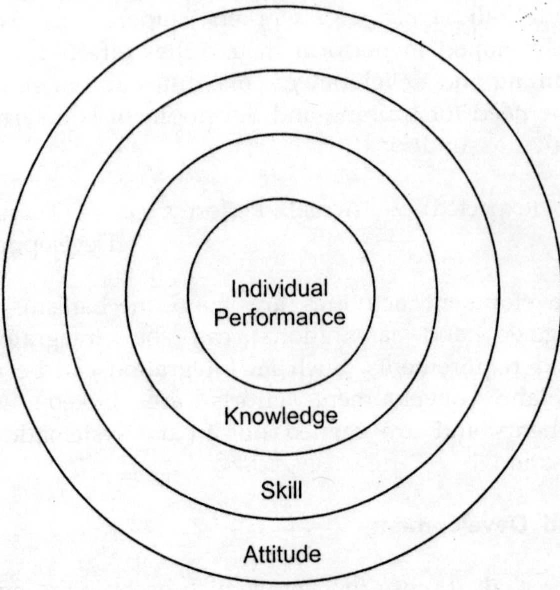

Development

Development has a broader meaning. It's aim is to grow or improve the overall personality of an individual. It is continuous process and is on the initiative from individual. Development is to meet an individual's future needs. Efforts towards development often depend on personal drive and ambition. It helps individual's in the progress towards maturity and actualisation of their potential capacities. It is long-term.

Any training and development programme must contain inputs which enable the participants to gain skills, learn theoretical concepts and help acquire vision to look into the distant future. In addition to these, there is a need to give ethical orientation, emphasise on attitudinal changes and stress upon decision-making and problem-solving abilities.

Development is whole process by which employee *learns, grows, improves* his abilities to perform variety of roles within and outside the organisation. He acquires socially desirable *attitudes* and *values.*

Management Education

Management development is aimed at improving one's abilities to perform professional management tasks. It involves learning on-the-job through experience, formal training programmes and several other approaches including self-development.

IMPORTANCE OF TRAINING AND DEVELOPMENT

A question is frequently asked why employees need training? Some objectives of training are as under:

- Training is required for improving *performance* on the job.
- Training is essential to keep pace with *technological* advances and avoid obsolence.
- To cope with changing environment such as competition.
- Training is needed for promotion to higher jobs, i.e. for *future role* succession.
- Training is needed for dealing complexity of *organisation problems,* e.g. coordination and integration of activities for achievement of goals.
- For *tackling human problems,* i.e. imparting training in human relations.
- Training helps to harness *human potential,* i.e. creativity.
- Training for creating favourable attitudes and motivation of employees.
- To train for better adjustment to the organisation and commitment to work.
- To train employees in the company culture.
- Training of employees is required for achieving organisation's efficiency, growth and to reduce costs.

In fact no organisation can ignore the training needs of its employees without seriosuly inhibiting its performance. Benefits of training accrue to supervisors, trainees, external customers (i.e. the end users of the company's products or service) and it contributes to organisation effectiveness.

Does Training Pay

A recent survey conducted by NFO India in association with HT Careers has highlighted:

- Impact of *well-designed training* programmes is increasingly being felt at work places and companies have gradually begun to ask for more such interventions.
- The focus on return on investment and systematic learning has increased.
- One has to look at training not just as a capital investment and

asset building for the future but *also* as an employee motivation and retention tool. Taking care of the training needs of an employee reinforces his/her interest in the job. It contributes to job satisfaction and even creates new roles or functions for existing employees.

To Conclude

Training seems very limited and restricting. Life is all about improvement and improvement is done through transformation. Transformation—whether of the organisation or of individuals—always help liberate and enable people. Training is to bring about the transformation in people's hearts and minds. (Ashutosh Pande).

Reference

Ashutosh Pande, "Perspectives on Training Need Assessment, Training and Management", New Delhi.

CHAPTER

2

The Training Process

Training process is an integral part of human resource management and organisation. The Fig. 2.1 outlines the inter-related steps in training process.

FIG. 2.1

Model for Training Process

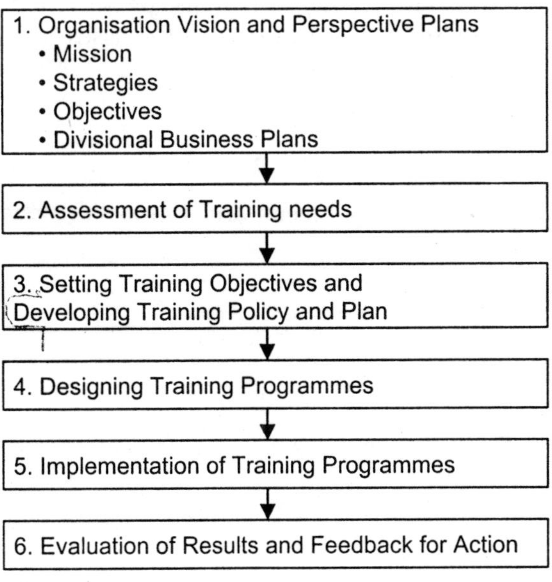

(1) ORGANISATION VISION AND PERSPECTIVE PLANS

The initial step in the training process is linking the organisation's vision, mission, strategies and objectives (overall and division-wise for thrust). Training activities have to contribute to the corporate goals by increasing the effectiveness of work being carried out in particular parts. The contribution can be seen to have two main aspects:

(a) Achieving the *immediate need* related to organisation's strategic problems.

(b) Training to be based on long-term plan and to preparing employees for *new challenges* (futuristic need) of the people and the organisation. Training function has to play proactive role even in changing the culture of organisation. Training can contribute towards strategic direction of the organisation by designing and implementing in creative way training programmes which move people in that direction.

(2) ASSESSMENT OF TRAINING NEEDS

Knowledge, skills and attitudes are the three criteria around which all job are based. A training need is a gap between the knowledge, skills and attitudes desired and already possessed by the employees. An individual needs training when his performance falls short of standards, i.e. when there is performance deficiency. Inadequacy in performance may be due to lack of skill or knowledge or any other problem, e.g. uninspiring supervision or some personal problem of the employee. The problem of performance deficiency caused by absence of skills or knowledge or attitude can be remedied by training. Fig. 2.2 illustrates the assessment of individual training needs and remedial measures.

FIG. 2.2

Assessment of Training Needs and Remedial Measures

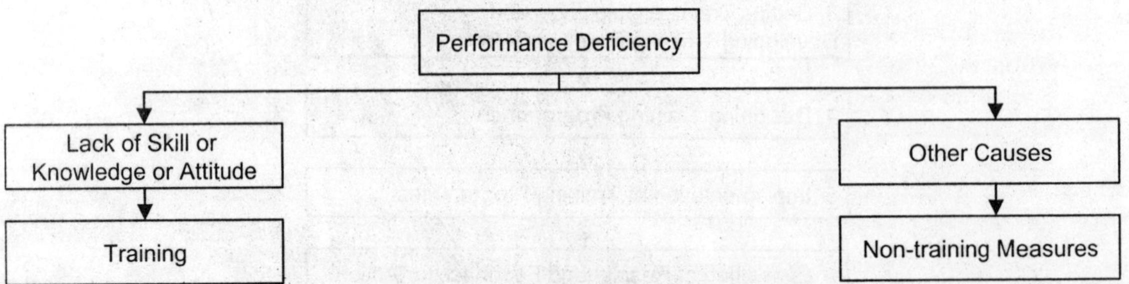

Occurrence of Training Needs or Whether Training is Needed?

Three major areas in which staff display such gaps, i.e. they don't meet the job requirements. These are: (a) when their performance in their present position does not match up to the required standards, (b) when the requirement of the job changes due to the changing circumstances, and (c) when the present job ceases to exist or the job holder changes jobs, therefore creating new 'gaps' in the new job.

Future Needs

(a) The following *future needs* will force the company to train, or retrain its employees:

- Expansion
- Reorganisation
- New Methods
- New Equipment
- New Products
- Retirements
- Promotion
- Seasonal Variations
- Change in Layout
- Special Jobs
- Changes in Manning Levels
- Attritions
- Organisation Culture
- Organisation Development

Existing Problems

(b) Training need is also indicated from such *problems existing* in the organisation:

- standards of work performance not being met;
- accidents;
- excessive scrap; incidence of errors or faults in a job are high;
- frequent need for equipment repair;

- high rate of transfer and turnover;
- too many low ratings on employee evaluation reports;
- many people using different methods to do the same job;
- excessive fatigue, fumbling, struggling with the job;
- bottlenecks and deadlines not being met.

Various Sources

(c) *Various sources* from which evidence of training needs may be gathered are as follows:

- Informal observations;
- Appraisal reports;
- Suggestion system;
- Group discussions;
- Questionnaire or check list to trainees or to supervisors;
- Attitude survey;
- Tests;
- Interviews with union officials;
- Selection or exit interviews;
- Analysis of reports relating to costs, turnover, grievances, etc.;
- Employee counselling.

Organisation Level Needs

(d) Some other methods to identify *the organisation level needs or for group of employees* are as under:

- Organisational goals and objectives;
- Organisation climate surveys;
- Exit interviews;
- MBO or work planning systems;
- Quality circles, TQM;
- Customer survey;
- Consideration of current and future changes.

(e) Change of Role

(i) Some years ago a medium sized manufacturing company called in some industrial Engineering consultants with the object of improving organisational performance. They interviewed the supervisors and discovered that the amount of time they actually spent on supervision was minimal. They, therefore, told the supervisors what their jobs should really entail, and said that as from Monday morning they would no longer have to involve themselves directly in the practical work of the department or the keeping of records. In other words, their duties would be solely supervisory. Two of them said they would rather go back on to the shop floor as they were skilled operators before elevation as supervisor.

The message for the training department is clear. Every individual who is promoted to a position of supervisory responsibility generates training needs, and every effort should be made to equip such employees with the skills to carry out their new responsibilities adequately.

(ii) Frequently one group will not communicate with another simply because it does not understand the language used. An accountant may avoid going near an engineer for fear of being confused with science. Ironically, the engineer may avoid contacting the accountant for the very same reason—financial jargon means nothing to him. There would, therefore, appear to be substantial need to help specialists understand each other's language in the interests of their working together for the common good. So the need for programmes such as finance for non-finance personnel, etc.

(iii) There is a common misconception that engineers and scientists do not make good managers. This seems from the fact that they are seen to be very much occupied in things, as distinct from people. They are deeply involved in and committed to their technical activities and may not therefore see what is going on around them. This is no reason to assume that they will not make good managers if they choose to move into the management ranks. The important thing is to recognise that this is so and thus to ensure that the machinery is available to enable them to cross that bridge and to be suitably trained for the new position.

The analysis of training needs is one of the most important stages in the training process. Clearly defined training needs may be established before training is commenced. The importance of analysing the true needs cannot be over-stressed failing which the training department loses credibility.

Edifice of Effective Training System

(f) Ashotosh Pande observes that "the edifice of effective training system is based on systematic training need assessment. As can be seen from the Fig. 2.3, performance on the job is dependent on both accuracy of role perception as well as on-the-job abilities such as knowledge, skill and attitude."

FIG. 2.3

Performance on the Job

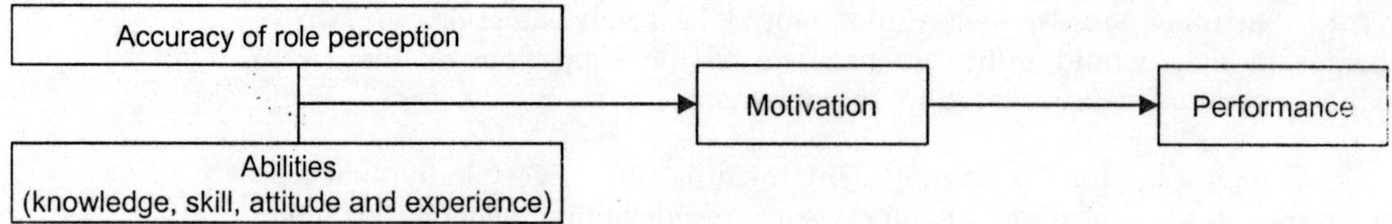

"Apart from the accuracy of role perception and abilities, successful performance on the job is also dependent upon motivation of the individual employees in an organisation. The following must be taken into consideration for assessing the training needs of any organisation."

(i) Vision and Perspective Plans

A proactive approach to training need assessment for any organisation has to clearly look into the training requirements from a future perspective and not merely to deal with day-to-day performance problems of the employees. The long-term vision of an organisation may envisage plans for expansion, modernisation, technology upgradation, improvement in systems and procedures, etc. Such developments over the years would require considerable inputs/services from various functions or departments. The following aspects are generally considered important by many organisations in today's competitive environment:

- Reviewing and updating individual and departmental objectives.
- Re-training and re-deployment for effective utilisation of man-power.
- Training for computerisation.
- Multi-skilling for flexibility of deployment.
- Appraising and helping employees to improve their performance.
- Career development prospects and opportunities for the employees.
- Training and continuous learning experience.

- Developing team skills and empowerment for improved performance.
- Encouraging employee participation for maintaining harmonious industrial relations.

(ii) Accuracy of Role Perception

With the changing requirements of an organisation, the role of various functions or departments also changes. Vision and future perspective plans provide important inputs for the evolving role of a function or department in an organisation; however, vision and future perspective needs to be analysed at organisational level, and accuracy of role perception is to be viewed at departmental level.

One of the most important causes of performance-related problems is lack of clarity of *role perception*. Accuracy of role perception refers to what employees think they are required to accomplish on the job and how. Many managers, clerical staff and workers in most Indian organisations have acquired formative experience in a non-competitive, low-tech era, where the pressure for improving quality and increasing productivity was minimal. There may not be sufficient clarity regarding their changing role in a competitive environment. Since setting goals and standard is the function of top and senior level managers, the responsibility for bringing out accuracy of role perception is also with the top and senior level managers.

Discussions with top management are important to understand the changing roles and responsibilities of departments or functions in the light of new problems and opportunities being faced by the organisation. Departments have to redefine their roles and responsibilities to strengthen their functioning and contribute effectively towards organisational requirement in a fast changing and competitive business. Since systematic training need assessment is a time consuming and costly exercise, it is therefore important that the training needs assessed remain valid for at least 3-5 years. Further, it should also be possible to adapt and fine tune as a result of feedback of participants and their user departments.

All KPAs be first determined at departmental level and exercise be carried out at various levels to determine the relative weightage of KPA at different levels. The analysis should also include standard of performance or results and key tasks and skills for achieving these results.

FIG. 2.4

Job Position

KPAs	Area	Weightage	Key Task or Activities / Critical Skills	Results or standard of performance

(iii) Abilities

Accuracy of role perception is a prerequisite to understand the abilities that are required of the job-holders to fulfil their role responsibilities effectively. Besides knowledge, skills, experience and attitude required for the desired performance on a job, abilities also include commitment to certain core values. The organisation may like to inculcate certain core values for facilitating a certain culture, which is important for its survival and growth.

Although training requirements differ from organisation to organisation, however certain broad generalisations are possible. Whether the training is driven mainly by *role defined skill needs* or on more general competencies, and *personality aspects* will depend to a great extent on the type of business environment in which the firm operates. The more complex and dynamic the environment a firm is maintaining, the more training and development needs to *focus on general competencies rather than role defined skills.* It is difficult to define what knowledge and skills will be required where and when in advance.

(iv) Motivation

Despite having the *right awareness of one's role and responsibilities* and also the *related knowledge* and *skill/experience*, an employee may remain short of expected performance because of lack of motivation. Motivation is the drive that energises, sustains and directs a person's behaviour and it derives from perceived relationship between behaviour and the fulfilment of values and/or needs. It is important because knowing why behaviour occurs and why it is directed towards one of countless possible goals allows considerable progress in improving an employee's job performance. When talking of motivation, it is important to *balance the motivation* of individual employees as wellas organisational needs and priorities. From the perspective of motivation it is important to design programmes in such a creative manner that the participants find it personally meaningful for their own development as well as for upgrading professional skills for achieving organisational objectives.

In some cases training is being used as a means of rewarding employees by nominating them to residential programmes at exquisite locations like Shimla, Leh, Manali, etc. While this may not harm, however, in order to make this training effective, it is important that *nominations be made after careful assessment of training needs* and the participant may also be asked to *take up a specific project in his work area* after the completion of training. If the training is a costly affair involving foreign training the HR department may also work out Return on Investment (ROI) from the training programmes and the subsequent implementation project.

(v) Identifying where Training is Needed?

The training need can arise at any of the following three levels:

- The Organisation
- The Activity
- The Individual

This identification can be done by detailed analysis:

1. Organisation Analysis

This entails analysis of following factors:

(a) Understanding of short-term and long-term *objectives* of the corporate and analysis of each department goals.

(b) Any review of organisation structure or diversification plans.

(c) Analysis of culture or organisation climate.

(d) Human resource future plans such as, identified through attitude surveys, i.e. change in leadership styles, team-building, etc.

2. Tasks or Role Analysis of Positions

- This is known through skills, knowledge required to perform the job through job content information.
- Deficiency in methods of performing job or performance standard required. This information provides lead for meeting training gaps.

3. Man Analysis

To know the individuals who need training. This can be known in various ways:

- Appraisal records.
- Through administrative tests.
- Interviews with supervisors regarding persons needing training in improving, inter-personal relations, waste control, weak in job performance, etc.

(vi) Training a Critical Mass of Employees

Once training needs have been clearly identified, the organisation's leaders should decide which employees will receive the training. Aniruddha

Bannerjee emphasises that to *create change, a critical mass of employees* needs to be involved. Getting a lot of people on the same wavelength accelerates the drive to the goal. Employees will make the new process 'the way we do things here'.

Newly promoted and newly hired members of a group should receive all the training that was provided to the original group. It is also vital that managers receive more or less the same training that is provided to the group that he will be managing. Nothing kills new learning as fast as the failure of the boss to understand and support it. Therefore, it is advisable that senior management and senior executives either also get trained in the same module or arrange to get some related training. Training is important because it adds to a particular mass of trained manpower, value that is not measurable by normal parameters. A well-trained mass becomes 'critical'. It is this 'critical' mass of employees that is usually required to push a company out from a state of inertia.

Training has to be customised to meet the needs of individuals as the organisation requires. However, trainers may sometimes also carry out assessments which may indicate a requirement of a particular set of levels in the organisation to focus on general competencies. Some details are presented as under:

(a) For the *senior management* team at the strategic level the most important skills are more general in nature. *Conceptual and meta skills*, which make the team members continuously open to learning and also internalising this learning for making the best use of opportunities, working out *strategic alliances* (issues) for competitive advantage, fostering innovation, adopting new approaches, improving systems and creating an environment of continuous growth and development in the organisation, are of critical importance. Apart from this *up-to-date professional knowledge in their field, leadership and inter-personal skills* are also quite important for senior level positions in an organisation.

(b) Since senior management is occupied with *strategic issues* most of the time, *middle level management* needs to take the responsibility for *managing day-to-day operations*, more or less in an independent manner. This means that the middle management level should be thorough and up to date *on all technical matters related to its functional area*. The other skills that are important for them are *interpersonal skills*, use and *application of computers, communication and presentation skills*, etc.

(c) At the *supervisory level* and for positions having a larger span of control, *interpersonal skills* and *group facilitation* are the keys to success. This of course must be supported by *sound technical skills, knowledge of systems and procedures* for smooth running of day-to-day operations.

(d) As we go down the hierarchy—up to the operator level—we need employees with *increased task-specific skills.* However in today's context employees at all levels have a dual role—one, that of a *disciplined doer, and, second, that of a creative thinkers.*

Many organisations have adopted modern management practices such as Kaizen and other *small group activities to tap the creativity* of employees for solving various problems. In such an environment we need to prepare all employees to make their informed decisions, use good judgment and willingly assume more responsibility for higher organisational performance. Employees at all levels, therefore, need to be skilled in *systematic data collection and analysis, problem-solving tools and techniques* and *teamwork and cooperation to be able to contribute* effectively, in addition to the technical skills pertaining to their jobs.

The above listing does not mean that the abilities and skills that are important at one level are not at all required at another. Fig. 2.5 summarises training inputs for different categories of employees. The inputs do not remain constant, as time goes by, there will be a greater emphasis on certain inputs at the cost of others. This however indicates that priorities change depending upon the level of the employees in the hierarchy. For working out the exact training requirements it is necessary to look for and at the gaps between the demands of the job and the *present abilities of the employee.*

FIG. 2.5

Training Inputs Across Employees

Inputs	*Operatives*	*Lower-level managers*	*Middle-level managers*	*Top-level managers*
Specific job skills	Yes	—	—	—
Motor skills	Yes	Yes	Yes	Yes
Interpersonal skills	Yes	Yes	Yes	Yes
Education	—	—	Yes	Yes
Development	—	—	Yes	Yes
Ethics	—	—	Yes	Yes
Attitudinal changes	Yes	Yes	Yes	Yes
Decision-making and problem-solving abilities	—	—	Yes	Yes

(vii) Training Needs Analysis

A training needs analysis is basically a data-gathering process used to identify and compare an organisation's level of actual level of performance to the projected (desired) level of performance.

The difference (discrepancy) will identify the immediate and/or long-range training need. The "performance" can be interpreted to new managerial (behaviour) skills or technical (production) skills required to mean do a job. Fig. 2.6 illustrates the interrelationship of these two dimensions.

FIG. 2.6

Defining Immediate/Long-Range Training Needs

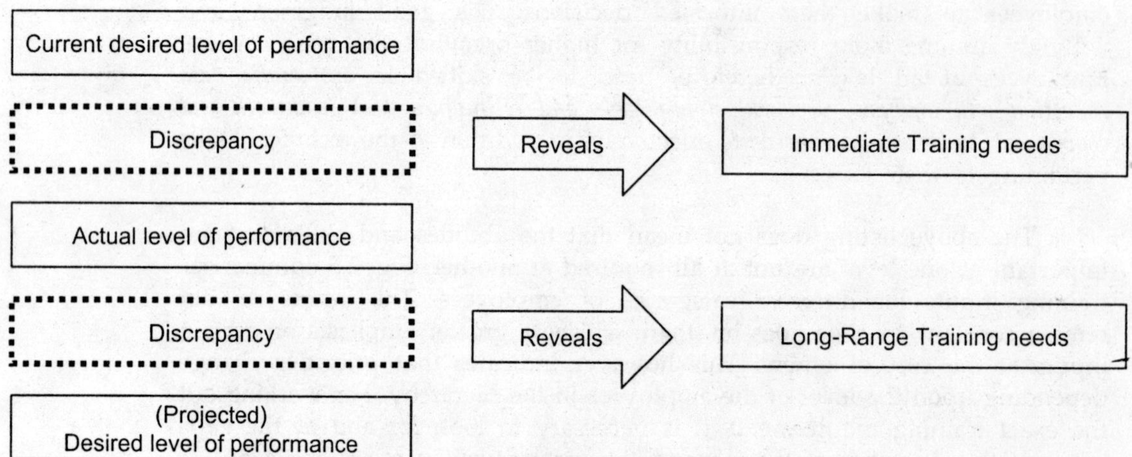

To conclude analysis of training needs (TN) is an important prerequisite for any training programme or event to be effective. However, training must be result-oriented. The resources invested in training must be targeted at fulfilling training needs, keeping in mind the limited budgets and the aim to provide cost-effective solutions. The focus should be at areas requiring training and development, promising a positive return on investment. Other benefit of need assessment is that trainers are able to pitch their course inputs closer to the specific needs of the participants. Need assessment helps diagnose the causes of performance deficiency in employees so as take remedial action.

After the training needs are assessed it is desirable to prepare *statement of training needs* for employees in all departments. This statement will provide gap between existing and required level of knowledge, skills and attitudes. Here we isolate problem areas which are amenable to be resolved through training effort.

(3) SETTING TRAINING OBJECTIVES AND DEVELOPING TRAINING POLICY AND PLAN

After assessing training needs for the organisation, training and development objectives are to be established. These objectives are essential for designing training programmes. Objective can help in measuring the training programmes effectiveness. Such objective should be tangible and measurable. It is easy to evaluate skills in terms of results, etc. But not in case of behavioural objectives. However, some beahviour standards can be planned and then evaluated. See also chapter on training policy.

(4) DESIGNING TRAINING PROGRAMMES

For developing and structuring training or development programmes some essential elements are:

- Choice of participants or trainees,
- Getting trainers/faculty,
- Duration of training programme,
- Training methods, and
- Training material, etc.

These constituents of training programme are covered in irem (5) conducting training programmes.

Normally training programmes are relevant in following five areas:

(i) For *new employees.*

(ii) For *performance* improvement.

(iii) To equip trainees to tackle *operational problems* of the organisation/job.

(iv) *Employee development* for future responsibilities.

(v) For organisation development to meet changing environment.

Clearly defined objectives are a vital step in training activities.

(5) CONDUCTING OR IMPLEMENTING TRAINING PROGRAMMES

Conducting a training programme requires considerable effort and coordination. Some organisations have from line department *programme director* and *programme coordinator* from training department.

(a) The Trainer

The choice of faculty is critical to the success of training progarmme. His specialised. knowledge on the subject and his experience and skills are reflected in handling working sessions. He should be able to put across particular message and concepts involved in the event of last moment drop out of a faculty member. Director of programme should be capable filling the gap. He must be able to divide the job into logical parts, so that he may take up one part at a time. He must understand the value of training in relation to job objectives. He must be patient and encourage questions from the trainees.

(b) The Trainees

The trainees should be from fairly homogenous group with respect to experience, knowledge and potential for learning so as to avoid disparity in the group. So proper selection of trainees is important for organisation to gain results. The trainees to be sounded about objective to be achieved.

(c) Curriculum

Curriculum should be *relevant* to trainee's level and job to be performed.

(d) Training Material

Training material should be relevant. Handouts to be properly indexed and even distributed in advance. This will enable trainees to understand the subject quickly and can remove their doubts by asking questions.

(e) Methods and Techniques

Methods and techniques should contribute to maintaining interest and high degree of participation. Choice of any method of training such as case study, game, discussion, presentation, tests, etc. will depend upon the objectives of the training programme.

(f) Duration of Training Programme

Duration of training programme will normally depend upon the skill to be acquired, the trainees learning capacity of trainees. The use of effective visual aids helps to reduce the training time.

A checklist for improving impact of training programme is annexed. These guiding points will assist at the time of introduction and conclusion of the training programme.

(g) Timing and Sequencing

Timing and sequencing of sessions are suitable with regard to training objectives. Duration of each session for two hours is adequate to maintain interest. There should be not more than four sessions per day.

(h) Location

Venue for training should be room with ventilation, free from noise and disturbances and to be comfortable. U-shaped seating arrangement is preferable for interaction among participants. Podium can be utilised by the speaker, surrounding of place should create training environment.

(i) Physical Facilities and Training Equipment

OHP, Whiteboard, Indicator, Flowers, etc.

(j) Checklist

Coordinator to prepare checklist for effective follow-up of training programme.

	Item	*Due date*	*Remarks*
(i)	Date of programme		
(ii)	Course approval		
(iii)	Last date for receipt of nominations		
(iv)	Programme preparation		
	Programme printing		
	Programme distribution		
(v)	Enrolment—circular to be issued		
	Enrolment—receipt of nominations		
	Enrolment—reminders		
(vi)	Speaker—selection		
	—Conformation		
	—Reminders		
(vii)	Reading material		
	—Preparation		
	—Printing		
(viii)	Accommodation booking (including food, drinks)		
(ix)	Teaching equipment		
	Evaluation Forms, etc.		
(x)	Misc. items—photographer		
	Pens, pads, name cards, felt pens, flip charts		
(xi)	Post training work		
	Payment to be settled		
	Evaluation processing		

(k) Transferring the Training to the Job

A. Bannerjee states that, "Perhaps the most important consideration is how the learnings and insights from the training will be integrated into each individual's day-to-day job. There are several ways to accomplish this. Among the most productive are having *participants address their real-life workplace challenges* in the training programme's skills exercises. These exercises will give the participants fresh ideas about ways to meet their goals.

Another approach consists of scheduling the training so that there are *workdays in between the training sessions.* Participants can practice and solidify the skills they learned during their workdays, and then develop those skills further on the last day of training. *Personal action plans also can help transfer skills to the job.*

Depending upon client interactions, many trainers can provide these clients with a three-step process aimed at transferring training. The first consists of materials given to participants at the end of their training programme. This kit of reinforcement tools may include visual stimuli (charts, posters, desk calendars, desk planners and others) that participants can put on their desks to constantly remind them to *use the skills.* The second step in that process is a *special training programme* for graduates of the training programme. This further *develops the acquired skills.* As the final step, selected employees at the organisation are *certified to teach a follow-up programme* that further reinforces skills and continues to encourage transference of the skills to the job.

Managers of the employees who are receiving the training should understand the trainee and be committed to supporting and *reinforcing the new learnings.* This means being able to answer employees' questions about the skills being taught, allowing extra time for the new process to be implemented, praising and rewarding the use of new skills, and in other ways *creating environments* in which the new ways can take hold.

Senior management can play a significant role in making the training provide maximum value. This can be accomplished by taking ownership of the programme. The CEO or another top executive can make it clear that the training programme has top-level support by appearing just before the programme."

(6) EVALUATION OF TRAINING

It is essential to determine the effectiveness in terms of achievement of training objectives. Results of evaluation enable trainee to assess is progress. Positive feedback from trainer is helpful.

Criteria for evaluation of training has to be according to objectives of the programme or multiple criteria to be used.

Methods

(a) Evaluation after training programme feedback from participants to be obtained through *questionnaire*.

(b) From the feedback discussion with the participants.

(c) Feedback *from faculty* regarding the interest, involvement of participants.

(d) Feedback from managers/boss after trainees go back on job and work for some time relating to knowledge behaviour, attitude on the job and productivity, etc.

(e) Administer test after training programme.

Thus evaluation would provide useful information about the effectiveness of training as well as about the design of future training programmes. Such a monitoring will enable to modify its future training programmes. For detailed evaluation methods see in separate chapter.

A. Banerjee further adds that "Ultimately, training must be judged by its *impact on the organisation*. This requires hard data on measurable objectives, such as increased sales, market share, reduced operating costs, lower rates of absenteeism, or whatever other objective the training was designed to achieve. Although other forces may affect these measurable criteria, it is nonetheless important that training to be tied to corporate objectives all the way through to the payoff stage.

'Taking the temperature' during and immediately after the training is also important. If the trainer antagonises the employees in some way, if there is too much information to absorb, or if the material or the approach is off-target, this needs to be known immediately.

Participants and their managers should be involved in the evaluations in ways more meaningful than filling out little checklists at the end of the day. Group evaluation sessions and discussions not only reinforce what was learned, they also underline the serious purpose of the training and stimulate employee ownership of the results.

Training is not a panacea, it cannot eliminate core problems like low capitalisation or a product line that does not meet customers' needs. Training can provide extraordinary improvements in the organisation. The key to getting the best return on investment from training is to view it strategically rather than tactically."

A Systematic Approach to Training

At the end of this chapter we give an outline of a systematic approach to training in Fig. 2.7.

FIG. 2.7

Model for a Systematic Appraoch to Training

I. Obtaining of Corporate Objectives

Linkage of training with corporate objectives and strategies

II. Identification of Training Needs

Organisation Analysis	• Identification of organisation *objectives, needs, growth potential* and *resources*.
Task/Role Analysis	• Identification of *knowledge*, *skills* and *attitudes* required.
Manpower Analysis	• Identification of *target population* and performance analysis.
Statement of training need	• Identification of *gap* between existing and required level of knowledge, skills and attitudes. • Isolate problem areas amenable to resolution through training.

III. Training Objectives and Plan of Training

Setting training objectives	• In terms of behavioural changes.
Develop measures of job proficiency	• In terms of output/results.
Develop training policy, plan, procedures, records	

IV. Design, Conduct and Evaluate

Plan and design training programmes	• Course construction • Arrange resources
Conduct training programmes	• Individual • Group • On-the-job
Follow-up and Evaluation	• Carry out evaluation against objectives set

V. Obtain Feedback and Action

Validate	• Against measures of job proficiency
Ensure feedback of results	
Revise training if necessary	

References

Aniruddha Banerjee, "Employee Training: Strategic Approach to Better ROI", Training & Management, Feb. 2004.

Vinit Taneja, Rima Taitly and Reni Rajan, "The Trainer", Training & Development, Oct. 2003.

Ashutosh Pande, "Perspectives on Training Need Assessment", Training & Management, New Delhi.

CHAPTER

3

Learning

Learning is concerned with bringing about relatively permanent changes as a result of experience. This can be done through direct experience, by doing, or indirectly, through observation. Regardless of the means by which learning takes place, learning cannot be measured *per se*. We can only measure the changes in attitudes and behaviour that occur as a result of learning. These are four.

We shall discuss the following aspects about learning:

(i) Basic principles or factors affecting the learning process.

(ii) Trainer's role in trainees' learning.

(iii) Theories of learning.

(iv) Experiential learning.

(v) Online learning.

(vi) Programmed learning.

(I) BASIC PRINCIPLES OR FACTORS AFFECTING THE LEARNING PROCESS

Some basic psychological principles or factors affecting learning are given below:

1. Learning Curve

We chart out the progress of learning in any skill and present it graphically in the form of learning curve. Skill in typing is shown below:

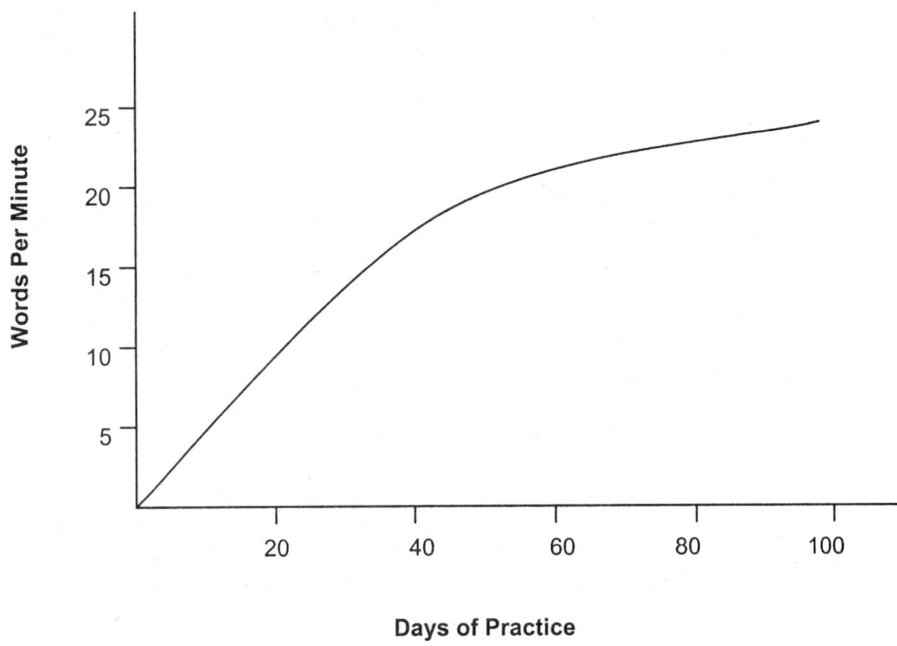

- First there is *rapid rise* in learning,
- Second characteristic is the tendency of curve to *rise less and less rapidly*, and
- Finally *levelling off*—plateaus—flattening of curve.

Learning curve is essential aid for trainers in understanding the *learning process*. Learning curves can be altered by devising right methods of training and can well reflect their effectiveness. It is clear that learning rarely takes place at a constant rate. It varies according to difficulty of task, ability and physical factors of individual.

2. Knowledge of Results (KR) or Feedback

The rate at which the trainee learns depends upon the feedback of results. Positive feedback is more effective than negative. This is also termed as reinforcement.

3. Accuracy and Speedy Performance

The speed of work can come only if job is learned with accuracy. Practice and motivation, can help, after a task has been accurately learned. Trainee must be encouraged to practice the activity, i.e. repetition.

4. Another Learning Principle is that of Distributed or Spaced Practice

Short practice periods, interrupted by *short rest periods* generally result in great economy in learning than *long practice periods* as well as lengthening of rest intervals. Spaced learning sessions give better results than lengthy learning sessions.

5. Previous Learning Facilities

One more principle of learning/training is that *previous learning facilitates* our present learning. For instance, after learning to drive one make of car, there is usually little difficulty in learning to drive any other make car. Thus, *transfer* of training helps in training courses. Practice makes a person perfect. Here one can associate new knowledge with the already possessed.

6. Role of Motivation is Crucial in Learning

Learner must know that whatever he is learning is going to be of great use to him. When a person is promised or that he will *get promotion* if he completes certain course. Individual learn's very fast under such motivated conditions. *Stimulus* must be known and understood by the trainees. Trainee should have motivation for learning and those should be selected who have such desire.

7. People Learn Step by Step, from known to unknown and simple to complex as shown on the next page.

8. Part *versus* Whole Learning

Generally, the smaller the amount of new material presented to the trainee at one time the quicker and effectively will he learn. Individual components of a job can be broken down into easily understandable steps to ensure that this overloading does not occur.

9. Logical Sequence

Information which is given in stages in a logical sequence are much more easily remembered than random presentation. Clear, sequential presentation of material and visual aids organised into efficient memory cues are helpful.

10. Depth of Impression

Recall is closely associated with the depth of impression of the past experience. Charts, diagrams and statistics for example, can be more easily learned with the help of graphic presentation.

Learning Stages—Simple to Complex

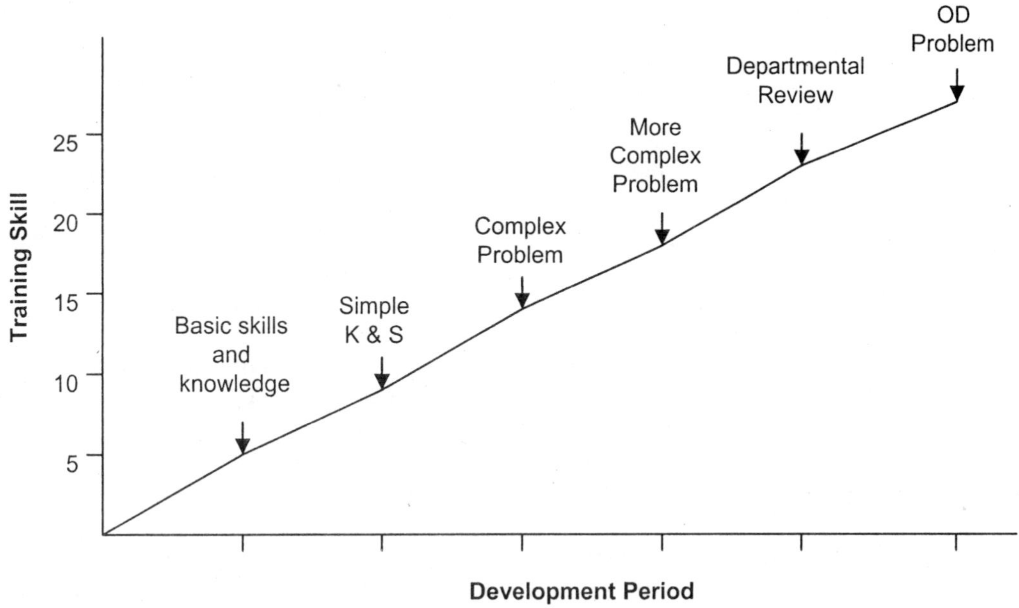

To conclude, training and development programmes are more likely to be effective when they incorporate the following principles of learning:

- Employee motivation,
- Recognition of individual differences,
- Practice opportunities,
- Reinforcement,
- Knowledge of results (feedback),
- Goals,
- Schedules of learning,
- Meaningfulness of material, and
- Transfer of learning.

(II) TRAINER'S ROLE IN TRAINEES' LEARNING

The trainer's task is to take up will to learn trainees, to optimise training opportunities and to help the trainee to met his own and corporate goals. To do this the trainer must have an understanding not only of how people learn, but of the psychological factors which influence learning, particularly current thinking on motivation in the instructional field.

(a) Goal Setting

The goal is a primary factor in the effort people put into their learning. So the trainer must be able to understand the goals at which his trainees are aiming, and to be able to point out other goals that the trainees may have over-looked. *Intrinsic 'goals'* are so called because they satisfy some inner desire, giving a sense of accomplishment which derives from doing something one always wanted to do, is obviously a powerful motivational force which helps the trainer enormously, his main task being to harness and channel the strong desire for knowledge in such trainees. Extrinsic motivation refers to the need for external goals being set as a reward for effort, e.g. money, praise, incentive bonus, prestige or better working conditions. The trainer's work here is centred on arousing interest in the extrinsic goals, pointing out benefits of their attainment and sustaining effort during training by reminding and giving feedback, encouragement and reward. Both types of motivation are important to the learning process.

(b) Need Satisfaction at Work

The trainer must have a basic knowledge of the needs that are satisfied during working hours so that he can pitch his instruction at appropriate goals. A working knowledge of motivational theory is also useful in the important business of gaining rapport with the trainee. It is important to view trainees, as individuals whose needs will vary with age, circumstances, background and time. However, a broad grouping of needs is a useful start. One grouping of needs satisfied by work can be termed social needs, the desire to conform be part of a team, relate to others and meet group objectives. Some of these needs are satisfied at work, mainly in group tasks, and one of the trainer's duties is that of *team-building*. The needs of many people at work can be seen in the context of personal fulfilment. The testing of one's abilities, the pride in achievement and the growth that comes from meeting challenges and achieving objectives gives meaning to many jobs at all levels of society. It is the analysis of a trainee's needs and the joint progress through learning towards his personal targets, that form realistic, adult attitudes to the fulfilment goals from the trainer's point of view.

(c) Incentives to Greater Efforts

Encouragement and feedback are great incentives, if given promptly. Praise is important to the trainee in terms of ego needs and should be given freely to trainees who produce good performances. The whole process of learning can be geared to setting challenges, friendly competition and adequate rewards in the right 'climate', i.e. where the trainer has built a rapport based on mutual respect. Price in results, the sense of craftsmanship is another area where the trainer sets standards' of quality arid performance. The need to meet the trainer's standard, i.e. the level of expectations can be a powerful motivator in some cases, particularly where groups are working in friendly competition. One of the major incentive in some cases but it is particularly strong in the young. The trainer's role here is often that of pointing out career opportunities in a realistic manners ensuring that such advancement goals are within the grasp of the trainee's abilities. Problems in transfer of learning occur when trainees have to move from a training centre situation to the real working area.

(d) Trainer-trainee Relationship

Learning is fun when presented in a stimulating, enthusiastic way by a trainer who genuinely cares about the relationship between him and his trainees. There is however a two-way responsibility, no trainer can maintain this climate on his owns since he depends upon his *trainee's attainments to fulfil his needs.* This understanding of mutual needs is important since the role of the trainer and the trainee revolves around it. The trainee needs the nurturing presence of a respected Fig. who provides him with a structure for his learning, monitors his performance and evaluates fairly. For the satisfaction in his works the trainer needs the attainment of successful performance by his trainees in a cheerful and willing manner. The trainer acts in many ways as a model, especially to young trainees. They see in him the embodiment of professional attitudes towards their work, and, consciously or unconsciously shape their behaviour towards his. Many trainees will remember their trainer long after they have forgotten the tasks that he taught; an illustration of the special relationship with young people that the trainer enjoys. With this privilege goes ensuing responsibilities, with regard to personal habits, approach to the jobs and personal mannerisms. Objectively, fairness and acceptance, of the rules are important factors in the psychological make-up of the successful trainer, and he should not be too much of a tyrant, for his is a powerful position. Conversely, he must not be too lax in his attitude or he will fail to give the learner a sense of challenge. 'A good trainer' finds the middle course, and will be rewarded by moments of genuine self-fulfilment for his efforts.

(e) Anxiety in the Learning Process

No one learns when they are fearful since this freezes performance and reduces the level of perception by the process of sensory inhibition. The very situation of learning something new arouses apprehension in many, since it is associated with past failures, fears of the training centre and doubts about future capabilities. The learner is vulnerable, since we are often rated in the world according to our skills or qualifications and it is obviously 'not O.K.' if we possess none of these attributes, or inappropriate ones.

The first step is his *manner, a friendly approachable* style with a straightforward *integrity*. The use of *appropriate humour* is an important factor, since laughter is a release of pent-up anxiety. An interest in the trainee as a person, with a *caring approach* to his progress is also important. This supportive attitude helps in clarity of demonstration and provides a climate for constructive tolerance of mistakes.

(f) Age and Capacity for Learning

All three parts of the learning mechanism are affected by advancing years; the *senses* become dulled. *Cerebral decay* is a function of brain cells dying off and not being replaced and the *effect or processes* are reduced as a result of increased inactivity. An Important factor in learning in older employees is the *relatedness of new material* to knowledge already possessed; generally the closer new skills are similar to those abilities acquired in the past, then the easier will be the assimilation of new material. Another important aspect is the relationship between age and the increased fear of the learning situation. Mature trainees will suffer from an understandable reluctance to enter the challenging atmosphere of learning something new, especially if it is many years since the last formal acquisition of new skills. It is obvious from the foregoing that the trainer will have to be especially aware when dealing with older employees if he is to help them to undergo the change that is part of the training process.

To Sum up trainers should:

- Treat all learners as individuals and get to know them as people learn at different speeds.
- Use friendly manners and be approachable and straightforward during training.
- Try to put people at ease, no one learns when he is/are nervous.
- Remember you area model as well as a teacher; trainees will imitate your behaviour as well as your skills.
- Find out the goals of each learner; use them in the development of the training programmes. Remember intrinsic goals are usually better than extrinsic ones.
- Learning does not stop at bare mastery. It must process as life long process.

(III) THEORIES OF LEARNING

There are various concepts of learning. These are given as under:

(i) One is the *cognitive view*. Its proponents argue that an individual's *purposes on intentions* direct his actions.

(ii) The other position is the *environmental perspective,* whose proponents believe that the individual is acted upon and that his behaviour is a function of its external consequences.

(iii) A more recent approach blends both of these theories. According to it, learning is a *continuous interaction* between the individual and the particular social environment in which he functions. This is called the *social-learning theory*. This theory acknowledges that we can learn by observing what happens to other people and just by being told about something, as well as by direct experiences. Since much of training is observational in nature, this theory would appear to have a considerable application potential.

(iv) The *influence of models* is central to the social learning view-point. Research indicates that much of what we have learnt comes from watching models such as parents, teachers, peers, motion picture and television performers, bosses, and so forth. Four processes have been found to determine the influence that a model will have on an individual.

(v) Experiential learning, is learning from experience or learning by doing challenging activity. Experiential learning as the term implies is learning from experience or learning by doing and what it does is to get an individual or a group of people involved in fun, yet challenging activities which are designed to bring out specific learning processes.

"The participants' interest and hands-on involvement in the activities ensures that individuals take ownership of their learning. This in turn contributes significantly to the transfer of learning back to the workplace."

The approach to the experiential learning process utilises the participants' own experiences and their reflections about that experience, rather than the lecture and theory method, as the means of generating understanding. This gives rise to useful insights which result in new or changed knowledge, skills and behaviour patterns.

Due to its holistic approach this training methodology has met with universal appeal.

Experiential learning however is still in its infancy in India. "Experiential learning has started happening very slowly over the last five to eight years."

Methodology of Experiential Learning

Some training consultants design and customise Experiential Learning Programmes for Corporates and particularly for cross-functional teams. Some call these as out-bound HR training programmes.

Experiential learning programmes require participants to be engaged in either indoor or outdoor activities. In fact, the experiential learning 'laboratory' is an environment different to the participants' usual surroundings. The idea being to take them away from their usual, familiar places of work or home and put them in an area where they can experiment, be challenged and think about new concepts.

For example, top functionaries from a corporate who "trekked tough terrain, crossed a river and played games" in an adventure tour organised by a training agency.

And what was the impact of those activities. "Well the bonds that were formed between people (participants) were strengthened and are still very strong.

At the end of the day, however, what remains unchanged is the fact that all these people learn from experience. From the games they play, "It's what you are not able to achieve in a classroom setting, that we do outdoors through the Outdoor Management Development Programme. Supposing you have to cross a river along with six fellow members, it would call for team work, depending on the other members and how you are able to communicate," Soin elaborates.

"These experiences are distinct from a "classroom" and "books" approach that rely on transferring knowledge and concepts that only touch the surface of a person's behaviour."

"Games offer safe experimentation. Instead of just theorizing, participants can learn through a series of mental, emotional, intellectual and physical challenges."

"You have to work as a team with everyone complementing each other instead of moving individually." Experiential learning programmes are now getting popular.

Perhaps the greatest challenge most organisations face today is in getting ordinary people to do extraordinary things. Think about it and you will find that in most corporates, the key to long-term survival lies in sustained innovation and creativity. Something your ordinary work may find difficult to do.

So how do you, as his superior, get him to put in that extra spark? Well, one way of doing this would be to send him on an experiential learning programme.

(IV) ONLINE LEARNING

There is lot of information around on computer—Online Learning. But question is how we can learn better from computer screen. B. Dublin states that online is here to stay. Computers will continue towards being part of our everyday learning environments. But still it is in infancy. It's dangerously easy to get carried away which the technology and have all sorts of wonderful things to look at on screen. We need to face up to the fact that however powerful the technology may be, the target is still to cause learning in human brains. People want to learn, and learn by doing, and learn through feedback and make sense of it all. Computers and communications technologies are tools that can help us to do this, but we have to use them wisely for what they are good at.

Ask questions when selecting online learning materials—

- Is it really, really, relevant?
- Does it really cause learning to happen?
- Does it give learners plenty of practice and activity?
- Does it give learners real feedback when they've done something?
- Does it make the most of letting people learn by making mistakes?
- Can learners get backwards and forwards easily?
- Can human support be built in easily?
- Can a trainer or tutor be contacted when needed, face to face or by e-mail?
- Can learners talk to each other and explain things to each other face to face or by e-mail?
- Does it make the most of people learning at their own pace?
- How long does it hold people's attention?

Concentration spans of the human species are in minutes rather than hours.

These questions have to be answered in the positive before a training model can come up and successfully impart learning. Modules in workshops which use e-learning should also look at these pointers in order to provide learning which is fun, relevant, interesting and most of all, which contributes to an overall increase in knowledge.

(V) PROGRAMMED LEARNING

Programmed learning or Programmed Instruction is one of the innovations in teaching technology developed in recent years. The material to be learned is prepared in such a way that it can be presented to the learner in a series of sequential steps. These steps progress from simple to more complex levels of instruction. The information to be taught is presented in a form known as a PROGRAMME. The person who writes the programme is called the PROGRAMME WRITER or PROGRAMMER and the people for whom the programme is written are referred to as the TARGET POPULATION. Programmes are generally presented in the form of a book. "HOW TO READ A BALANCE SHEET" brought out by ILO is an excellent example of Programmed Instruction.

Features of Programmed Learning

(a) The student works his way through a course by a series of small steps.

(b) The actively responds by answering questions on solving problems.

(c) The correctness of his response is immediately established. It is an accepted fact that learning is the highest where feedback is quickest. One of the disadvantages of the modern training systems is that the student does not get a quick feedback. On this ground this is an effective method. Where necessary, he is also provided with additional information to correct his answer.

(d) The learner works toward predefined goals.

The biggest vantage of this method is that the *learning takes place at the student's own pace*. He proceeds from frame to frame. If his response is correct, he immediately gets information indicating that his *response was correct* and he can proceed to the next step. If his response as incorrect, he is instructed to restudy the material. It is thus possible to guide the progress of a student in an orderly manner just as a tutor would do. It is absolutely essential that the trainee is *highly motivated* to continue learning.

References

P.N. Singh, Training for Management Development, Ed. Craig and Bittel, Training and Development Handbook.

An Introductory Course in Teaching and Training Methods for Management Development, Published by ILO.

Article by Dhananjay H. Rawal, "Programmed Instruction" (1979).

P.P. Rao, HRD through In-House Training.

Nalini Menon, H.T. Careers, New Delhi, 11.9.2003.

Barthomello Dublin, "Evaluating Online Training", Training and Management, November 2002.

CHAPTER

4

Life Long Learning

One common characteristic of successful companies which have survived for a century or longer is that these have adapted to change. Take the case of Tatas, they have diversified in hi-technology areas. These companies have always had a fresh approach to business and believed no industry could escape radical changes. So they prepared for it and adjusted appropriately. Says Satish Khanna that "People and corporations have always recognised that change is the only certainty." We see now degree of change is very fast due to it and internet revolution. Yesterdays style, technology and approach can act as a hindrance. The organisations must encourage the next generation of changes in their industry, by experimenting and innovating with new ideas. Satish Khanna adds that "the most important thing is an organisational mindset that welcomes and encourages change." Similarly, professionals and employees have to keep their skills sharpened, relevant rather ahead of times. Many professionals resist change and new practices. It has to be appreciated that what you consider your strength at one stage of your career, can become a liability unless it is suitably upgraded or changed. Instead being rule driven and rigid, one has to have flexibility and openness to new ideas and innovations.

So we have to be ready to grab the opportunities that arise from change, whether technological, social or legal. We must learn from our forward looking colleagues and benchmark them in keeping update and relevant. We should be alert and aware of global environment and reinvent ourselves. So learning has to be a *continuous process* even if you had long back retired from active service. Satish Khanna adds that never lose ability to learn. Be eager to receive wisdom flowing from any body, regardless of his status of hierarchical position. The capability to learn is what differentiates us from animals. Remain a student forever. Know yourself and you will be able to know the world. Knowing our minds is the route to enlightenment. We shall discuss new methods of keeping ourselves as continuous learner.

(I) CONTINUE VALUE ADDITION FOR SUCCESS IN CAREER AND LIFE

We mention here the views of Dr. P.N. Singh regarding how to add value to yourself.

One of the best way of career planning is to do continuous value addition by investing in one's own development. It should be remembered that all development is self-development. By acquiring skills, which are in demand in the market a person can increase his value. As an example, a graduate who learns computer operations, adds value to himself. When a drop out from school learns car driving, he adds value to himself.

Therefore, we should help ourselves to continuously keep on adding value to us. Once we do that, we will not have to chase jobs. Jobs will chase us.

Add Value to Yourself

- The knowledge and skills needed in the new millennium will be different. One such skill needed will be computer literacy. Therefore, you have to clearly understand skills needed in future and prepare yourself by acquiring these skills.
- You should make an estimate of the supply-demand scenario in the future. Skills in short supply should be acquired. This will automatically enhance your value.
- There is some relationship between your aptitude and professional success. You have better chances of succeeding in professions where your aptitude is. Choosing a profession in line with your aptitude will certainly add value to you.
- Two programmes you must attend at the appropriate time. A good public speaking course during your college days and an equally good course of leadership during the first five years of your career. This will be an important value addition to you.
- Please take rotational assignments at regular intervals to broaden your experience. This is the best way of value addition in the organised sector. Somebody can claim to have 20 years' experience. It may really be one year's experience multiplied 20 times. There is little value addition here. But, if that experience

were four blocks of 5 years each in different assignments, real value addition would have taken place.

- We should review our resume every year to see what we have added value to ourselves and incorporate in it. This process will keep you alert for acquiring new assets.

(II) GENERATE A SELF DEVELOPMENT PLAN

Personal development planning (PDP) is an effective tool for developing a constructive approach to acquiring skills and knowledge throughout your working life so that there is a continued sense of achievement.

The accelerating pace of technological change, complexity of information, and the shifts in pressures created by competition are imposing increasing demands on mangers to review their skills and capabilities and develop their potential. It is important for a person to know exactly what would be most pertinent to his development.

The new security in employment consists of not complacency but loyalty, to oneself, to one's own potential and skills.

Self-development is the result of and entails, constant nurturing, shaping and improving an individual's abilities, knowledge, and interests to ensure maximum adaptability and effectiveness. Moreover, development must also imply reducing obsolescence of employee skills. It is about enabling individuals to improve and *utilise their full potential* at each career stage and not just the upward movement.

A personal development plan (PDP) results from prioritising your goals, the things you want to achieve or the position you wish to be in, the short or long-term. To accomplish the plan, you need to identify the skills, knowledge, and competence to be developed/achieved. This helps to define the appropriate development plan to meet those perceived needs. Scheduling and timing is important but cannot be too regimented. Self Development Plan (SDP) allows for an introspection and assessment of your own achievements. It can lay the basis for:

- Re-appraising your goals and ways to attain them.
- Refreshing those technical skills that outdate fast.
- Building-up and refining transferable skills (such as self-awareness, developing leadership qualities, ability to learn, adaptability and flexibility to change, empathy, good time management).

- Willing and continual learning.
- Gaining contentment from a sense of achievement.
- Helping to ensure employability and endurance in times when very few jobs can be guaranteed.
- Achieving a position where you can harness the opportunities into stepping stones for success, which may arise or which you can make happen.

SDP is an on-going and cyclical process; once you are start there's no stopping. Once you have decided about where you are going, you will keep assessing yourself, thus, propelling yourself forward constantly.

Start with your SDP by identify the aim/objective of your development process needs to be identified. You may be able to do this all by your own. If not so, do not hesitate to rope in your colleagues, for enabling you to do so. It involves:

- narrowing down to an area of your interest,
- recognising your potential within the chosen sector,
- analysing and gaining a measure of what you are good at and interested in, and
- taking a realistic account of the organisational facts you encounter and associating your plans with organisational demands to the extent possible.

Try to reflect on:

- your private life and family, work and money, constraints and obstacles to mobility, now and in the future and on the value system that you have evolved out of all this for yourself, and
- various aspects of the work and see how far they fit in with your own value system.

Your career goals and aspirations determine your development needs. Having assessed yourself prepare a roster of the skills or knowledge you will need to acquire, update or improve.

Once you have identified the gaps, set yourself development objectives. These can be called as SMART: Specific, Measurable, Achievable, Rotational, Timely. Try and include an element of challenge in them so that you can deliver your best and carry yourself on to new ground. The key stage to the self-development cycle is review of accomplishments achieved through development plans.

It is important to revise your plan periodically. A plan that does not evolve and adapt is probably not being followed. After all, when the surrounding world isn't static, how can your SDP not be dynamic?

(III) DEVELOP SOME EFFECTIVE STUDY HABITS

Study is the application of a systemic effort towards achievement of specific goals. Formal education only facilitates self-education. Education is not a one time process. It has to be there throughout one's life. Thus, education is lifelong process. The following points help in effective study:

- Distinguish between reading and understanding, i.e. equip with wisdom.
- Clearly distinguish between mere fact from conclusions. The study consists of the process of acquisition of knowledge and process of reasoning.
- Hard work is very important but it can produce gains only if it is properly and intelligently oriented.

(IV) OVERCOMING GENERATION GAP: GROW AND CHANGE TO KEEP PACE WITH TEENAGERS

We shall share here some golden rules on parenting by Sudha Gupta:

Teenage is an age of contradictions, when the bodies, minds and emotions of children grow at different rates. This is the time when it becomes very important for parents to *upgrade their thinking* and re-evaluate their relationship in order to respond to the changing needs of their teenager:

- To keep in step with their teenager, parents must constantly look for *new insights and new ways* to relate to them. You have to adapt and change right along with your teenager. Your relationship can no longer be that of just parent-child. It must evolve into a parent-friend or a friend-friend relationship.
- Remain up to date with what is happening in your child's life. Keep an account of his activities. Ask your child to help you understand his age group, such as why they feel, act or dress in a certain manner. If your child feels that you are asking because of a sincere desire for understanding, he will definitely respond well and develop a *closer understanding* with you.
- Respect your child's individuality. Understand that he is maturing and is developing insights and understanding. Seek his opinions and views on important things and *discuss with* him the issues that affect your family's life.

- Earn his confidence by being confidential. Don't behave as though you have always been perfect and never made a mistake when you were his age. Talk to him about your *own teenage trials.* This will encourage him to confide in you in turn. And never, never betray his confidence in public.
- *Guide rather than intrude.* Sometimes when your teenager confides something, your first impulse could be to barge in and take charge. But control yourself. *Guide him towards the solution* of his problem rather than solving it for him. Give him breathing space.

Remember, however your teenager behaves, deep inside he still *depends on you for love and support.* If you only show negative expectation and find fault all the time, then this is what he will respond to. But if you *show positive expectation, supporting and encouraging him* all the way, then there is no reason why the teen years should be a problem for you and your teenager.

(V) BE WILLING TO LEARN FROM MISTAKES AND DEVELOP GLOBAL PERSPECTIVES

Our mindset consciously analyses and learns from mistakes. The process of recognising and admitting mistakes is largely internal. It is process of self-examination and discovery. In order to evolve as a person, it is important to be receptive to learning from any source and to cultivate a learning attitude. So be a willing seeker, good listener, keen absorber and genuine student of any one who can teach you. Satish Khanna emphases, "Learn how to stay a student throughout life, and take advantage of teachers who are always around you."

Further, it is important to visualise totality of organisation vision, mission and global perspective to work towards acquiring knowledge and competencies. We normally see small parts and understand only small bits and pieces of big picture. Once you visualise big picture and understand the context of an event or decision, you can be much more effective. We have to develop strategic framework to attain world-class status, i.e. by being multi-skilled, core competency, flexible, willing to adapt, focus on ethical standards and creativity.

(VI) UNDERSTAND MEANING OF LIFE AND GEAR TOWARDS THAT

Aim is to achieve big things in life. We should understand the meaning of life. Satish Khanna has termed it as developing "MPS Strength". Mental, physical strength makes people complete and balanced.

- Be physically fit, strong and capable of staying ahead in the daily race.

- Be mentally agile, alert and capable of holding up under demanding and successful conditions.
- Be a spiritually developed, aware and evolved person with the capability to understand meaning of life. This is necessary for satisfaction and happiness. So actively live life and work hard for success. Respect quality of life, be a family person to love and be loved, good, friends and personal relations, explore nature and enjoy its seasons. Relax when you need to and live life meaningfully.

References

Dr. P.N. Singh, "Continue Value Addition is the Key to Success", Article in *Training and Management*, Nov. 2002:33.

Satish Khanna, "Future Manager", Tata McGraw-Hill Publishing Co. Ltd., New Delhi.

Sudha Gupta, "Golden Rule on Parenting", *Hindustan Times*, 25 Jan. 2003.

Create a Self-Development Plan, "Breakthrough", Feb. 2002.

S.K. Bhatia, "Stay Life Long Learner", in Boost Your Professional Career, Deep & Deep Publications Pvt. Ltd., New Delhi.

UNIT II

THE TRAINING METHODS

CHAPTER

5

The Training Methods—Approach

There are numerous training methods. The choice of a method or a mix of methods depends on various factors. According to Mirza S. Saiyadain it depends on considerations as under:

(a) The purpose of training is an important consideration in the choice of methodology. Knowledge can be provided by traditional methods of training like lectures, and discussions skills and attitudes have to be developed by experiential methods of training like in-basket, T-group, etc.

(b) The nature of contents often determine the nature of methodology. A concept can be clarified through a lecture while the operation of machine may best be demonstrated.

(c) The level of trainees in the hierarchy of the organisation also determines the nature of methodology. In fact, techniques like in-basket management games, etc., are designed for managerial levels and hence cannot be effective at workers level.

(d) Finally, all organisations have to be concerned with cost factors. Cost considerations have to be taken into account while deciding on methods of training. However, cost consideration should not override the quality consideration

Mirza S. Saiyadain further adds that, "all methods of training should satisfy the following criteria otherwise their effectiveness could be questioned:

(i) They should provide for active participation by participants. Lack of participation by trainees may limit learning to only listening the trainer and not getting the benefit of sharing experiences.

(ii) The training method should also provide participants constant feed-back on their performance. The realisation that one is learning constantly or one has not been able to improve upon the previous performance is a useful motivation to put in necessary efforts.

(iii) The method should be able to facilitate transfer of training contents to real life situations. The methodology should be such as to provide participants linkages between what is done in classroom and what is its relevance to actual on-the-job behaviour. This is an important consideration without which learning would remain theoretical."

An analysis of the relative effectiveness of training methods is given in Fig. 5.1.

FIG. 5.1

The Relative Effectiveness of Training Methods

Training Methods	*Knowledge acquisition rank*	*Changing attitudes rank*	*Problem-solving skills rank*	*Interpersonal skills rank*	*Participant acceptance rank*	*Knowledge retention rank*
Case Study	2	4	1	4	2	2
Conference (Discussion)	3	3	4	3	1	5
Lecture	9	8	9	8	8	8
Business Games	6	5	2	5	3	6
Films	4	6	7	6	5	7
Programmed Instruction	1	7	6	7	7	1
Role Playing	7	2	3	2	4	4
Sensitivity Training	8	1	5	1	6	3
Television Lecture	5	9	8	9	9	9

Source: Based on Personnel/Human Resource Management by Leap and Crino.

According to David A. Decenzo and S.P. Robbins, "There is no training method that is right for all situations. A number of trade-offs must be made when actually making the choice of techniques and putting the programme together—costs, time, and capacity of the trainer or trainees. A comparison of training methods with learning criteria and costs is given in Fig. 5.2.

FIG. 5.2

Comparison of Training Methods with Key Learning Criteria and Cost Estimates

Method	*Learning Criteria*			
	Feedback of Results to Trainee	*Permits Practice During Training*	*Transfer of Learning to Job*	*Estimated Cost Per Trainee*
Apprenticeship programmes	Yes	Yes	High	Mod.-High
Job instruction training	Yes	Yes	High	Moderate
Classroom lectures or conferences	Varies	No	Low	Low
Films	No	No	Low	Low
Simulation exercises				
Cases	Some	No	Low	Moderate
Experiential exercises	Yes	Yes	Moderate	Low
Computer modeling	Yes	Yes	Mod.-High	High
Vestibule training	Yes	Yes	High	Mod.-High
Programmed instruction	Yes	No	Moderate	Moderate

* Elizabeth Gorovitz, "Employee Training: Current Trends, Future Challenges," *Training and Development Journal*, August 1983, p. 28.

We have covered the training methods under followings headings in separate chapters:

On-the-job Training Methods.

Off-the-job Training Methods—Knowledge Based.

Off-the-job Training Methods—Simulation Based.

Off-the-job Training Methods—Experiential Based.

CHAPTER 6

On-the-Job Training Methods

The most widely used methods of training take place on-the-job. On-the-job training places the employees in an actual work situation and makes them appear to be immediately productive. It is learning by doing. For jobs that either are difficult to simulate or can be learned quickly by watching and doing on-the-job training makes sense. (David A. Decenzo and Stephen P. Robins, HRM.)

In this chapter we shall cover the various on-the-job training methods:

(i) Job Instruction Training (JIT),
(ii) Coaching,
(iii) Job Rotaton,
(iv) Job Enlargement, and
(v) Syndicate Method.

(i) Job Instruction Training (JIT)

Job Instruction Training (JIT) was part of the training within industry program. JIT proved highly effective and became extremely popular. JIT consists of four basic steps: (1) preparing the trainees by telling them about the job and overcoming their uncertainties; (2) presenting the instruction, giving essential information in a clear manner; (3) having the trainees try out the job to demonstrate their understanding; and (4) placing the workers into the job, on their own, with a designated resource person to call upon should they need assistance. The sequence of these activities is shown in Fig. 6.1. Under this productivity significantly improves and rejects are reduced.

FIG. 6.1

JIT Instruction/Learning Sequence

Basics of Instruction	*Essential of Learning*
Prepare • Break down the job • Prepare an instruction plan • Put the learner at ease	Motivation
Present • Tell • Show • Demonstrate • Explain	Understanding
Try out • Have the learner "talk through" the job. • Have the learner instruct the supervisor on how the job Is done. • Let the learner do the lob. • Provide feedback both positive and negative. • Let the learner practice.	Participation
Follow-up • Check progress frequently at first. • Tell the learner whom to go to for help. • Gradually taper-off progress checks.	Application

Source: Leon Gold, "Job Instruction: Four Steps to Success", *Training and Development Journal*, September 1981, p. 29.

(ii) Coaching

Coaching is again on-the-job training of individual by the supervisor in the area of specifically defined tasks. This technique is more appropriate for orientation of new employee and for helping disadvantaged employees to learn specific jobs. The supervisor must have interpersonal competence and be able to establish helping relationship with the trainee.

(iii) Job Rotation

Job rotation is one of the technique of job design through which human needs are satisfied.

Need: To overcome undesirable aspects of job, i.e. boredom, dissatisfaction and declining productivity.

Action: Moving employees from job to job into a job for a short period of time and then out again. Such as night shift, as in hospitals, police, fire departments.

Benefits:

- Reduces boredom and monotony.
- Exposes the employee to a broader perspective of entire production process. He performs different job of similar nature.
- Employees become competent in several jobs rather than only one.
- Knowing a variety of jobs improves the employee's self-image, provides personal growth, and makes the employee more valuable to the organisation. Job rotation also improves inter-departmental cooperation as employees become more understanding of each other's problems.

(iv) Job Enlargement

Need: Jobs either getting over simplified, specialised and routine and thus become monotonous.

Worker feels bored and dissatisfied. This leads to absenteeism and turnover.

Action: It involves expanding the number of tasks or duties to a given job. Enlarge jobs by *adding tasks* of similar nature and skill. It is horizontally enlargement. For example, tightening 4 nuts and 4 bolts instead of one. And also to do additional assignment to go to store.

Example: Despatcher, Addresses, tickets, list go to post office, liaison with courier services, etc.

Benefit:

- *Provides* variety in skills and tasks.
- *Autonomy* in work completion.
- *Worker is responsible* for entire piece of work. Task identity.
- Worker can get *feedback* on job performance.
- Can contribute to employee motivation.

(v) Job Enrichment

Like job rotation and job enlargement, job enrichment is also a technique of job design.

Need: Workers do not visualise how their work contributes to the organisation goals.

Action: It is vertical change in loading, i.e. supervisory tasks are added involving—planning, organising and controllong of jobs.

Example: Plant worker also to be engaged in selling the product (corn flakes).

- *Empowerment* is a by-product of job enrichment, similarly more autonomy is there in task completion.
- Job enrichment adds *status to* owe's job and thus is motivating and satisfying factor.

Benefit:

- Workers are *enthused* about their contribution.
- They realise their jobs are *more meaningful* to them and their *attitudes toward* their job improves. They get awareness of their resutls.
- Leads to reduced absenteeism, reduced rejects.
- Morale high turnover reduced.

However, negative outcome is, that unions resist as it adds to additional responsibility.

(vi) Syndicate Method

According to P.N. Singh, "Working in a small group to achieve a particular purpose is described as a syndicate method. The essence of the syndicate method is that participants learn from each other and contribute their own experiences to the fullest.

This method is suitable for training and development of executives with considerable experience. It is not so useful in the case of management students without any experience.

The Methodology

(a) The participants are divided into group consisting of about ten participants. These groups are called "Syndicates".

(b) Each Syndicate functions as a team that can represent various functional as well as interest areas.

(c) The Syndicates are given assignments which have to be finished and a report submitted by a specified date and time.

(d) By rotation, each member of the syndicate becomes the leader (Chairman), for completing a specific task or an assignment.

(e) Each assignment to a Syndicate is given in the form of a "Brief". This is a carefully prepared document by the faculty.

(f) Generally, each Syndicate is required to submit a report which is circulated to other Syndicates for critical evaluation.

(g) Team leader of each Syndicate is required to present the view of his team on the task assigned to them at a joint session of all the groups.

The Syndicate methods has some merits:

- It secures a very high level of involvement from the participants.
- For the practising managers, their own experience is the starting point in the Syndicate method.
- The Syndicate method also gives the participant a practice in communicating with his colleagues and understanding them."

To conclude, Syndicate method involves a group of people who pool ideas, examine and share facts, test assumption, and draw conclusions, all of which contribute to improve job performance. It is a planned conference and, therefore, one major requirement is that all participants have the necessary background and knowledge to take an active and meaningful role in the conference.

Syndicate works like a management team of an organization, performing a specific task. The Syndicate method enables the participant to acquire a proper perspective on his job.

Reference

P.N. Singh, 'Training for Management Development', Suchandra Publications, Mumbai.

CHAPTER

7

Off-the-Job Training: Knowledge-Based Methods

Off-the-job training covers a number of techniques—classroom lectures, tutorials, conferences, penels, films and programmed instruction.

Lecture

Lecture is traditionally the most formal method of instruction and usually consists of verbal explanation or description of the subject matter with or without illustration. Usually during lectures the trainee is passive, listening and watching in silence without interruption. However, its advantages are:

(i) It can be used to give an overall view of the subject matter as introduction.

(ii) The presentation of new techniques and procedures of which the trainees can have no previous knowledge.

(iii) The stimulation of interest in a new direction, line of thought or development.

(iv) Teaching complex information which can be precisely worked out before hand even to the exact word.

The lecture method forms a quick measure for providing facts to a large number of individuals at a point in time. It may improve attitude but fail to develop skills. Lectures can be effective if they are planned and prepared in advance and the group is ready to listen. However, lectures are criticised for lack of participation on the part of trainees.

However, a group discussion after the lecture, the trainee can learn to express themselves and clarify ideas on the topic.

(ii) Tutorials

Tutorials are usually one-to-one or one-to-two-or-three at the maximum in trainer/trainee ratio. Tutorials are the final link in the lecture, group discussion when individual problems are ironed out as explained below:

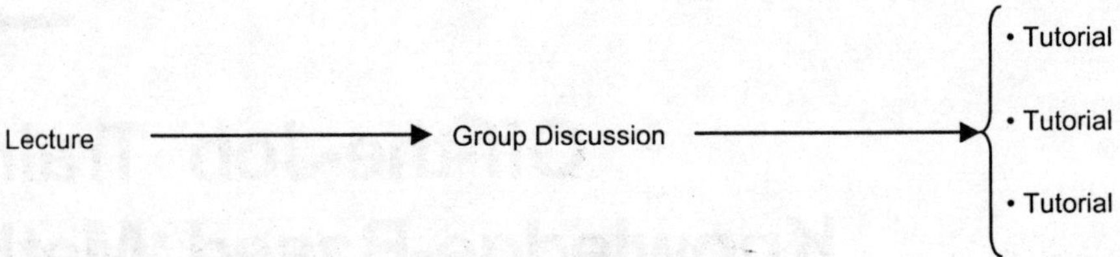

(iii) Conferences, Panels and Buzz Sessions

Conferences, projects, panels and "buzz sessions" involve group participation. Conference method is suitable for a group consisting of 12 to 25 members who are required to discuss and share a problem common to them. Although it provides little information, it may encourage analytical thinking. A conference may be of two types—guided and unguided. Both types of conferences necessitate the role of a leader and should not exceed two hours in duration. The conference provides a pooling of ideas to solve problems. The conference leader should encourage discussion, stimulate competition, enhance ego and reflect the feelings of participants. The conference method is used to help employees develop problem-solving skills. Group *discussions* and Meetings are the two common techniques often made use of in organizations. The chairman or the trainer leads discussion, involves trainees in attempting to solve problems and in arriving at decisions. The conference leader must have the necessary skill to lead the discussion in a meaningful way without losing sight of the topic or theme. The conference method or group discussion effects changes in the participants through modification of their experiences due to sharing and reshaping of their views, thinking and attitudes.

The Panel

The *panel* method provides a substitute for the conference method where the group is large. The efficacy of this method lies with the panel leader whose role consists in moderating, clarifying points, controlling, questioning and summarising the discussion.

Buzz Sessions

Buzz sessions involve a break-up of a conference group in several small group of four to five participants. Each small group discusses the problem and reports its views to the entire group subsequently. (R.S. Dwivedi)

(iv) Films

Motion pictures can be a useful training technique. They can provide information and explicitly demonstrate skills that are not easily presented by other techniques. Motion pictures are often used in conjunction with conference discussions to clarify and amplify those points that the film emphasized.

(v) Programmed Learning

A form of individual study, the programmed learning is more suited when non-motor skill or knowledge is to be learned by a large number of trainees. The trainer monitors trainees' independent progress through the programme. This method is governed by the principle of *positive reinforcement* developed by B.F. Skinner and allows the trainee to learn through a series of small steps in phases and at his own pace. Reinforcement, in simple terms, means rewarding a correct response and punishing a wrong response. Thus, one important feature of programmed instructions is that it provides immediate feedback of whether the participant has answered correctly or not. To facilitate this the instructions are designed in such a way that all future learning depends on acquisition and retention of previous learning. First, basic understanding is provided. Subsequently, questions are designed based on this basic learning. If the response is correct he goes to the next stage. If it is not, he is asked to go back and start again. The instructions are nothing but carefully planned sequential knowledge which moves from simple to complex levels. The major advantage of this method is that the trainee can adjust his learning at a pace and rate suitable to him. Today, a number of programmed books are available in such fields as Sciences, Statistics, and Computers. They preserve several advantages of face-to-face learning by use of printed pages and without the need of a tutor.

CHAPTER

8

Off-the-Job Training—Simulation Methods

In this chapter we have covered various simulation methods as under:

(a) Role Play,

(b) Case Study,

(c) Vestibule Training,

(d) Business Game/Management Game,

(e) Simulated Management Game (SMG),

(f) In-Basket Exercise, and

(g) Action Learning.

In this category real-work instances are taken for training to take place. Some of the examples (of methods) winch fall under this category are role playing, case method, management games, etc. Role playing is one method where action is involved. Learning takes place when individuals try to improve their job performance by actually doing something about the day-to-day job problems. A hypothetical or real situation is created where each person plays his or somebody else's role. Case method is another type where an actual situation is written for discussion. Each participant of the training programme is asked to read it and then discuss and analyse the situation. The purpose of the method is not to find one solution but many dealing with the situation, each of which is equally plausible given all the facts that are available in the case. This method provides the trainees practice in problem-solving and decision-making. Another type of training method under this category is management games which uses simulation of a business situation for learning. Here the trainees are divided into teams belonging to the management of competing organisations. After the simulation, operating and policy decisions are taken, and processed. Thereafter, the implications are fed back. These games are played in many rounds. There is yet another simulation method called in-basket method which is a simulation of manager's in-trays consisting of reports, mail or any type of item that comes to his in-tray. In the learning situation, the learner is required to read the item, analyse the problem and determine a course of action much in the same way as he would do in his work situation.

(A) ROLE PLAY

Meaning

Role Playing generally focuses on emotional (mainly human relations) issues rather than actual ones. The essence of role playing is to create a realistic situation, as in the case study and then have the trainees assume the parts of specific personalities in the situation. For example, a male worker may assume the role of a female supervisor, and the supervisor may assume the role of a male worker. Then both may be given a typical work situation and asked to respond as they expect others to do. The consequence is a better understanding among individuals. Role playing helps promote interpersonal relations. Attitude change is another result of role playing. Case study and role playing are used in management development programmes.

In this method the instructor assigns parts taken from case materials to group members. The situation is usually one involving conflicts between people. The role players attempt to act the part as they would behave in real life situation, working without a script or memorised lines and improvising as they play the parts.

Importance

(a) Learning is facilitated by active participation rather than passive listening of lecture.

(b) Attitudinal changes are effectively accomplished by placing persons in specified roles. It trains a person to be aware of, and sensitive to the feelings of others. This information serves as a feedback of the effect his behaviour has on other people. The development of empathy an sensitivity is one of the primary objectives of role playing. It has been shown in a number of experiments that the very act of arguing for another view, even if it is purely an exercise, exposes the person to some of its virtues which he had previously denied. Thus, a supervisor might play the role of a subordinate, a salesperson the role of a customer, and a nurse's aide the role of a hospital patient. It is learning through observations and feedback about their effectiveness and weakness.

(c) Each person is able to discover his own personal faults as to how often these hurt others.

(d) Role play permits training in the control of feelings and emotions.

Steps in Role Playing Process

According to Dr. P.N. Singh, it involves three phases as under:

(a) The Warm-up

To warm-up to get the trainees participate in a constructive manner with minimum anxiety and maximum motivation.

(b) The Enactment of Role

Before conducting the role play-enactment, the trainer should carry out the following: (a) Read general information. (b) Those who have volunteered to role play are given briefing sheets and sent out of the room with the instruction not to communicate amongst themselves. (c) The instructor should clarify all the doubts that Role Player might have. (d) Role players take their positions facing the class. (e) To begin the role play, the trainer sets the scene by restating the identity of the roles being enacted and making a brief statement about what has just happened.

(c) Post-enactment Discussion

Reaction to role play should be obtained first from the person who has the skill burden, then from other participants and finally from the audience.

Video tapes are often used to record role play situations and can be later shown back to the role players. It can be used by trainer to point out the trainee's mistakes later.

To conclude, Role playing is mainly useful for training in behavioral dimensions Careful designs to highlight trouble spots in participants' lives, role briefing of players, and allowing sufficient time after each play for its discussion are very important.

(B) CASE STUDY

A 'case' provides a decision-making situation. The student uses this "case" data to identify the problem, analysis, diagnose and solve it. Case method is excellent method for developing analytical skills.

A case is an objective description of a "real life" business situation in which executives take action and are responsible for results. Cases are designed to illustrate problem issues.

Case Study is a written description of an actual situation in business which provokes in the reader the need to decide what is going on, what the situation really is or what the problems are and what can and should be done.. Taken from the actual experiences of organisations, these cases represent attempts to describe as accurately as possible, real problems that managers have faced. Trainees study the cases to determine problems, analyse causes, develop alternative solutions, select the best one, and implement it? Case study can provide simulating discussions among participants, as well as excellent opportunities for individuals to defend their analytical and judgemental abilities. It appears to be an ideal method to promote decision-making abilities within the constraints of the limited data.

According to P.N. Singh, Analysis of case can be done in 4 stages:

(i) Define the Problem in the Case

Each case represents a real-life business situation. Buried in each case are a multitude of business and management problems. There may be more than one major problem presented, but each case problem should be explicitly placed in order of importance. Trainers should act as facilitators in such a way that students are able to clearly identify the problem. It may be advisable to group the problem into two categories : major and minor ones. However, the trainer should never identify the problems and then ask students to discuss.

(ii) Laying objectives for problem solution objectives should be explicit so that decisions and actions are achieved.

(iii) Identify Alternative Course of Action

Each alternative win have its strengths and weaknesses, and those should be made explicit. None will be 'perfect', but—by keeping the objectives an standards in mind—one or two approaches can be chosen. There is no "right" or "wrong" solution; the merits of a case analysis depend on the depth of analysis as well as the decision reached.

(iv) Taking Decision and a Plan Action

It is important the student's decision should be directed at the problem and A's examine consequences of the decision.

The teacher should stimulate discussion and not curb it. Faculty can intervene when absolutely necessary. Student should not be prejudiced which he may be unaware. Much of the work in analysing cases can be done by group discussion.

Case method improves student's skills in problem-solving, analysis and communication. There is nothing absolutely "right" or "wrong". Cases are powerful instruments for business education and it is increasingly being adopted.

It is relevant to quote here the views of Ishwar Dayal who emphasise that case method is very important for education in professional management. In my understanding, a "professional" programme should impart at least three things:

- Knowledge that is relevant to the profession, in this case it woud be *general management*.
- Application of this knowledge in (the diagnosis, analysis and intervention) *work situations*, where the above competencies are developed in laboratory-like situations under expert guidance.
- A set of *ethical principles* that the student must follow later in his job. Over the years, with more refinement, the case method was adopted by many leading B-schools the world over, particularly those supported by Harvard.

During a case discussion, the teacher's contribution lies in identifying cases relevant to all the modules that he or she wants to cover with students and then provide her own insights into the final resolution of the case. Sometimes, teachers also arrange supplementary reading material to facilitated discussion and some heated interaction.

An average student takes about two to three hours to prepare a "case". Then there is some class-room discussion, wherein other students also interact and are invited to present their opinions on the case. This is an important phase as it allows the first student to examine his position *vis-a-vis* other's positions. This also develops a team spirit in students and they are able to reconcile divergent positions to arrive at well thought-out final decisions on the case.

To conclude, in words of P.L. Rao, it is excellent means of promoting self-awareness, developing empathy towards other people's points of view and gaining knowledge by doing is the case study. It is a highly active method of training, with maximum involvement of all the senses and student interest is usually high, especially if the case history is based upon a series of actual events.

The real advantages of this case method are in attitude formation and change. It is extremely useful for illustrating important principles about business life, e.g. the possibility of several solutions to a problem and the consequent reduction of narrow-mindedness, the frustration of situations in which no one tells people what to do, and the advantages of integrating knowledge obtained from a number of foundation disciplines, etc.

(C) VESTIBULE TRAINING

Vestibule training utilises equipment which closely resemble the actual ones used on-the-job. However, training takes place away from the work environment.

A special area or room is set aside from the main production area and is equipped with furnishings similar to those found in the actual production area. The trainee is then permitted to learn under simulated conditions without disrupting ongoing operations. A primary advantage of vestibule training is that it relieves the employee from the pressure of having to produce while learning. The emphasis is on learning skills required by the job. Of course, the cost of duplicate facilities and special trainer is an obvious disadvantage. Vestibule training allows employees to get a full feel for doing tasks without "real-world" pressures it tends emphasise on learning rather than production. A vestibule school may be started when the training work exceeds the capacity of the line supervisors.

(D) BUSINESS GAME/MANAGEMENT GAME

Meaning

Business game is a training technique in which participants consider a sequence of problems and take decisions. It is a simulation which consists of a sequential decision-making exercise structured around a hypothetical model of an organisation's operations in which participants assume roles in managing the simulated operations. (P.N. Singh)

A management game has been described as a dynamic training exercise utilising a model of a business situation. In these games participants are divided into various teams which are placed in competition with each other in resolving some problems information about which is supplied to all teams. The game illustrates the value of analytic techniques such as the use of mathematical models to arrive at optimum solutions. (P.C. Tripathi)

Importance

Management games are commonly used in M.D. Programme. As a person learns more by doing something and also it is relevant to the situation in the business world. Managers fight for what is good for their respective departments and not for what is good for the organisation. Business games help in reducing such conflicts and lay emphasis for the growth and good of an organisation. So managers should take a systems approach of management rather than sectarian function-based approach. Other advantage of business games are that these are helpful unchanging attitudes. Such games are absorbing, and thus provoke interest of the participants.

Learning may be more effective. Business game may be functional game or for the total organisation results.

Conducting of Business Games

First step is to brief the group with instructions and clear their doubts. Faculty should give feedback to maintain tempo. He should explain results achieved. This will encourage competition. Manager's should be asked to take decisions within time schedule. The game should be closed when the learning objective has been achieved.

Role of the Faculty

Faculty must have complete understanding of the game and should clearly explain the game to participants. He should give feedback quickly. The game must be compared with real life sitautions. Business games is not to be taken as a game, but as a simulation of real life situations with the clear objective of learning.

To conclude, business game is a powerful tool and are good for emphasising the importance of long range planning. It should be more used in management development programmes.

(E) SIMULATED MANAGEMENT GAMES (SMG)

Dr. Vinod Dumblekar states that decision-making ability comes in the form of simulated management games (SMG). SMG is now becoming popular as a management training tool. The credit for popularising this training tool, goes to All India Management Association (AIMA) which has been organising annual national level competitions for corporates since 1992.

We reproduce here extracts from an article titled "Games Manager's Play", *Training and Management Journal*, New Delhi, January 2002.

(i) Training Process in SMG

(a) Participating teams are from the same or different organisations.

(b) The games administrator explains the objective/purpose of the game, apart from the rules of the game.

(c) May involve pre- and post-games measures to evaluate the level of understanding through the game.

(d) Maximum intervention from the administrator.

Behaviour Simulation Games

These focus primarily on the processes of interpersonal relations, on *how* decisions are made, and with what consequences, rather than on the substance of the decisions.

Games have set rules and predictable results. Often their design is hidden in order to highlight a behavioural process and to dramatize its effects.

The facilitator has a wide range of critical roles in simulation sessions. One moment he provides expertise, the next he is theory-builder and teacher: he organizes and manages the session and facilitates its process. Both process learning and cognitive learning can result from a good simulation session. The most common shortfalls occur in the processing or debriefing of participants after a game or exercise.

(ii) Purpose of SMG

SMG provides the vital link between theory and practice in a unique manner. A management simulation game provides a unique *learning opportunity* in two formats. In competition mode, it can be used for *testing and display of the business management skills* of participants. Competitions generate enormous friendly enthusiasm and the primal urge in participants to find new abilities within themselves.

In purely training mode, participants imbibe business concepts through the medium of *decision-making with strategic intent*. This forces them to recognise, understand and respond to business situations. In both the formats, it covers a plethora of concepts and problems—almost all the contents of a typical MBA course—in just two days. It ensures faster learning and long-lasting take away. Organisations find these Games to be cost effective and attuned to the real world.

(iii) Learning Involved in SMG

Since simulation games are interactive and *recreate the real-life business* scenario, they provide an interesting backdrop for participants to learn about various issues in management. They sensitise the participants to the nuances of *collective decision-making* across functional departments and to the process of *coordinated strategy* formulation in a competitive environment. Lack of control over men and material in real-life corporate settings can create frustration among lower and middle level executives and can adversely impact their confidence levels. Simulation games can avoid that by putting them in a boardroom simulator, "It not only expands, but *explodes your imagination and decision-making abilities,*" says Prof. Dumblekar. "Moreover, you can test your understanding of critical management concepts in real-life situations at virtually no cost," he adds.

According to Prof. N. Dhillon of MDI, who is presently engaged in developing an online version of the game with Dr. Balaji, "They also teach the participants to effectively read environmental cues, develop an overall strategy, understand nuances of relations between operational decisions, appreciate the *need of teamwork,* see *business as a whole.*"

Other skills that learns from these games include: new management methods, recognising opportunities and threats, perceiving competition, thinking and planning ahead, integrating your decisions with those of others, seeking consensual decisions, top-down enterprise view and business leadership approach.

(iv) Advantages of Simulation

A discoverer seldom forgets what and how he discovered something. The biggest advantage simulation management games provide is, you *learn by making mistakes*—something akin to a discovery. "And this is permanent learning," says Prof. Dumblekar.

Training by simulation games holds distinct advantage over conventional methods of learning like seminars, class-room lectures, project reports, etc. Firstly, since the evaluation is done by the computer—purely on the basis of data that is punched in by the competitors themselves—there is *no subjectivity* or 'human element'—something that often creeps in project evaluation. Secondly, "this is an entire two-year MBA packed in two days," says the professor since it tests all your theoretical concepts in real-life situations with real competitors.

(v) Futuristic Scope of SMG

According to Dr. V. Damblekar, "In the distant future we would need to capture intangible problems such as corruption, ethics and politics, and tailor such games for senior executives. There is rich scope in issue-specific games covering topics such as Corporate Government or Business Process Re-engineering, Mergers and Acquisitions and several other areas."

In fact, SMG provide a vital link between theory and practice in a unique manner.

(F) IN-BASKET EXERCISE

The in-basket is a simulation of a manager's workload on a typical day. The name is derived from the famous IN and OUT trays found on the table of an executive.

(a) *In-Basket*: In-Basket or In-Tray technique involves simulation of a series of decisions a trainee might have to make in real life. The manager presented with pack of papers and files in a tray containing administrative problems and are asked to take decisions within specified time limit. The decisions taken by several managers are recorded and compared with one another. Learning occurs as trainees reflect and evaluate the decisions taken on priorities, customer's complaint, superior's demand, irrelevant information and the like. Usually feedback is provided so that manager can appraise his results.

(b) The limitation on time is the most important fact of the whole exercise as it simulates the real life situation, where a manager is always expected to take a timely action. This stress on time introduces realism and stress in the situation. In order to complete the assignment in time, the player is forced to:

(i) set priorities; and

(ii) delegate some of the work to his subordinates.

(c) The participant's role does not end with merely suggesting solutions. He has to take action as has to be done by a manager in the real life. He has to write notes and memos to complete the exercise.

(d) The In-Basket game also includes a procedure which allows players to explain their actions.

Benefits

(i) The biggest advantage of this method is that it is rooted in the real life situation of the corporate world.

(ii) It effectively enhances skills in decision-making and problem-solving.

(iii) The In-Basket exercise can be designed to focus on the activities that are part of all managerial positions. It can also be designed to emphasise certain specific aspects of performance. For example, if the objective is to enhance human relations skills, the In-basket material can be loaded heavily with inter-personal conflict situations, materials related to other areas being kept to the minimum.

(iv) This method has been found particularly advantageous in assessing specific dimensions like Written Communication Skills, Sensitivity, Risk Taking, Initiative, Planning and Organising, Management Control, Use of Delegation, Problem Analysis and Decision-making. The In-Basket exercises have been used very widely by Assessment Centres. These centres uses primarily to select people from within for higher positions. It leads to high involvement.

(G) ACTION LEARNING

Action Research or Action Learning involves three processes: A change process based on systematic collection of data, feedback of data to the client group and selection of a change action based on what the analysed data indicate. The employees and groups that are involved become a source of pressure to bring about the change. It is problem focussed.

In action research, change agent is usually an outside person who is involved in the total change process from diagnosis to evaluation. The process action research consists of five steps: analysis, feedback, actions, to correct the problem that are identified and evaluation.

Action-learning or Action Research is another simulation method where relationship is established between learning and doing. In action learning programme, this aspect is given importance. In this method, managers of one organisation go to another organisation to tackle the problems identified in the adapted organisation and to implement the solution. In India, the Bureau of Public Enterprises (BPE) introduced this method in some public enterprises like oil companies, aircraft manufacturing companies, fertiliser companies, BHEL, etc. (Bakshi, 1979). Over 82 such companies have introduced this programme with some degree of success.

Action learning is based on the fact that manager (fellow) learns while diagnosing the problem, reviewing it, and then actually implementing the solutions. The concept of action learning was developed by Prof. R.W. Rewans.

Action Research as an Intervention to Organisation Change

In tackling OD problems, OD change agent adopts action research perspectives. Indeed action research model originated in OD. Action research is a data-based problem-solving model that replicates the steps involved in the scientific method of inquiry (French and Bell, 1991: 98). The action research mode basically involves a systematic process of diagnosing problems through data collection and analysis, feeding the data back to members of the management team, discussing and findings, planning collaborative action and implementing proposed solutions. It is basically problem focused, action-oriented, cyclical (leads to change as well generation of knowledge) collaborative and experimental. It improves learning of action researcher and builds capabilities to tackle future problems. This action research process is explained in Fig. 8.1.

FIG. 8.1

The Process of Action Research

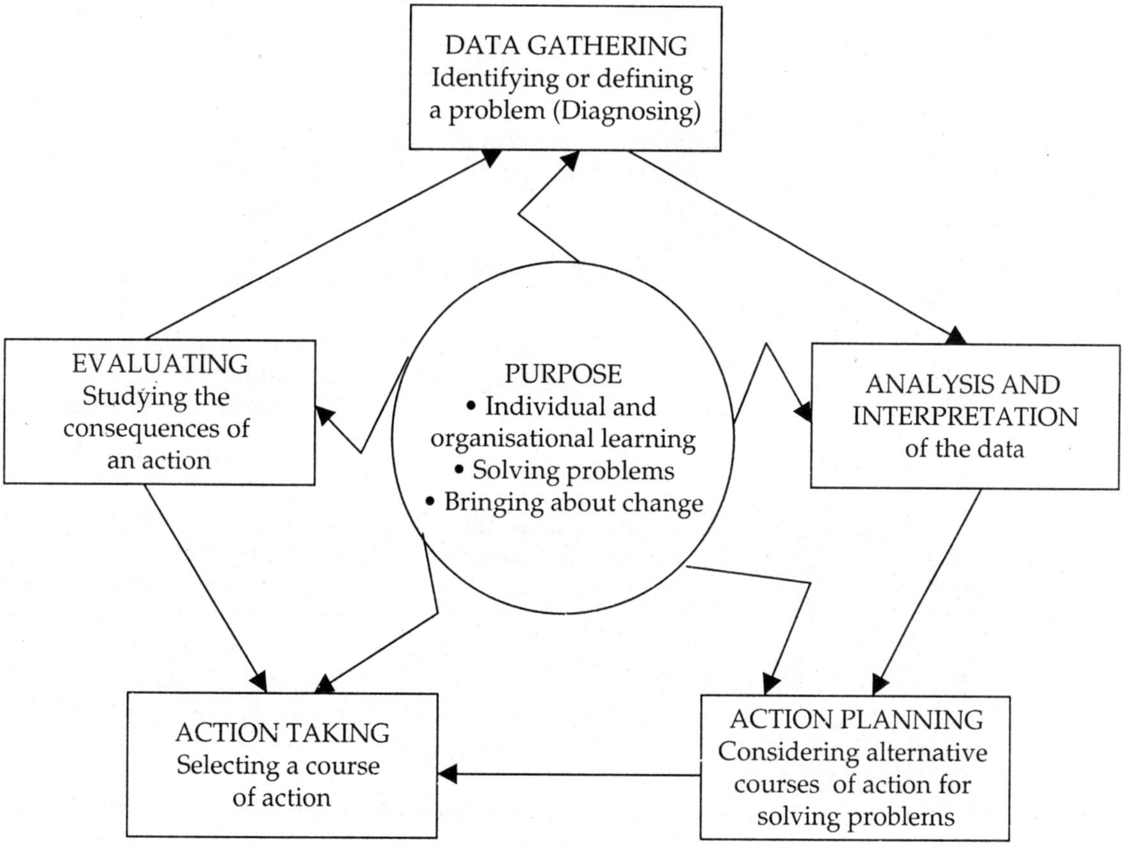

Source: Adapted from Susman and Evered (1978) by E. Sendil Kumar and S. Ramnarayan.

Action research is used to actually solve the problems faced by the organisation. Action research involves not only participation but also attempts to tap the competencies of the employees. This serves dual purpose of contributing to successful change efforts and also fulfils employees needs for greater involvement.

We can *compare* pure research and action research in terms of focus in different aspects as in Fig. 8.2.

FIG. 8.2

Comparison of Pure Research and Action Research

Stage	*Pure Research*	*Action Research*
1. Initial focus	Research starts with theory or hypothesis to be tested.	Some practical problem arises and focus on how to solve it.
2. Initiation	By reacher.	Organisation first realises it has problem and then initiates investigation.
3. Methodology	Designing an experiment and collect data, precisely to plan. Experiment is completed before data is analysed.	It proceeds with series of steps: ❑ Diagnosis ❑ Analysis of data ❑ Recommendations for action ❑ Acton taking ❑ Evaluation ❑ If necessary, rediagnosis. There is no rigid plan.
4. Results	Done for publication and read by scientists.	❑ The audience is practitioner. ❑ Publication in co. report or a case study. ❑ Findings shared with the participants.

REFERENCES

P.N. Singh, Training for Management Development, Suchandra Publication, Mumbai.

R.N. Tripathi, Human Resource Development.

Robert L. Craing, Training and Development Handbook, A Guide to Human Resource Development.

Ishwar Dayal, Case Method, *Hindustan Times*, Careers, 19.11.2003.

P.L. Rao, "Choosing the Right Method", HRD Through in-House Training.

CHAPTER

9

Off-the-Job Training—Experiential Methods

Following methods are covered under experimental group:

(i) Sensitivity Training,
(ii) Transactional Analysis,
(iii) Fish-Bowl Exercise,
(iv) Johari Window,
(v) Counselling,
(vi) Empowering,
(vii) Interviewing,
(viii) Self-development, and
(ix) Out-Bound Learning.

(I) SENSITIVITY TRAINING

Sensitivity training uses small number of trainee, usually fewer than 12 in a group. They meet with a passive trainer and gain insight into their own and others' behaviour. Meetings have no agenda, are held away from workplaces and questions deal with the "here and now" of the group process. Discussions focus on "why participants behave as they do, how they perceive one an other, and the feelings and emotions generated in the interaction process." Sensitivity training is a group training method that uses intensive participation and immediate feedback for self-analysis and change. In this participants remain involved and enthusiastic participants have to make positive efforts to learn out this experience.

The objectives of sensitivity training are to provide the participants with increased awareness of their own behaviour and how others perceive them; greater sensitivity to the behaviour of others, and increased understanding of group processes. Specific results sought include increased ability to empathise with others, improved listening skills, greater openness, increased tolerance of individual differences and increased conflict resolution skills. The drawback of this method is that once the training is over the participants are themselves again and they resort to their old habits.

Sensitivity training can go by a variety of names—laboratory training, encounter groups, or T-group (training groups).

(II) TRANSACTIONAL ANALYSIS

It introduced over two decades ago by Berne and further popularised by Hanris and Jongewald, Transactional Analysis (TA) provides an individual with a practical and useful method for analysing and understanding human behaviour. In fact, it is a method of analysing a transaction. A transaction is nothing but a social interaction between two more people who encounter each other. In every social interaction, there is a *stimulus* provided by one individual and a *response* to that stimulus given by another individual. This stimulus-response relationship between two individuals is a transaction.

Analysis of any transaction can be done by analysing the ego states of an individual. Berne says that every normal individual functions from three ego states—parent, adult and child. An ego state is a system of feelings accompanied by a related set of behaviour patterns. Each ego state can be described as under:

Parent

The parent ego is nothing but a huge collection of recordings in the brain of an individual of attitudes and behaviours imposed on him in his early years (roughly first five years) from various external sources, primarily his parents. The characteristics of this ego are to be over-protective, officious, distant, dogmatic, etc. Verbal clues that a person is operating from the parent ego state are his use of such words as 'always', 'never', 'should', 'ought', etc., when he uses language of threat or tries to resolve conflict by force. There are physical clues also like raised eyebrows, pointing an accusing finger at somebody, and so on.

Child

The child ego is also a collection of recordings in the brain of an individual of attitudes, behaviours and impulses which come to him naturally from his own seeing, hearing, feeling and understanding as a child. Characteristics of a person acting in the child state include being curious, impulsive, sensuous, affectionate, dependent, fearful and depressed. Verbal clues that the person is operating from the child ego state are the use of words like "I wish", "I guess", "I do not care" and so on. There are physical clues also like temper tantrums, attention seeking, giggling, coyness, silent compliance, etc. The child in us is likely to lead us to behave as dependents, as competitive and to approach conflict resolution through avoidance or smoothing.

Adult

This ego state consists of reality testing, rational behaviour and decision-making or problem-solving analysis. An individual in this state processes, verifies and updates the data which he has received from the other two states. In other words, this state is a shift from the "taught and felt concepts" to "tested concepts". Adult data is gathered as a result of an individual's ability to find out for himself as to what is the difference between life as it was taught and demonstrated to him (parent), life as he felt, wished or fantasied (child) and life as he figures out by testing (adult).

The functioning of the adult-ego state does not try to do away with parent and child data. Rather it examines these data and tries to update them in the reality of the external world. The adult in an individual shows itself in a variety of ways. Phrases like "I see", "I think", "It is my opinion", words with an emphasis on data collection, e.g., why, where, when, who, how, what, and an emphasis on data processing and problem-solving are the indicators of the adult-ego state in an individual.

All of us evoke behaviour from one ego state which is responded to by the other individual from any one of these three states. This gives rise to three types of transactions: complementary, crossed and ulterior.

A *complimentary transaction* is one in which the stimulus and response ego states are complementary to each other so that the communication between any two individuals runs along parallel lines between them (Fig. 9.1). Thus, the parent in one individual is responded to by the child in the other or the adult in one is responded to by the adult in the other. In this type of transaction both parties feel satisfied.

FIG. 9.1

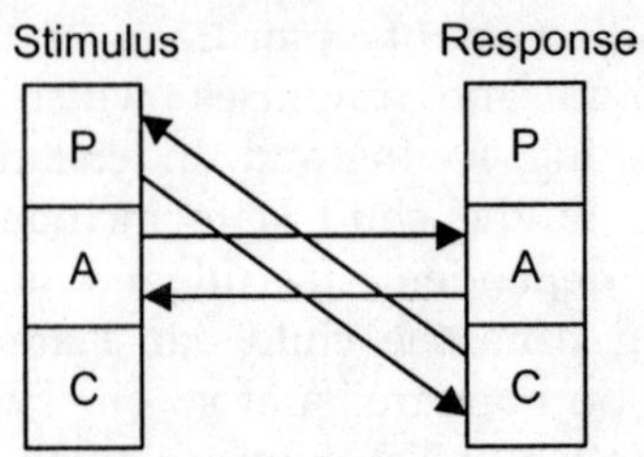

Example:

(a) Employee: I cannot do this job myself. Please help me. Will You? (Child-Parent)

Supervisor: Sure, I am coming just now. (Parent-Child)

(b) Supervisor: Have you finished the job? (Adult-Child)

Employee: Yes, I finished it long back and it has already been delivered to the assembly line (Adult-Adult)

When communication runs along *crossed lines* between individuals, the transactions are *crossed*. In this communication further transactions stop.

Example:

Supervisor to Employee: How many pieces have you made by now ? (A-A)

Employee to Supervisor: Do not disturb me. When I complete the whole work I will let you know. (P-C)

Ulterior transaction has double meaning. On the surface level it is a clear adult message but it also carries a hidden message. For example, husband while sitting on the dining table may find the table dirty. If he writes on the table "I Love You" to be read by his wife he is of the surface using his adult ego state but his ulterior motive is to hint her that she has not cleaned the table. In other words, his message is proceeding from the parent state and his wife must respond to it from her adult state by cleaning the table.

Thus, TA gives an insight into the fundamentals of human psychology and helps to improve interpersonal relations.

Task of the Trainer

The primary task of the trainer is to interpret group behaviour in terms of ego states in which the participants are operating in the 'here and now' situation.

The trainer must as far as possible operate from an adult state and not get personally involved in transactions between participants.

Finally, the trainer must have a specialist's knowledge of the theory and practice of T.A. which must be clarified before he starts interpreting behaviour.

(III) THE FISH-BOWL EXERCISE

The fish-bowl exercise is yet another experiential method of training involving the active participation of trainees to enhance their learning experience. It is essentially used in providing skills in understanding human behaviour. It effectively uses group interaction to develop in the participants a degree of self-awareness.

Objectives of the Fish-Bowl Exercise

1. To inculcate in the participants the discipline of observing others and on the basis of this, provide objective and constructive feed-back.
2. To learn about oneself, one's behaviour and personality as seen through the eyes of others and consequently to overcome weaknesses and improve upon strengths.

The aspects to which the fish-bowl exercise can be put to effective use are: individual and group behaviour, content of communication, roles individuals play in groups, inter-group conflicts, level of participation, dynamics of group problem-solving and decision-making and, inter-personal relations.

Method of Conducting the Exercise

The exercise can involve upto 25 participants seated in two concentric circles (one inner, the other outer). The inner circle is the target group, members of this group will either discuss a pre-selected topic or move towards completion of a group task. After the discussion by the members of the inner group, which may extend upto half-an-hour, the outer group is asked to comment on the content and more importantly the dynamics and group process of the inner group members. The trainer in this case shall only act as a facilitator and guide the participants and the processes towards constructive results.

Feedback may be provided using either of the two basic techniques mentioned below:

- Each member of the outer group observes all members of the inner group on all aspects of group dynamics.
- Each member of the outer group observes all members of the inner group on a specific dimension of group process.

Participants must learn to provide feedback with clarity and precision.

(IV) THE JOHARI WINDOWS

The Johari Window is a conceptual model for increasing personal effectiveness. It was developed by Joseph Luft and Harry Ingham (the name Johari combines their first names). As shown in the following Fig. 9.2 this model divides an individual's personality into 4 parts. That part which is known both to the individual and to others is called 'Arena' That part which is known to others, but not to the individual is called 'Blind'. Thai part which is known to the individuals but not known to others is called 'Closed'. And that part which is not known both to the individual and to others is called 'Dark'.

FIG. 9.2

	Known to self	*Not known to self*
Known to others	Arena (e.g. name, age, family, job, physical appearance, etc.)	Blind (e.g. certain mannerisms about which the individual does not know but others know)
Not known to others	Closed (e.g. an individual may hide his anger and not let others know about this)	Dark

The implication of this model is that in order to make oneself effective in interpersonal relations one should expand one's arena. Alternatively, one must try to reduce the other three areas. 'Blind' can be reduced by receiving feedback from others. 'Closed' area can be reduced by self-disclosure. Nothing much can be done about the dark area. It can be reduced by special psycho-analysis techniques only.

Points to be Remembered at the Time of Giving Feedback

(a) Feedback should be descriptive and not evaluative. Thus, instead of saying "You are not a good speaker" say "In the last 10 minutes you have repeated the same statement four times".

(b) Feedback should be data-based and specific and not general based on mere impressions. Thus, instead of saying a person, "You are in the habit of interrupting others" say "You have interrupted A, B and C". Recent examples of behaviour are better than old ones because they are more vividly recallable.

(c) Feedback should first be checked for its correctness with the perceptions of other persons in the group.

(d) Feedback should be well-timed. This means two things. First, it should be immediate. Second, it should not be given in a circumstance where it is likely to be perceived as an attack or criticism. It should be given in private.

(e) Feedback should include only those things which the receiver might be expected to do something about. There is obviously no point in calling such defects to the receiver's notice which he cannot improve upon, e.g., physical impediments.

(f) Feedback should not be more than what the receiver can handle at any particular time.

Points to be Remembered at the time of Receiving Feedback

Negative feedback should be patiently owned and examined by the receiver rather than met with some form of defensive behaviour.

Some forms of *defensive behaviour* commonly used by the feedback receiver are as follows:

- Quickly accepting or denying the negative feedback.
- Quickly finding reasons or justification for some behaviour (rationalisation).
- Projecting one's own resentment to the feedback giver.
- Expressing anger for getting negative feedback on some weaker person (displacement).
- Cutting interaction with the feedback giver (withdrawal).
- Showing aggression toward the feedback giver.
- Being humorous.
- Competing with the feedback giver by proposing alternate theories and other ways of interpretation of his behaviour.
- Pairing with other persons who have also been given similar negative feedbacks.
- Brushing aside the feedback with a cynical attitude.

(V) SELF-DEVELOPMENT

To an increasing degree, people are *turning towards self-analysis* not because they suffer from depressions, phobias or comparable disorders but because they feel they can't cope with life. Or they may feel that factors within themselves are holding them back or injuring their relationships with others."

These lines were written by Karen Horney about 50 years ago and are applicable even today. For instance, in the current business environment, people are spending a great deal of time, effort, energy and money in developing/sharpening their personality/skills. Personality development and grooming are the current buzzwords. Scores of institutes have mushroomed in the market purporting to teach how to speak better English and attain leadership qualities in order to build a dynamic personality. In this context, it is important to understand that all development and learning can be achieved through systematic and concentrated efforts.

(i) The *desire to learn* must come from the core of a person. The challenge is to create a *desire to learn* and then utilise this desire to create a sense of action in the individual.

(ii) We strongly believe that *good managers are made* and not born. They are fashioned by business experience and the realities of the workplace. They grow in stature and managerial skill largely from their *encounters with people and problems*, and not from merely studying the notes and theories catalogued in textbooks.

(iii) We learn, grow and develop by way of observing, practising, thinking, re-thinking, experimenting and continually questioning the self. Worthwhile answers emerge from the heat of the action, by *dealing with the* course of real business events as well as the problems and personalities of those involved in them.

(iv) So an effective development of an individual is a combination of exposure to *theory and action-oriented* business situations. Theory creates conceptual clarity awareness and knowledge and practical experience provides application orientation, confidence and maturity in dealing with complex situations.

(v) We would recommend that an effective *course on personality development*/business communication (written and oral) is a must for every executive/manager or even today's businessman. A good course revolves around:

(a) *Behavioural training*, for example self-awareness, assertiveness, positive thinking and a positive mindset.

(b) *Technical training* revolves around writing, reading, listening and speaking.

(c) General-grooming revolves round giving respect, correct mannerisms and dress sense, personal hygiene and personal habits.

These inputs, if imparted and acquired in a systematic manner, will definitely facilitate an individual in improving his outlook and managing his self in a professional, ethical and mature manner.

(VI) OUTBOUND LEARNING PROGRAMMES

All learning is action-based (experience) an outdoor-based training programme provides the team with powerful and tangible outcome on interpersonal and intrapersonal levels. The key benefits are better self-concept, confidence, an understanding about leadership, team working and willingness to take risks, stress handling, creativity, negotiating, communication, problem-solving, decision-making, trust-building.

Reasons of Outbound Learning Programmes

An outbound experience provides a huge opportunity to simulate real life situations. Naturally, reflecting on such experiences can offer deep understanding of self and team issues. "When experienced facilitators observe behavioural nuances of participants and provide the right kind of feedback, it creates insights for the group, making them powerful learning experiences", explains V.J. Rao, group vice president, learning, Tata Management Training Center. The use of role plays and simulation exercises is common in classroom training. Outbound learning ia about 'real-playing' not 'role playing'. Outbound programmes work on the principle that when a team is thrown together in wilderness, where they have to find for themselves and meet challenges together, there is growth in many directions. Some experiences could be adventure sports—night trails, rock climbing, river crossing, treasure hunting, rafting. Participants go along with articles such as ropes, toy guns, compasses and walkie-talkies, etc.

Concept of Outbound Learning

- People generally have more resources and are more capable than they think they are.
- A small heterogeneous group is capable of coping with significant physical and mental challeges.
- Learning is more successful when problems are presented rather than solutions or methodologies.
- Stress and shared adventure serve as important catalysts in the discovery process.

- The single most important factor that determines a person's future is his idea of self.
- Significant, long-lasting learning can be achieved through an intensive, short-term experience.

Source: Wildertrails Adventure Club.

When outbound programmes are well planned and perfectly executed is perceived as a serious learning initiative. The success of the outbound programme is measured by its relevance back in the workplace and whether the learnings are actionable. Retention of learnings is longer and it gets internalised much faster.

Phillips Software Centre has actively employed outward bound learning as an intervention to impart organizational culture and values in the teams across the organization. The exercises are designed in such away that the participants are able to understand the values better and reflect on how they have been demonstrating it in the workplace. Says Ramakrishna:

> "The leadership has ensure that when the participants return, things don't slip back. Care should be done to do this while the enthusiasm is still there, the fires burning and the learning fresh."
> "The team leader plays an important role in reviewing the learning. He must demonstrate commitment by showing appreciation when members exhibit right behaviours as well as alert the team of deviations."

References

Berne E., Transactional Analysis—A New and Effective Method of Group Theory, *American Journal of Psychotherapy*, 1958.

Harris, T.A., I am OK, You are OK: A Practical Guide to Transactional Analysis, New York: Harper & Row, 1967.

James, H. and Jongewald, D., Born to Win, Reading, Mass: Addison Wesley Publishing Company.

P.C. Tripathi, HRD, Sultan Chand & Sons, New Delhi.

Rakesh Seth, *H. Times Careers*, Jan. 2004.

Human Capital, October 2003, New Delhi.

CHAPTER

10

Training Methods, Training Climate and Training Techniques Checklist

We present here formal training alternatives which are cost effective ways to improve performance.

(a) Using Experienced Employees for "day-to-day" Training

Many managers value allowing highly skilled workers to share their knowledge. To make sure these human resources are tapped, implement any of the following programmes:

(i) Create Informal Support Teams

Assign groups of two, three, or four, each containing an experienced worker. (Size of group assignments will depend on the number of highly skilled employees available.) Arrange:

- Weekly troubleshooting meetings.
- Biweekly brainstorm sessions.
- One-on-one skill training sessions.
- Pre-arranged Q and A time over the phone.

(ii) Organize "Development Meetings"

Schedule large or small meetings containing a mix of employees from the same division or department, or who do similar jobs. Before the meeting, tell experienced employees to think of "lessons they learned the hard way", or shortcuts, organizing systems, planning techniques, etc. they use to help them do their job well. Be prepared to facilitate a discussion that will subtly draw out this information for more inexperienced employees to hear and apply.

(iii) Show and tell using new product samples or products.

(b) Creative Alternatives to Formal Training

(i) Using cassette programme or home study and discussion for performance improvements.

(ii) Taking advantage of professional societies may offer a variety of inexpensive development opportunities including:

- Luncheon speakers
- Self-study materials
- Brief training sessions on current topics
- Special events.

(iii) Field trip to companies and expose students to students to situations.

(iv) Audio-vedio representations by business executives to relate their experiences.

(v) Inviting guest speakers to classroom as to make contact with business professionals.

(vi) Another innovative method is holding faires for solving company problems.

(vii) Summer projects in industry bring students to working world and business environment.

(viii) Class projects—when students' team can work on problem-solving situations with a company in which they identify research problem.

(c) Modular Programmes for Development

ILO has designed a modular programme for supervisory development. The programme provides training content and material for supervisory functions and skills for the trainers. Trainer can compile his own training programme to meet the needs of supervisors in the organisation.

(d) Walk about

This is an innovation in training, i.e. "Walk about" introduced by Asian Institute of Management, Manila. Prof. M. Gibbons intended walk about for MBA students so that they get a chance to design and implement a managerial learning into experience, i.e. "involve doing something and not just studying about it."

(e) Debates

Debates to develop oral communication skill and ability to reason. Students can be assigned in teams and represent different view points.

(f) Summarising

Students can summarise and analyse articles relating to particular aspect of study and make presentations.

(g) GRID Seminars

Grid Seminars developed by the famous duo Drs. Robert Blake and Jane Mouton have become very popular all over the world. The objectives of the Seminar are as follows:

(i) understand the Grid styles of supervision;

(ii) experience productive 9, 9 teamwork;

(iii) develop skills of solving problems with subordinates;

(iv) clarify personal values and convictions about effective supervision;

(v) perfect your skills in using the Grid approach for solving problems of supervision; and

(vi) increase personal motivation to do the best possible job of being effective.

Training Climate is Important

Climate, ambience, tone—whichever the word, the phenomenon it labels is pervasive. Also, it tends to perpetuate itself, carrying the quality of the relationships forward in the programme. One trainer sets a task. The group accepts it eagerly, perhaps as a challenge, and works hard. Another trainer sets the same task. The group resist it. When the climate is favourable, nothing goes wrong in the programme, when the climate is sullen, it is almost impossible to do anything right.

Fig. 10.1

Favourable Training Climate: Roots and Effects

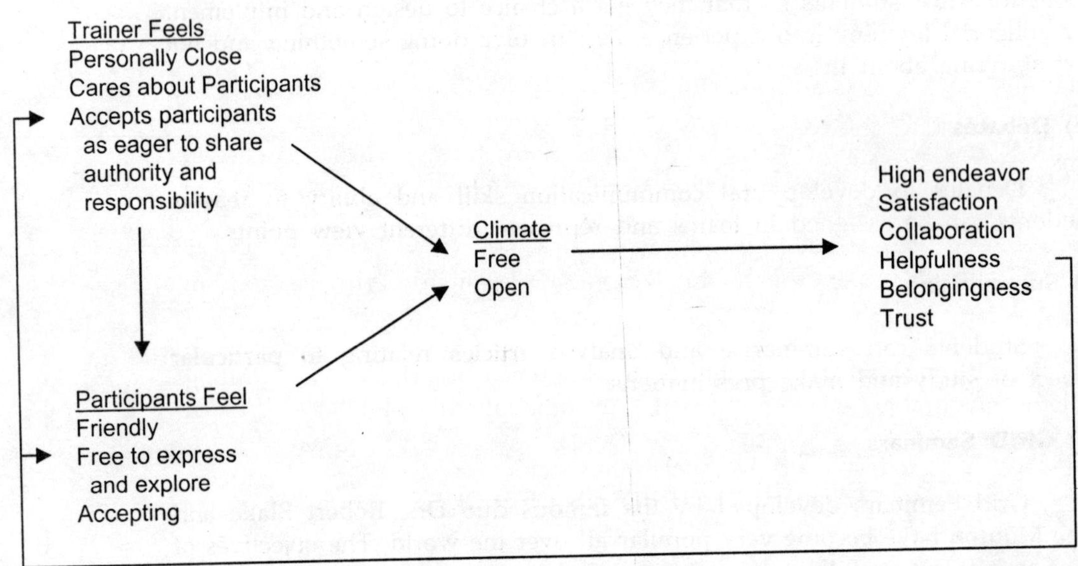

Fig. 10.2

Unfavourable Training Climate: Roots and Effects

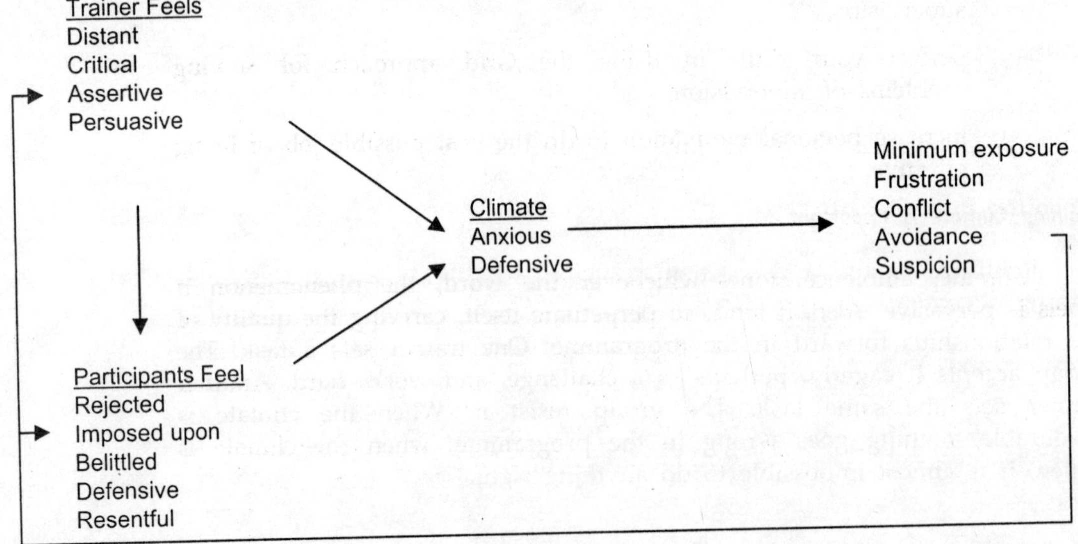

A favourable climate develops when a trainer moves close to participants as a person, cares about their needs and difficulties, accepts them as valued people, and is eager to share the tasks of constructing and running the best possible programme. Participants respond to this with friendly feelings, feel free to express themselves openly and to explore new directions, and accept difficulties and errors as unintended. These shared feelings of freedom, closeness, and enthusiasm characterize the climate favourable to learning and lead readily to high endeavor and satisfaction, eagerness to collaborate, sensitive and perceptive giving of help, greater openness and sense of belonging together. These feelings are then carried forward. This scheme can be summarized in a flow diagram, as presented in Fig. 10.1.

A climate unfavourable to learning is similarly summarized in Fig. 10.2.

It is easy to see that an unfavourable climate interferes with training while a favourable one facilitates it. An unfavourable climate is full of interferences, static.

TRAINING TECHNIQUES CHECKLIST

We can use training techniques checklist at least 4 to 5 different techniques in every session, to keep things lively.

Ice Breaker

A quick way to help everyone get acquainted; establishes a precedent for participation and discussion; establishes rapport; sets positive expectations.

Lecture

Shares a lot of information in a brief period; builds a foundation for later application; defines and outlines key concepts.

Handouts; Printed Materials

Reinforce lecture and discussion; help pace the programme; extend learning beyond the classroom.

Question and Answer

Clarifies and amplifies lecture material; encourages participation; allows learners to be self-directed; stimulates thinking.

Group Discussion

Uses the learner as a resource; lets participants get acquainted; develops a sense of group identity; elicits questions.

Group Problem-solving

Lets learners utilize what they know; establishes a sense of purpose; builds a team atmosphere; creates an emotional investment in the outcome they create.

Paired Discussion

Uses the learner as a resource; builds trust between participants; allows for more disclosure and individual involvement; great when time is limited.

Warm-ups

Quick to facilitate; fun and light-hearted; prepare learners for involvement in a specific learning activity; often point out the need for learning the subject matter.

Self-report Instruments

Let the learner self-evaluate privately; build self-assessment and self-monitoring skills; offer a referral tool for checking awareness.

Case Studies

Give participants a chance for in-depth exploration and application of a concept; encourage problem-solving.

Role Playing

Offers a safe environment for learning new skills, places, group members at an even level; forces participants to understand concepts and techniques presented.

Demonstration

Shows and tells; lays the foundation for skill development, generates questions; presents an overview.

Energizers

Offer a brief diversion; create a physical relief value for the body and mind; great for recharging the groups energy level.

Recorded Report Outs

Recorded information on a flip chart sheet or overhead conserve as a resource; participants have a chance to learnt from everyone.

Simulations

Offer participants a chance to generalize personal behaviour in real-life situations; encourage individual involvement.

Closure Activity

Summarizes and sets the stage for action; sets expectations on-the-job application; facilitates the transfer process; makes learners responsible for using what they've learned.

These four questions help us decide which training techniques to use:

- Who is our audience?
- What is our purpose?
- How much time do we have?
- Which approach will best meet our needs?

Reference

Developing the Group and Climate, Training for Development, USA.

CHAPTER

11

Evaluation of Training

The last stage in the training and development process is the evaluation of results of training. Since huge sums of money are spent on training and development, how far the programme has been useful must be judged.

We shall cover in this chapter as under:

1. Need for evaluation of training.
2. Principles of evaluation.
3. Criteria for evaluation.
4. Techniques of evaluation.

I. NEED FOR EVALUATION OF TRAINING

(a) The main objective of evaluating the training programmes is to determine if they are accomplishing specific training objectives, that is, correcting performance deficiencies.

(b) A second reason of evaluation is to ensure that any changes in trainee capability are due to the training programme and not due to any other conditions. Training programmes should be evaluated to determine their lost effectiveness.

(c) Evaluation is useful to explain programme failure, should it occur.

(d) Credibility of training and development is greatly enhanced when it is proved that the organisation has benefited tangibly from it.

(e) Finally, Evaluation is critical not for assessing quality of training, but also to see that future changes in training plan should be made to make it more effective, and achieve goals of the organisation.

2. PRINCIPLES OF EVALUATION

Evaluation of the training programme must be based on the following principles:

(i) Training faculty must be clear about the goals and purposes of evaluation.

(ii) Evaluation must be continuous.

(iii) Evaluation must be specific.

(iv) Evaluation must provide the means and focus for trainers to be able to appraise themselves, their practices, and their products.

(v) Evaluation must be based on objective (quantitative) methods and standards.

(vi) Realistic target dates must be set for each phase of the evaluation process.

(vii) Evaluation must be cost effective.

3. CRITERIA FOR EVALUATION

HR professionals should try to collect four types of data while evaluating training programmes: measures of reactions, learning, behaviour change, and organisational results:

(a) Reaction measures reveal trainees' opinions regarding the training programme.

(b) Learning measures assess the degree to which trainees have mastered the concepts, knowledge and skills of the training.

(c) Behaviour indicates the performance of learners.

(d) The purpose of collecting organisational results is to examine the impact of training on the work group or the entire company. (K. Awasthappa)

(4) TECHNIQUES OF EVALUATION OF TRAINING

The evaluation can take place at various level as under:

4.1. First techniques intended to measure *changes in individual* levels of:

(a) Knowledge,

(b) Skills, and

(c) Attitude

4.2. Next, criteria for evaluating increase in *effectiveness* at the *individual, team* and the *organisation level.*

4.3. Finally, some aspects of comparing the *cost of training and outcomes*.

These several techniques are being used by organisation. These can be grouped as under:

4.1. Techniques to Measure Changes in Individual Levels

(1a) Measuring Changes in Knowledge

(i) Open ended questions, e.g. essay type.

(ii) Short answer, e.g. define, calculate, describe.

(iii) Objective test items, e.g. select the correct alternative.

(iv) Multi-choice questions.

(v) Gain ratio. There are some situations where it is worthwhile to pre-test as well as post-test knowledge. Gain ratio will be an estimate of the effectiveness of the programme.

(1b) Measure of Skills

(a) Inspection at the end of test final product.

(b) Stage test and also test of final product.

(c) Profiling skills at various levels such as—semi-skilled, skilled, highly skilled.

(d) At assessment centre 1st and 2nd time. The effectiveness of the programme can be assessed after second attendance at the assessment centre.

(1c) Evaluation of Attitude and Behaviour

An attitude is a tendency or a pre-disposition to behave in certain ways in particular sitautions. Attitudes cannot be measured directly, but are inferred from the things people say or are seen to do so. Changing some-one's attitude to something may well change what they say or do. But this will depend upon particular situation also. Some techniques are:

(i) Reaction of trainee to the programme at the end.

(ii) Learning reviews, i.e. what they have learned at the end of the day or what they particularly useful?

(iii) Behaviour analysis of trainees during training programme may be an important indicator of the effectiveness of the training.

(iv) End-of-event questionnaires for feedback.

(v) Noticing change in attitude by asking questions (before and after the programme).

(vi) Semantic—differentials before and after the programme on a topic on seven point scale.

(vii) Repertory grid—asking each participant what their concept is of good interpersonal skills, etc.

(viii) Behaviour scales in pre- and post-training appraisal format.

4.2. Criteria for Evaluation of Effectiveness

Criteria for evaluation can be individual, team and organisation levels:

(a) Individual Change in Effectiveness

(i) Improvement *in skill* (productivity) reflected in performance appraisal after training.

(ii) Higher *self-efficiency* (self-perception and confidence) score before and after the training.

(iii) Goal setting and action planning during training for transfer of learning back to work.

(b) Changes in Effectiveness of Teams

(i) *Problem-solving* and action planning for tackling the problems in quality circles.

(ii) Improvement of *inter-personal* skills in the group.

(iii) Role identification model. By increasing understanding of: (a) Functional role, or (b) Team role, i.e. *helping relationship* of team members for achieving the objectives. This helps team members to recognise and use their team resources.

(c) Changes in Organisation Effectiveness

(i) Evaluation of effectiveness in terms of productivity, flexibility and absence of organisation strain.

(ii) Blake and Mouton Grid which seeks the simultaneous

achievement of high production-centered and high people-centered methods.

(iii) Cameron's (1980) classification of organisation effectiveness:

(a) Goal directed.

(b) Resource acquiring—comparison with competitors.

(c) Constituencies (groups such as customer, suppliers who have stake in the organisation responding to demands and expectations of the groups. Such as assessing customer complaints or company image survey, or customer satisfaction.

(d) Smoothness of internal processes, e.g. little conflict and no strain and smooth and integrated working of departments.

(iv) TQM model of nine elements such as:

(a) *Through the enables*: leadership, policy and strategy people management, resources and processes.

(b) *The results*: Customer satisfaction, people satisfaction, impact on society, and business results.

4.3. Comparing the Cost of Training with Outcomes

(i) Cost effectiveness analysis as basis of comparisons.

(ii) Cost benefit analysis—that benefits from training are more valuable to the organisation than cost of training.

(iii) Impact analysis from stakeholders.

(iv) Value added to employees and they are able to work more effectively after training.

4.4. A format to evaluate a training is at annexure (P.C. Tripathi).

4.5. A case study which shows visible results in improving the participants new qualities is at annexure (Mirza S. Sayiyadain)

References

Mirza S. Sayiyadain, "Human Resource Management", Tata McGraw Hill Publishing Company Ltd., New Delhi.

P.C. Tripathi, "Human Resource Management", Sultan Chand & Sons, New Delhi.

K. Aswathappa, "Human Resources and Personnel Management", Tata McGraw Hill Publishing Co. Ltd., New Delhi.

UNIT III

ORGANISATION DEVELOPMENT INTERVENTIONS

CHAPTER

12

Organisation Development (OD): Concept

Organisations are facing numerous challenges and threats to its effectiveness and profitability from turbulent environments, global competition, changing customer needs, ever changing technologies and emerging employees aspirations. Keeping the organisations survive and grow is the real challenge. Organisation development is the discipline designed to improving organisations and people in them through planned change.

Organisation Development (OD) offers an approach to bringing about a positive change in organisation efficiency and effectiveness. OD is a process of planned change organisation-wide to increase organisation effectiveness through changing the methods or process by which work is done.

OD takes organisations to higher levels of performance by excelling. It aims at building internal competencies and teams in the organisation. It focuses on behaviour and uses various behavioural tools.

OD has been *defined* in many different ways. In general terms, it is an effort to improve an organisation's effectiveness by dealing with individual, group, and overall organisational problems from both a technical standpoint and a human standpoint. At the heart of OD is a concern for improving the relationships among the organisation's personnel.

OD is a powerful *change strategy*. It uses *"process consultation"* where the consultant works with the leader and group to diagnose and enables them to solve their own problems. It is participative, collaborative and problem-focused approach. OD taps the experience and expertise of members as they work on their problems to generate solutions.

We shall discuss organisation development under following headings:

(i) Theme of OD.

(ii) OD characteristics.

(iii) How to know organisation is having problems?

(iv) The process of organisation development.

(v) OD interventions.

(I) THEME OF OD

OD emphasis is in *improving organisation effectiveness* and *culture*. For this OD focus is three-fold, i.e.:

(a) by improving *organisation processes*;

(b) redesign the *organisation structure* to make it function better; and

(c) change organisation as a *system*.

(a) The *organisation processes* refer to how things get done in organisations, i.e. work climate, the methods for arriving at results. Important processes include communication, problem-solving and decision-making, conflict resolution, openness, trust, mutual trust, collaboration, allocation of rewards, human resource practices and continuous learning. It involves a fundamental change in an organisation culture as termed by Warner Burke.

(b) The *organisation structure* refers to how individual tasks are designed and how these tasks are integrated in a coherent manner. Right structures promote responsibility, innovation and initiative whereas other structures curb such behaviours and are rigid, inefficient. Redesign of organisation structure is an active area of experimentation of OD.

(c) The *system perspective* highlights that organisation elements are interdependent, interrelated and cause multiple effects. Change in any element of the system (strategy, structure, task, technology, processes and culture) will cause changes in other elements. The primary goal of OD programmes is to optimise the whole system by ensuring that elements are harmonious and congruent.

In nutshell, as the environment changes, the organisation must adapt by using above approaches programmes and innovative interventions, which involve the entire organisation transformation (W.L. French and C.H. Bell).

(II) OD CHARACTERISTICS

OD may be referred as:

(i) *systematic*, long-range, planned, *change* effort,

(ii) organisation-wide,

(iii) managed *from the top*,

(iv) to increase organisation *effectiveness and health*,

(v) through planned interventions,

(vi) using *behaviour* science knowledge and *action research*, and

(vii) with the use of external consultants.

Seven characteristics (French and Bell, 1990 and Backhard, 1969). OD is not a one time affair, but a lengthy process of meeting the challenge in continuous basis.

(III) HOW TO KNOW ORGANISATION IS HAVING PROBLEMS?

One way of getting some feedback on the organisation at large is to examine its organisation climate. Organisation climate is determined by knowing the attitudes and perceptions the employees have about the organisation's leadership, products, pay, employee benefits, discipline, policies and goals.

In measuring organisational climate, we are interested in learning about the *informal* organisation, which is analogous to the part of an iceberg that rests under the water. Fig. 12.1 depicts the organisational iceberg:

(a) The *formal* aspects of the iceberg are those that are *readily observable*. Job definitions, span of control, forms of departmentalisation, organisational goals, policies and systems and efficiency measures laid by the organisation are all examples. We can see these things, and they are oriented toward structuring the organisation.

(b) On the underwater part of the organisational iceberg are the *informal* aspects. These are *hidden from view* and are oriented to socio-psychological processes and behavioural considerations. They include power, influence, interpersonal and inter-group relations, group norms, perceptions of trust and openness, value orientations, superior-subordinate relation and employee satisfaction.

The major differences between *formal* and *informal* organisational aspects are that the formal aspects are visible, and also that if there is something wrong with the formal aspects, we can adjust them. If someone is

Fig. 12.1

The Organisational Iceberg

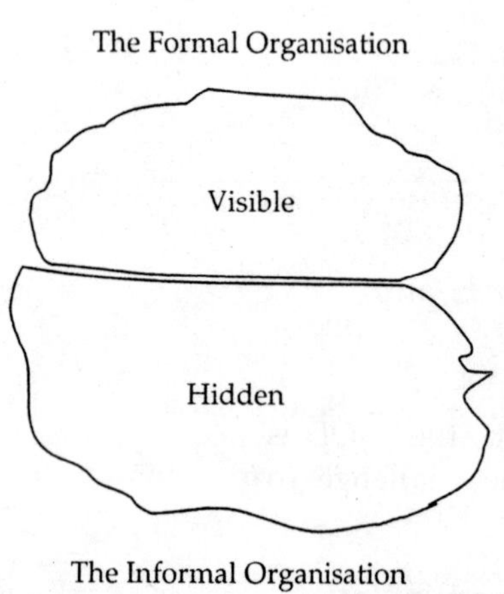

Formal Aspects
Job Definitions
Job Descriptions
Forms of Departmentalisation
Span of Control
Operating Policies
Efficiency Measures

These are readily observable and oriented to structural considerations

Informal Aspects
Power and Influence
Interpersonal and Group Relations
Group Norms and Sentiments
Perceptions of Trust and Openness
Value Orientation
Employee Satisfaction

These are hidden from view and oriented to social-psychological process and behavioural considerations.

Source: Adapted from James A.F. Stoner and Charles Wankel, "Management", Prentice Hall of India Pvt. Ltd., New Delhi.

inefficient, we can find out why and try to deal with the problem. However, if there is a lack of trust and openness in the organisation, how does one identify this problem before it begins to create trouble? One is seldom able to do this. Usually we do not know what is going on in the informal organisation until problems begin. However, there are ways of measuring organisational climate and dealing with a trouble situation before it becomes too serious. The catchall term used to describe this process is *organisational development*.

(IV) THE PROCESS OF ORGANISATION DEVELOPMENT

Lewin (1947) conceptualised social change as occurring in three phases: (a) unfreezing, (b) changing, and (c) refreezing. Typical OD processes implemented by one leading Indian company is presented in four stages summarised in Fig. 12.2.

(i) The Diagnostic Phase Involves

- Client's top management to recognise the problems and have awareness of the need for change in the organisation.
- The engagement of change agent or consultant by client organisation.

FIG. 12.2

Four Stages of OD Process Model
(Adopted by Prof. Abad Ahmad in Bharat Heavy Electricals Ltd., Bhopal)

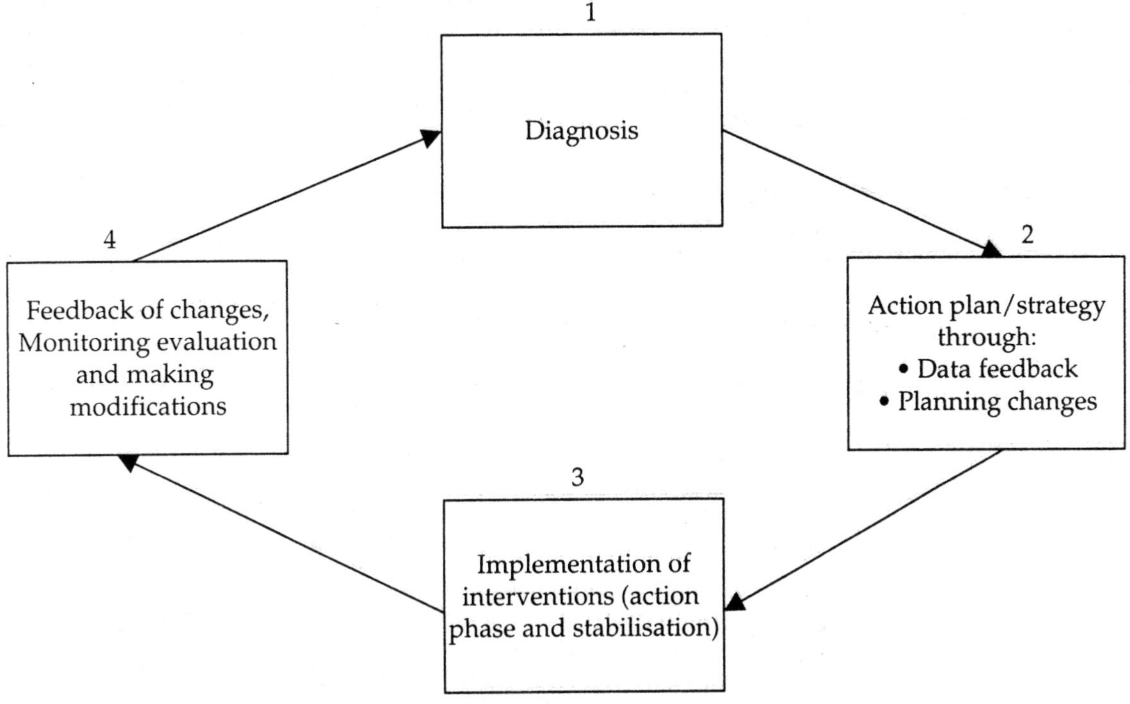

- Diagnosis in OD is a collaborative process which involves the client system and consultant's joint collection and analysis of data. Emphasis is on continuous and participative diagnosis.
- OD consultant may make use of tools such as questionnaire (survey) and interview schedules (consultation meetings).
- In brief, OD diagnosis attempts to analyse the current state of the organisation in terms of various structures, systems and process in order to identify actual and potential strengths and weaknesses.

(ii) Action Plan/Strategy Development

- Sharing of joint diagnosis of problems by the consultant and client team to the top management in an OD workshop.
- In this workshop top management jointly develops action plans and strategies in the form of interventions (e.g. team-building and OD grid, etc.) to bring about changes or improvement.

(iii) Action and Stabilisation Phase—Implementation of Interventions

- Implementation of action plans—changes through intervention.
- Long drawn series of actions that may last several months such as grid OD intervention of Blake and Mouton.
- This phase of interventions of OD process takes place under conditions of unfrozenness, mobilising efforts which is necessary for changes to have an impact.
- Allowing changes to stabilise and to permeate the culture of the organisation. To ensure that the positive element of change programme are diffused to other parts of the organisation.

(iv) Feedback of Changes, Evaluation and Making Modification Phase

- This phase consists of monitoring and reviewing the progress of the actions by collecting feedback about the changes introduced.
- Making modification in case need arise. Mid-course corrections.
- In case some new problems are revealed in the collection of data (survey/consultation process) another phase is commenced.
- In the event of achievement complete success, it has to be ensured client team is competent enough to maintain the changed system without the support of the consultant, as there is tendency among organisations to revert to their original states. Consultant can thus withdraw.
- In nutshell, OD practitioners, both internal and external consultants may counsel decision-makers on an individual basis, work to improve working relationships among the members of working group or team, work to improve relationships among interacting and interdependent organisational groups; and gather attitudinal data throughout the organisation and feed this data back to selected individuals and groups who use this information as a basis for planning and making desired improvements.

OD is a long range effort to improve and organisation's problem-solving and renewal processes, particularly through a more effective and collaborative management of organisation culture—with special emphasis on the culture of formal work teams—with the assistance of change agent and technology of applied behaviour science, including action research.

OD INTERVENTIONS

An *OD intervention* is defined as the set of *structured activities* in which selected organisational units (target groups or individuals) engage with a task(s) where *task goals* are related to organisational improvement. All the activities which are planned and carried in order to bring about improvements are called as interventions. These cover the action planning and implementations.

The *OD strategy* can be defined as an overall plan for relating and *integrating different organisational improvement activities* over a period of time to accomplish objectives.

Characteristics of OD Interventions

- An OD intervention focuses on *organisational process* apart from substantive content of an activity.
- An OD intervention *focuses on work team* as the unit of analysis and change towards effective behaviour.
- OD would view change as an *ongoing process* and would rely on a *collaborative management* of work culture.

Classification of Interventions Applicable to OD

Different writers have classified OD interventions under various headings. We shall mention the classification done by French and Bell; he has classified interventions as under:

(i) Process Interventions

These may relate to development of *individuals* such as sensitivity training, behaviour modelling, role playing, awareness expansion, training, feedback, coaching, monitoring, transactional analysis, etc.

Another category of interventions may also focus on the *group/team* development such as role analysis, role negotiation, team-building, process consultation, etc.

Some interventions may relate to *inter-group* problems such as confrontation meetings, mirroring, etc.

(ii) Structural Interventions

These are change efforts aimed at improving organisation effectiveness through changes in task, structural, technological and goal processes in the organisation. Technological/structural changes are re-engineering for product development and customer service. Organisation, in order to improve efficiency may merge several divisions or eliminate layers of management. These are self-managed teams, work redesign, Management by Objectives (MBO), Quality Circles, Quality of Work Life Projects (QWL), Collateral

Organisations, Physical Settings, Re-engineering and Total Quality Management (TQM).

(iii) Large Scale Systems Change

These include organisation transformation, or second order change or second generation OD interventions. These usually require a multiplicity of interventions and takes place over a fairly long period of time. For example, the five-year organisational transformation process at British Airways, as reported by Goodstein and Burke, included the following:

- Replacement of the top management team.
- Redefining the nature of the business from transportation to service.
- Diagonal task forces to plan changes.
- A reduction in hierarchical levels.
- Substantial downsizing of the workforce, including middle management, without lay-offs.
- Team-building (off-site) including role clarification and negotiation.
- Process consultation.
- Modifying the budget process.
- Top management commitment and involvement.
- Personnel staff trained to be internal consultants.
- Peer support groups.
- Performance-based compensation and profit sharing.
- Experiential training programmes for senior and middle managers including feedback on managerial behaviour.
- Open communications.
- Continuous data-based feedback on work group and organisational climate and management practices.
- A new appraisal system emphasizing both behaviour and performance.
- Continuous use of task forces.

Thus, wide variety of interventions were utilised in this large scale system change programme. Large scale system change can include:

(i) a reconceptualisation of the nature of the business;
(ii) the use of a parallel learning structure;
(iii) a reduction in hierarchical levels;
(iv) team-building including cross-functional teams;
(v) survey feedback;
(vi) extensive use of task forces; and
(vii) intensive leadership training.

TO CONCLUDE

Organisation development is about improving organisation performance. But it has dual focus of developing individuals also, who comprise the organisation. French and Bell in their monumental volume on OD mention that "basically, organisation development is a process for teaching people how to solve problems, take advantage of opportunities, and learn how to do that better and better over time". Thus, it is concerned with ways to increase the effectiveness of individuals, teams and the organisation as a whole. A major thrust in organisation development is improving organisational effectiveness by improving organisational processes.

References

R. Beckhard, *Organisation Development: Strategies and Models*, Addison Wesley Reading Mass, 1969.

French, Wendell L. and Cecil, H. Bell, *Organisation Development*, Prentice-Hall of India, New Delhi, 1973.

S.K. Bhatia, Management of Change and Organisation Development, Deep & Deep Publications Pvt. Ltd., New Delhi.

CHAPTER

13

OD Interventions and Classification

An *OD intervention* is defined as the set of *structured activities* in which selected organisational units (target groups or individuals) engage with a task(s) where *task goals* are related to organisational improvement. All the activities which are planned and carried in order to bring about improvements are called as interventions. These cover the action planning and implementations.

The *OD strategy* can be defined as an overall plan for relating and *integrating different organisational improvement activities* over a period of time to accomplish objectives.

1. CHARACTERISTICS OF OD INTERVENTIONS

- An OD intervention focuses on *organisational process* apart from substantive content of an activity.
- An OD intervention *focuses on work team* as the unit of analysis and change towards effective behaviour.
- OD would view change as an *ongoing process* and would rely on a *collaborative management* of work culture.

2. CLASSIFICATION OF INTERVENTIONS APPLICABLE TO OD

Different writers have classified OD interventions under various headings. We shall mention the classification done by three famous learned authors, i.e. first, French and Bell; second, Udai Pareek, and third, D.K. Shandilya, after this few more models for change are given:

1. First, French and Bell have broadly classified as under:

(i) Process Interventions

These may relate to development of *individuals* such as sensitivity training, behaviour modelling, role playing, awareness expansion, training, feedback, coaching, mentoring, transactional analysis, etc.

Another category of interventions may also focus on the *group/team* development such as role anlaysis, role negotiation, team-building, process consultation, etc.

Some interventions may relate to *inter-group* problems such as confrontation meetings, mirroring, etc.

(ii) Structural Interventions

These are change efforts aimed at improving organisation effectiveness through changes in task, structural, technological and goal processes in the organisation. Technological/structural changes are re-engineering for product development and customer service. Organisation, in order to improve efficiency may merge several divisions or eliminate layers of management. These are self-managed teams, work redesign, Management by Objectives (MBO), Quality Circles, Quality of Work Life Projects (QWL), Collateral Organisations, Physical Settings, Re-engineering and Total Quality Management (TQM).

(iii) Large Scale Systems Change

These include organisation transformation, or second order change or second generation OD interventions. These usually require a multiplicity of interventions and takes place over a fairly long period of time. For example, the five-year organisational transformation process at British Airways, as reported by Goodstein and Burke, included the following:

- ❑ Replacement of the top management team.
- ❑ Redefining the nature of the business from transportation to service.
- ❑ Diagonal task forces to plan changes.
- ❑ A reduction in hierarchical levels.
- ❑ Substantial downsizing of the workforce, including middle management, without layoffs.
- ❑ Team-building (off-site) including role clarification and negotiation.

- Process consultation.
- Modifying the budget process.
- Top management commitment and involvement.
- Personnel staff trained to be internal consultants.
- Peer support groups.
- Performance-based compensation and profit sharing.
- Experiential training programmes for senior and middle managers including feedback on managerial behaviour.
- Open communications.
- Continuous data-based feedback on work group and organisational climate and management practices.
- A new appraisal system emphasizing both behaviour and performance.
- Continuous use of task forces.

Thus, wide variety of interventions were utilised in this large scale system change programme. Large scale system change can include:

(i) a reconceptualisation of the nature of the business;

(ii) the use of a parallel learning structure;

(iii) a reduction in hierarchical levels;

(iv) team-building including cross-functional teams;

(v) survey feedback;

(vi) extensive use of task forces; and

(vii) intensive leadership training.

(iv) Interventions Based on Target Groups

Another way to classify OD interventions is by the primary target of the intervention, e.g. individuals, dyads, triads, teams and groups, inter-group relations and the total organisation. Details of these are explained subsequently.

2. Second, Prof. Udai Pareek has classified interventions into three groups. In first classification he has identified who take active role, participant or facilitator. He has divided these interventions into two groups: (Udai Pareek, 1998, *Organisation Development*, edited by S. Ramnarayan, T.V. Rao, and Kuldeep Singh, Response Books).

(a) Participant—Active Interventions

(i) Encounter groups.

(ii) Role playing.

(ii) Use of *instruments* for self-awareness through feedback.

(iv) Self-study and reflection.

(v) Awareness expansion.

(b) Facilitator—Active Interventions

(i) Psycho-dynamic methods.

(ii) Change motivation or individual orientation.

(iii) Training.

(iv) Feedback.

(v) Coaching and mentoring.

(c) Role Focused Interventions

Besides the above two groups, Prof. Udai Pareek has emphasised on role-focused OD interventions. Role-focused interventions provide certain benefits:

(i) *Attempts to build mutuality amongst the roles.* Giving and receiving help is possible in relationship of mutuality—which grows out of trust and perceptions of other's roles as well as one's own.

(ii) It encourages *new solutions to problems* and creativity. Emphasis is on attempting alternative ways of solving a problem by looking to problem from different angles.

(iii) *Confrontation of problems* by bringing to surface and attempt to search out a lasting solution instead of avoiding the problem.

(iv) *Joint exploration to evolve solution* by people themselves rather than expect any such solution from experts, etc. Exploration implies a joint effort at understanding the problem and weighing the alternative solutions.

Role interventions are aimed at generating data through work groups and solutions are achieved through process-oriented work on problems. Important interventions are:

(i) Role analysis.

(ii) Managing role stress.

(iii) Role negotiation.

3. Third, D.K. Shandilya has mentioned that there is wide range of OD interventions. They are basically centred around one or more of the following dimensions:

(a) *Target*: What organisational segment is planned to be examined and changed?

(b) *Focus*: What is planned to be changed? Is it the task system or behaviour, etc.?

(c) *Strategy*: How is the change planned to be brought about?

(a) Classification by "Target" of Interventions

Change is an organisation can be initiated both at the *individual* and *group* level. Behavioural processes also differ for two person group called Dyads and for three persons called Triads, a small group of let us say 10 persons where face to face interaction is possible between all members of the group, and a large group where face to face interaction breaks down. A significant dyad in an organisation is the Boss-Subordinate twosome. An organisational segmentation based on psychological processes of individual *vs.* group can target the following OD interventions:

- ❑ An employee.
- ❑ Boss-subordinate twosome called as dyads.
- ❑ A section or a department.
- ❑ Two departments interaction.
- ❑ Total organisation.

Different interventions are available for working with different segments. Role analysis for example, starts with an individual and moves on to twosome groups for role negotiation. Analysis of objectives can be carried out at any level starting from an individual. While third party peace-making is an example of inter-group intervention, a confrontation meeting is generally at the total organisation level. It is important to note that basically the focus of OD is generally at the group level, though in order to suit specific needs activities may have to be started at individual level.

French and Bell have given a comprehensive list of OD interventions based on target groups. These are explained in Fig. 13.1.

Fig. 13.1

Typology of OD Interventions Based on Target Groups (French and Bell, OD)

Target Group	*Interventions Designed to Improve Effectivenss*
Individuals	Life and career-planning activities Coaching and counselling T-group (sensitivity training) Education and training to increase skills, knowledge in the area of technical task needs, relationship skills, process skills, decision-making, problem-solving, planning, goal-setting skills Grid OD phase 1 Work redesign Gestalt OD Behaviour modelling
Dyads/Triads	Process consultation Third-party peace-making Role negotiation technique Gestalt OD
Teams and Groups	Team-building—Task directed —Process directed Gestalt OD Grid OD phase 2 Interdependency exercise Process consultation Role negotiation Role analysis technique "Startup" team-building activities Education in decision-making, problem-solving, planning, goal-setting in group settings Team MBO Appreciation and concerns exercise Socio-technical systems (STS) Visioning Quality of Work Life (QWL) programmes Quality circles Force-field analysis Self-managed teams
Inter-group Relations	Inter-group activities —Process directed —Task directed Organizational mirroring Partnering Process consultation Third-party peace-making at group level Grid OD phase 3 Survey feedback

Total Organization	Socio-technical systems (STS) Parallel learning structures MBO (participation forms) Cultural analysis Confrontation meetings Visioning Strategic planning/strategic management activities Grid OD phases 4, 5, 6 Inter-dependency exercise Survey feedback Appreciative inquiry Search conferences Quality of Work Life (QWL) programmes Total Quality Management (TQM) Physical settings Large-scale systems change

(b) Classification by "Focus" of Interventions

The change can also be aimed at different aspects of organisational functioning. These aspects include, objectives, structure, systems, processes, etc. Some examples of focus on OD interventions for various aspects of organisational functioning are as under:

FIG. 13.2

Focus on OD Interventions

Aspects of Organisational Functioning	*Interventions*
Objectives	MBO
Structure	Job redesign
Systems	Appraisal feed-back
Processes	T-group team-building

The behaviour patterns of interaction among members of the organisation are called 'processes'. Varieties of interventions exist for each type aspects of organisation functioning.

(c) Classification by "Strategy" of Interventions

Design of an intervention means the manner in which the change is to brought about in the organisation. Broadly, there are three basic strategies:

(i) *Power coercive strategy*, i.e. a change to be brought about by rewards and punishment.

(ii) *Empirical-rational strategy*, for example, people willingly change when they know that the change is in their own interest.

(iii) *Normative re-education strategy*, it relies on examining the attitudinal and value aspect of human behaviour.

However, OD programmes may use a combination of interventions using different strategies.

3. ORGANISATION DEVELOPMENT CHANGE TREATMENTS

Change treatments are actually the forms of intervention or the organisation development processes. In practice, the OD umbrella has come to include nearly every behavioural-based management tool. There has been a proliferation of new names applied to old techniques, some new techniques, as OD processes. Each change treatment is designed to bring about a change that will result in improved organisation performance.

Basically, change treatments will fall into general categories derived from the target of change or that part of the organisation that is treated. Although it can be argued that ultimately the target is always the same—the human element—the means to bring about performance changes can be quite different. Some change treatments deal directly with the development of individuals, while others treat a part of the work environment directly which in turn has an indirect impact upon personal performance. The following breakdown of change treatments into categories (see Fig. 13.3) describes the kinds of OD processes that are likely to be applied within each.

FIG. 13.3

General Categories of Change Treatments

Change Treatment Categories	*Possible Areas of Emphasis*
Personal Development	Interpersonal skills, beliefs, attitudes, communication skills, conflict resolution, leadership styles, decision-making, individual goal-setting.
Group Development	Team-building, intergroup processes, coordination of activities, conflict resolution, group problem-solving, group goal-setting.
Task Development	Formulation of task objectives, analysis of work-task situation, job design.
Structural Development	Organisational hierarchy, formal structure, formal interdepartmental relationship, relationship of jobs, formal communication networks.
Data Utilisation	Gathering data, analysis of data, feedback of data, data discussion.

It should be noted that there is a strong inter-relationship and interdependence between these categories. This, of course, means that some overlap is possible and categorisation of some processes would be difficult.

Wendell French and Cecil Bell have identified five major kinds of treatments that include some specific processes:

(i) Diagnostic activities,

(ii) Team-building activities,

(iii) Inter-group activities,

(iv) Survey Feedback activities, and

(v) Organisation Principle activities.

Training may be given to employees in the following:

(i) Contingency management,

(ii) MBO,

(iii) Leadership,

(iv) Communications,

(v) Problem-solving,

(vi) Motivation,

(vii) Management of conflict,

(viii) Interpersonal skills,

(ix) Behaviour modification,

(x) Technical skill, and

(xi) Management principles.

As mentioned above many types of interventions can be used by OD change agents. Some of these are directed toward the individual; role play and counselling are the most popular examples. Others are mere group-oriented, as in the case of team-building, survey feedback, system four management developed by Renesis Likert, and grid training closely associated with Robert Blake and Jane Mouton's managerial grid.

Reference

S.K. Bhatia, Management of Change and Organisation Development, Deep & Deep Publications Pvt. Ltd., New Delhi.

CHAPTER

14

OD Interventions based on Target Groups

Change in an organisation can be initiated at various levels. French and Bell have given a comprehensive list of OD interventions based on target groups (earlier chapter). We elaborate here few of those interventions:

(A) OD INTERVENTIONS FOR INDIVIDUAL

(i) These are such as *sensitivity training laboratory* or T-groups to increase *sensitivity* and skill in handling inter-personal relations. It refers to a method of changing behaviour through unstructured group interaction. Members are brought together where participants discuss themselves and their interactive processes, loosely directed by a behavioural scientist. The group is process-oriented, which means individuals learn through observing and participating when they express their ideas, beliefs and attitudes.

The objectives of the T-Groups are to provide the participants with increased awareness of their own behaviour, the way they effect others and how others perceive them and increase understandings of group processes. This is not popular now.

(ii) Other methods of *self-awareness* are leadership style; (PAA) passive, aggressive, assertive; listening; and communication are commonly used.

(B) OD INTERVENTIONS FOR TWO OR MORE INDIVIDUALS

(i) *TA—Transactional Analysis* is basically for analysing interpersonal behaviour and development of self-knowledge which comes through analysis of own behaviour. TA concentrates on style of communication between people. It teaches to send messages that are clear and to give responses tha are natural and reasonable. It reduces destructive communication habits o games.

(ii) *Third-party peace-making* activities can be conducted by a skilled consultant to assist two members to manage their interpersonal conflict through conflict resolution techniques. It can also be used as an inter-group intervention in a conflict situation. The facilitator obtains information from both the parties and transmits to the other party in a manner suitably the groups or their representatives come together to resolve the inter-group problems.

(C) OD INTERVENTIONS FOR TEAMS OR GROUPS

(i) *The Process consultation*. It helps in understanding the dynamics of their working relationship in the group. Its objective is to guide in the diagnostic and problem-solving skills. Process consultation is for an outside consultant to assist a manager to perceive, understand, act upon process events with which he has to deal. These might include work flow, informal roles and relationships among members and formal communication channels, decision-making, cooperation and competition. Consultant acts as a guide and helps manager to solve his problem. Primary goal of process consultation is to help solve problems by making manager aware organisation processes, their consequences and the ways by which they can be changed.

(ii) *Team-building*. Another intervention used is team-building as organisations are increasingly relying on teams to accomplish work tasks. Team-building utilises high interaction group activities to increase trust and openness among team members. The objective is to improve coordinative efforts of members that will result in increasing the team's performance.

The activities considered in team-building typically include goal setting and laying priorities of the team, developing of inter-personal relations among team members, clarification of each member's role and responsibilities and team process analysis.

(D) OD INTERVENTIONS FOR INTER-GROUP RELATIONS

Conflict situations between groups are identified and analysed. *Confrontation meeting* (mirroring) may be used for inter-department cooperation. Inter-group development seeks to change the attitudes and perceptions that groups have of each other. A popular method for improving inter-group relations is problem-solving. In this method each group meets independently to develop lists of perceptions of itself, the other group, and how it believes the other group perceives it. The groups then share their lists, after which similarities and differences are discussed. Differences are clearly articulated and the groups look for the causes of the disparities. The groups can now move to the integration phase, i.e. working to develop solutions that will improve relations between the groups. Basically, organisation mirroring is meant to give feedback to work group regarding how other group view each other. The aim of this intervention is to improve inter-group relations and increase organisational effectiveness.

(E) OD INTERVENTIONS FOR TOTAL ORGANISATION

Some interventions for total organisation are:

- *Presentation of survey feedback* to top management team helps members to determine action to be taken to solve the problems uncovered in the survey by use of questionnaire or through data collection. It refers to receiving new information about self, others, group or organisation dynamics. Information feedback has the potential to bring about constructive change.
- *Grid OD intervention* is used to bring about change in the entire organisation and improve organisation effectiveness. It is based on managerial grid of Blake and Mouton (1964). Various six phases of OD grid training are summarised as in Fig 14.1.

FIG. 14.1

OD Grid Training

Grid OD

(i) Training

(ii) Team development

(iii) Inter-group development

(iv) Organisational goal-setting

(v) Goal attainment

(vi) Stabilisation

(i) Laboratory-Seminar Training

The purpose of this is to introduce the participants to the overall concepts and materials used in grid training. In this first focus on training, e.g. *manager's styles*—training to managers is imparted so that high score on both, i.e. concern for production and concern for people is achieved which is desirable.

(ii) Team Development

Members of the same department are brought together to chart how they are going to attain 9, 9 position on the grid. In this emphasis is on improving both boss-subordinate relationships and team effectiveness. Here focus is laid on diagnosis meetings, task achievement, building relationships, role clarification and mutual expectations.

(iii) Inter-group Development

Here thrust is on improving coordination, cooperation, relieve tensions and solve problems jointly. Here focus is on group-to-group. Conflict situations between groups are identified and analysed.

Yet another intervention is practiced, i.e. third party peace making. It is designed as an inter-group intervention where OD consultant acts as a mediator in a conflict situation.

(iv) Organisational Goal Setting

Member agree upon the important goals for the organisation, in the manner of management by objectives.

(v) Organisational Goal Attainment

In this participants attempt another strategy used is to accomplish the goals which they set.

(vi) Stabilisation

Stabilise positive changes and identify new areas of opportunity for the organisation after evaluation of overall programme is conducted.

Choosing an OD Intervention

D.K. Shandilya has emphasised that there are basically three factors that influence the choice of OD intervention:

(a) *Potential* of an OD intervention to achieve desired results. It deals with the basic problem and is capable of solving it by its application.

(b) Intervention is *practical and feasible* in the situation.

(c) Intervention has the *acceptability* by the client system.

Reference

S.K. Bhatia, Management of Change and Organisation Development, Deep & Deep Publications Pvt. Ltd., New Delhi.

CHAPTER

15

Process OD Interventions

Organisation process refers to the methods for arriving at results. These interventions may relate to development of individuals. Another category of interventions may focus on the team processes. Some process interventions may relate to inter-group problems. While another lot may deal with organisation-wise issues such as culture. We have covered some process interventions in this section:

(i) behaviour modification (modelling),

(ii) encounter groups,

(iii) role playing,

(iv) administering instruments,

(v) self-study and reflection,

(vi) awareness reflection,

(vii) psycho-dynamic methods,

(viii) changing motivation,

(ix) training,

(x) feedback,

(xi) coaching and mentoring,

(xii) role analysis,

(xiii) managing role stress,

(xiv) role negotiation,

(xv) system four management,

(xvi) job expectation technique, and

(xvii) life and career planning.

These process interventions are elaborated:

(i) Behaviour Modification (Behaviour Modelling)

It is a programme where managers identify performance-related employee behaviours (to reduce errors, absenteeism, tardiness, and accident rates) and then implement an intervention strategy to strengthen desirable performance behaviours and weaken undesirable behaviours.

It uses application of re-inforcement theory to individuals in work setting. Reinforcement theory relies on positive reinforcement, shaping and recognising the impact of different schedules of reinforcement on behaviour. This is used by managers for changing employee behaviour (Robbins Stephen).

Behaviour modelling is also similar concept. It is based on social learning theory. Behaviour modelling has been shown to be an excellent way to make first line supervisor more effective and improve organisational performance. For example, many first line supervisors find it difficult to discipline employees. To learn this behaviour, they must see a link between successful disciplining and desired outcomes (like favourable recognition from supervisors) and must come to believe they can do it after practising the skills until they too are proficient (self-efficacy).

(ii) Encounter Groups

Interventions based on encounter groups are called as sensitivity training, laboratory training, training T-groups, and learning L-groups. Encounter groups aim to provide participants with intense experiences to help them their ways of interacting with others, their styles of self-presentation, their values, etc. The participants work in small groups of 10 to 12 persons for periods of about five days. These groups work without an agenda and only with facilitator's guidance. This helps on learning about self and others.

(iii) Role Playing

In role playing, people adopt the roles of others from real life and act them out. Role playing requires more detailed observation. Role playing is a conscious attempt to simulate roles played in real life such as in Ram Lila and other epics, children acting out roles of parents or teachers. Role playing develops certain competencies such as perceiving the feelings and ideas, learning skill of relating a situation, gaining better insight into inter-personal relations.

(iv) Administering Instruments

These instruments include—psychological tests, questionnaires, checklists and inventories. These instruments are increasingly being used in OD interventions. These instruments increase self-awareness and interpersonal effectiveness through feedback. These facilitate new behaviour and understanding concepts due to personal involvement in tests.

(v) Self-Study and Reflection

Learners are supplied study materials to acquire knowledge and skills. Often managers are required to prepare project assignments. Learners go through library work, documents or interview knowledge people. Thus, in this process, participants learn on their own as they are exposed to new ideas through reading. However, the main limitation of self-study is that it does not lend itself to development of social skills. It provides learners with knowledge and new information.

Reflection is higher form of self-study. Effective managers think and concentrate about what should be done to solve problems. Schon (1983) calls such persons 'reflective practitioners'.

(vi) Awareness Expansion

For coping with stress and burn out certain exercises such as—meditation, yoga, walking, jogging, boxing 'boss' effigies are recommended by OD practitioners. Such interventions expand individual consciousness. Similar steps are: (a) increasing awareness, and (b) making new decisions are involved in assertiveness training, gender sensitivity, prejudice and stereotype analysis.

(vii) Psycho-Dynamic Methods

In these interventions, individuals peep deep into the past (usually in childhood). These are based on psychological theories of Eric Bern and Freud. These interventions are conducted by trained specialists in these fields.

(viii) Changing Motivation or Individual Orientation

David McClelland (1976) has proposed a very effective intervention as motivation arousal. Facilitators help participants to analyse their fantasies as expressed by stories they write. The stories are analysed for the needs or motives they reveal (for example, achievement, power, affiliation). Each motive has an associated network of images. The participants become aware of these and make decisions to increase one need such as achievement, through games, action planning exercises. The intervention has proved very effective in prompting change in individuals.

(ix) Training

Training is most widely used OD intervention. Training is a means of developing or changing culture-training strategy has to be designed to move step by step from where organisation is, to where it 'should' go. Evaluation of training effectiveness after the training is important in view of training costs involved. Training is also used to improve individual knowledge skill and attitude. Training activities can be for imparting technical skills for task performance, or for improving inter-personal effectiveness, leadership qualities, decision-making, goal-setting, etc.

(x) Feedback

When feelings or perceptions are communicated to individuals about their behaviour, performance or personal styles, this information is called feedback. The purpose of feedback is to help individual to increase personal and inter-personal effectiveness. Giving feedback provides data about individual behaviour and its effect on others. Receiving feedback builds useful self-awareness among recipients and encourages them to change behaviour so as to increase their personal and inter-personal effectiveness.

Giving feedback can be made effective by insuring:

- it is descriptive than evaluative,
- it is focused on subordinate's behaviour rather than on his personality,
- it concerns behaviour that is modifiable,
- is specific and data-based rather than general and impression-based,
- provides data from the manager's own experience,
- reinforces positive new behaviour and what the subordinate has done well,
- suggests avenues for improvement,
- is continual rather than sporadic,
- is based on need and is elicited by the subordinate,

- is intended to help,
- satisfies the needs of both the manager and subordinate,
- is well timed, and
- contributes to the rapport between the manager and subordinate, and enhances their relationship.

The effectiveness of feedback depends as much on how it is received and used as it does on how it is given. If the feedback disconfirms the self-image of expectation of the recipient, dissonance is created. Dissonance produces either a confronting or defensive behaviour. The feedback recipient may reduce dissonance by reacting in either a defensive or confronting manner.

(xi) Coaching and Mentoring

Workers and managers alike *develop* themselves by interacting with those they admire and by building *trusting relationships* with people who nurture, support, and guide them. It focuses on establishing mutual *understanding and its confidentiality*.

When young people join organizations, they need guidance and support from experienced people whom they admire, can confide in, and receive advice from them. Such a relationship is called mentoring, and the senior person is called a *mentor*. The concept of *mentoring* centres around the emotional support and guidance given by an older, more experienced person to a younger, less experienced person called a *protege*. Mentors need not be, and preferably should not be, the protege's supervisor.

However, employees also need to develop trusting and supportive relationships with their supervisors, who can set challenging work goals, provide support to achieve them, help analyse barriers to higher performance, and plan goals for the future. This process is called *coaching*, defined as the help supervisors provide to their subordinates by analyzing and guiding on-the-job performance. While mentoring centres around general development and psychological well-being, coaching is linked to the analysis of job performance and identification of training needs.

Mentoring affords an opportunity for individuals to *share their concerns* and receive moral support and guidance for their development. Mentoring begins when a trusting relationship is established. Mentor's model behavioural norms for their proteges. They also listen to their proteges' personal and job concerns, help them search for solutions to problems, share relevant experiences, respond to their emotional needs without making them dependent on the mentors, and cultivate long-lasting yet informal personal relationships.

Mentoring involves support offered to a person by someone who is senior in competence experience, expertise, or position. Three processes are central to successful coaching and mentoring: communication, empowering, and helping.

Enlightened organisational leaders are now paying more attention to mentoring. Generally, high potentials young managers are assigned to mentors, who are senior in position and age and occupy senior positions. Mentors are selected from any department and have their interest, availability, and 'mentoring competence'. One mentor may have more than one proteges. The ultimate goal of both coaching and mentoring is to help employees attain psychological maturity and effectiveness as observed by Prof. Udai Pareek.

(xii) Role Analysis Technique (RAT)

Role refers in terms of expectations from the member. It requires that a role be defined by such expectations. This can be done through role analysis which may help evolve an agreed understanding of the main functions of a role (called 'key performance areas' or 'key result areas'), the critical attributes the role occupant should have or develop in order to perform the role effectively, and the discrepancy between the expectations and the performance. It is designed to clarify role expectation and obligations of individuals carrying out organisation tasks.

Role Analysis Technique (RAT), the individual expectations and obligations relative to others are discussed in a group with help of facilitator, to arrive at a consensus. Once this exercise is carried out for each member of the group, it is expected that it will lead to reduced conflicts and cohesiveness for higher productivity. Role analysis leads to role descriptions and identification of critical attributes and also finalisation of KPAs.

According to Dayal (1969), role analysis is a structured exercise to provide:

(a) an overall picture of what the role is supposed *to achieve* and the rationale for the existence of that role,

(b) the *contribution* of the role to the achievement of the *overall* departmental/business group/functional/company goals, and

(c) the *inter-linkages* to other related roles in the organization.

Role analysis helps the organization to:

- bring role clarity for the role occupants,

- bring clarity across functions between the related roles in the organization,
- bring greater understanding of the expectations from the focal role as seen by the members who are affected by the performance of the focal role,
- build trust, collaboration, team spirit and internal customer orientation,
- set clear objectives for planning of work, its monitoring and review,
- give and receive objective feedback on performance,
- facilitate realistic identification of training and development needs, and
- aid potential appraisal, career planning and succession planning.

(xiii) Managing Role Stress

Role is set of functions which an individual performs in response to the expectations of management and his own expectations about position he occupies. Some stress is needed for optimum performance but excess of it is dysfunctional. Stress can be due to boredom, unmanageable conflicts, overwork, ambiguity in expectations. Effective management of stress involves channelising stress towards productive purposes and developing strategies for coping with it.

(xiv) Role Negotiation

When executives of two departments unite towards a common goal (say manufacturing and sales), then they are interested in their effectiveness and require cooperation from the others. They are interested in a fair and negotiated way of working which will enable them to become effective. This process of negotiation is done through group work to develop ways of increasing collaboration and support for common goals.

The process normally involves of unfreezing phase, then negotiation phase (i.e. clarification regarding expectations and then finalisation of mutual contract). This may be followed up in another workshop to review and renegotiation after couple of months.

(xv) System Four Management (Likert's System Four Model)

This is a survey-based method of identifying how far an organisation is representative of theory 'x' or authoritarian culture, or how far it approaches theory 'y' participative culture. The diagnosis can then be a target-setting aid and review method.

(xvi) Job Expectation Technique

This approach can operate at the level of individual psychological contract, or in the performance appraisal and review level. The OD consultant can be helpful in observing and advising on process aspects.

(xvii) Life and Career Planning

In Development Centres individuals are assisted to review their strengths and weaknesses, their career aspirations and the organisational opportunities available. They also assess the capabilities and assess the training needs. In organisational downsizing external consultants are often employed to counsel employees about to be made redundant.

References

Udai Pareek, Articles in Organisations Development, edited by S. Ramnarayan, T.V. Rao and Kuldeep Singh.

Dayal, I., 'Role Analysis Technique in Description', *California Management Review.*

French, W.L. and Cecil H. Bell, Jr., 'Organisation Development', Pearson Education Asia.

S.K. Bhatia, Management of Change and Organisation Development, Deep & Deep Publications Pvt. Ltd., New Delhi.

CHAPTER

16

Structural OD Interventions

Structured interventions are change efforts aimed at improving organisation effectiveness through changes in task, structural, technological and goal processes in the organisation. Technological/structural changes are re-engineering for product development and customer service. Organisation, in order to improve efficiency and performance may merge several divisions or eliminate layers of management. Some of these interventions are:

(i) Job design/re-design.

(ii) Organisation design/re-design.

(iii) Teams.

(iv) Self-Managing Teams.

(v) Enhancing emotional intelligence in teams.

(vi) Quality circles and total quality management (TQM).

(vii) Quality of Working Life (QWL).

(viii) Management by Objectives (MBO).

(ix) Strategic management.

(x) Physical setting on basis of OD.

(xi) Parallel learning structures.

(xii) Excellence in organisation.

(xiii) Making six sigma initiative.

(xiv) Boundaryless organisation.

(xv) Role of Information Technology in enhancing organisation effectiveness.

(xvi) Creative organisations.

(xvii) Organisation designs for international expansion.

(xviii) Organisation designs and work cultures.

These interventions are explained in following pages.

JOB DESIGN/RE-DESIGN

Job designing has a significant impact on both the employees and the organisation. Poorly designed jobs often result in boredom and a subsequent aftermath of increased turnover, reduced motivation, low levels of job satisfaction, less than optimal productivity, and an increase in organisational costs. Many of these negative consequences could be avoided or minimised through the proper identification of significant job components. The job design process emphasises the design or re-design of jobs to incorporate factors which lead to the fulfilment of both employee and organisational objectives.

This approach combines the techno-structural as well as the social process needs of individuals and organisation. It is receiving renewed attention as IT and other features of the modern work environment impinge on the psychological as well as physical well-being of employees.

The Concept of Job Design

The term 'job design' refers to *the way the tasks are combined to form a complete job*. Job design is a process which integrates work content (tasks, functions, relationships), the reward (extrinsic and intrinsic), and the qualifications required (skills, knowledge, abilities) for each job in a way that meet the needs of employees and the organisation. Jobs differ in the way their tasks are combined, and different combinations create a variety of job designs in the organisation.

Objectives of Job Design

There are three objectives of job design:

(i) to meet the organisational requirements such as higher productivity, operational efficiency, quality of product/service, etc.,

(ii) to satisfy the needs of the individual employees like interest, challenge, achievement or accomplishment, etc., and

(iii) to integrate the needs of the individual with the organisational requirements.

Approaches to Job Design

There are various approaches to job design which are discussed below:

1. Scientific Management Approach

It attempts to simplify and standardise the jobs to efficiently perform the jobs by employees. F.W. Taylor, the father of scientific management stressed for proper selection, training and incentive to employees for achieving more productivity. Unfortunately, this approach did not give importance to human aspect and treated employees like machines. Psychological needs of employees were overlooked.

2. Behaviour Science Approach

Human relations approach advocated the design of jobs which facilitate social need gratification by the workers, including the use of non-authoritarian leadership styles by supervisors and the fostering of effective work groups.

3. Job Characteristics Approach

This approach focuses on job redesign, work structuring, job enrichment and so on to improve quality of worklife of workers. The job characteristics model of Hackman and Oldham states that three key psychological states of a job-holder determine his motivation, satisfaction and performance on the job. These states are:

- Experienced meaningfulness—the degree to which the job-holder experiences work as important and worthwhile.
- Experienced responsibility—the extent to which the job-holder feels personally responsible and accountable for the result of the work performed.
- Knowledge of results—information about how well he is performing the job.

When a worker experiences these states on the job, he feels motivated. He works hard to perform well to the extent these states are important to the worker. Therefore, motivation, satisfaction and performance should be integrated in the job design. These psychological states are generated by the following characteristics or dimensions of the job:

(i) Skill Variety

The degree to which the job requires the person to do different activities so that he can use a number of different skills and talents.

(ii) Task Identity

The degree to which the job requires completion of a whole and identifiable piece of work.

(iii) Task Significance

The degree to which the job has a substantial impact on the work and lives of others both inside and outside the organisation.

(iv) Autonomy

The degree to which the job provides freedom, independence and discretion to the individual in scheduling the work and in deciding the procedures to be used to do the job.

(v) Feedback

The degree to which the job provides the individual with clear and direct information about job performance and outcomes.

All the job characteristic dimensions have psychological impact on the workers. The first three dimensions affect whether or not workers view their jobs as meaningful. Autonomy determines the extent of responsibility workers feel. Feedback allows for feeling of satisfaction for a job well done by providing knowledge of results to the job-holder.

Re-designing of Jobs involves Concepts

In sum, the re-designing of jobs involves the following important concepts:

(i) Forming *natural work-units* basic work items and grouping.

(ii) *Combining tasks.*

(ii) Establishing *client relationship* so that employee can evaluate product or service he receives.

(iv) *Vertical loading,* i.e. planning and control involved in the job.

(v) Feedback to worker on quality and performance.

(vi) Forming of self-managing or semi-autonomous groups.

Techniques of Job Re-design

Further some *techniques of job design and re-design* are as under:

(a) Work simplification.

(b) Job rotation.

(c) Job enlargement.

(d) Job enrichment.

(e) Work improvement to achieve objectives of:

- eliminate wasteful motions,
- remove duplication of efforts,
- improve plant layout and machinery, materials, and
- improve processes, working conditions. (By Haynes and Massie).

Approaches to Job Re-design

No single approach to job re-design as mentioned above, can bring satisfaction to employees and meet organisation objectives. So there is need to have combination of approaches to job re-design as explained in Fig. 16.1.

FIG. 16.1

Approaches to Job Redesign

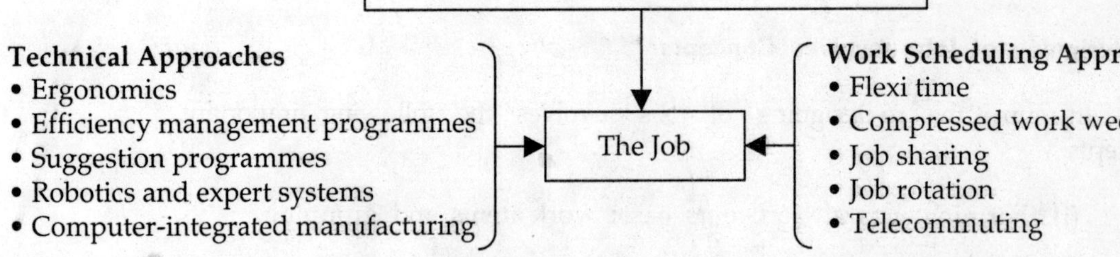

ORGANISATIONAL DESIGN/RE-DESIGN

This has been a major pre-occupation in the last decade, with most Western organisations striving to be leaner and flatter. It has been criticised as worst, a short-term cost-cutting exercise, but when accompanied by OD techniques to ensure culture-change and empowerment, can radically transform ailing organisations.

Organisation structure refers to the job tasks that are formally divided, grouped and coordinated. Organisations in which people work have important bearing on employee attitudes and behaviour.

Organisation designs (structure) constrains the employees and controls what they do. For example, organisations designed around high levels of formalisation and specialisation, strict adherence to the chain of command, limited delegation of authority, and narrow spans of control give employees little autonomy and effect their behaviour. In contrast, organisations that are structured around limited specialisation, low formalisation, wide spans of control provide greater freedom and encourage employee's behaviour diversity.

Stephen P. Robbins in "Organisation Behaviour" has stated that "strategy, size, technology and environment determine the type of structure for an organisation. Structural designs can be either: (a) *mechanistic* (high specialisation, rigid departments, clear chain of command, control, centralisation and high formalisation) or (b) *organic* (cross functional teams, free flow of information, decentralisation and low formalisation). The specific effect of structural designs on performance and satisfaction is moderated by employees' individual preferences". He has explained the determinants of organisation design and its outcomes in the Fig. 16.2.

FIG. 16.2

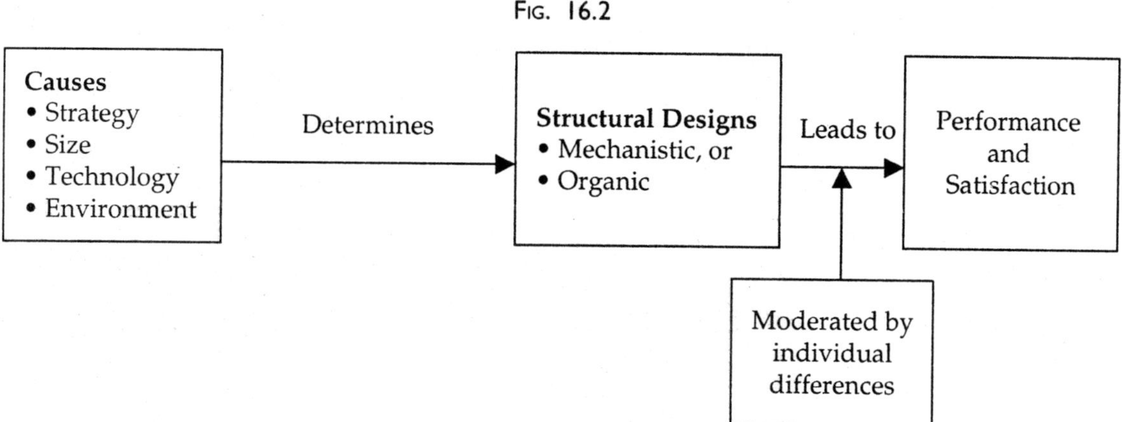

Re-design of Organisations Structure

The formal *bureaucratic* design can be an impediment to learning. However, by *flattening* the structure, eliminating or combining departments, and increasing the use of cross-functional teams inter-dependence is reinforced and boundaries between people are reduced.

Managements have been working to develop new structural designs that can make organisations more effective. Some of structural designs are: The *team structure* (the use of teams to coordinate work activities), the *virtual organisation* (a small, core organisation that outsources major business functions), the *boundaryless organisation* (that seeks to eliminate the chain and command and replaces departments with self-managing empowered teams), and the *famine organisation* (where members are valued as human beings, have informal relations, members measure their success in terms of service to others, expand members skills by offering new learning experiences, members are bound in a caring community, and information and power sharing by participating in decision-making. The other interventions are discussed in separate chapters.

Reference

S.K. Bhatia, Management of Change and Organisation Development, Deep & Deep Publications Pvt. Ltd., New Delhi.

CHAPTER

17

Process of Building Organisation Culture

Organisation culture is a *common perception* held by the organisation's members. Organisation culture is the shared understandings of norms, values, attitudes and beliefs of an organisation, which can foster or impede change.

It is a system of shared meaning. An understanding to employees of "the way things are done here". Organisation culture conveys the ways in which "people work and think".

Organisation culture may be referred to pattern of beliefs, values and learned ways of coping within an organisation. These are visible in structures and processes of the organisation and the ways its employees behave.

"An organisation's culture consists of the shared values and common assumptions held by the people within the organisation". In dynamic organisations, these values and assumptions drive behaviours that create value for the organisation's major stakeholders, be it customers, employees or other groups such as suppliers, etc. As opposed to developing individuals' resources, building a 'Cultural Identity' for the organisation is what Cultural Competency is all about. People are crucial for gaining organisational advantage. The environment and culture will stimulate individuals to perform in the desired manner.

The strong, widely recognised corporate culture is frequently cited as a reason for the success of such companies as IBM and Protector and Gamble. A company's predominant culture may change quite rapidly or be forced by competition into change. Vijay Sathe has shown that culture's durability and efficiency represent both an asset and a liability for an organisation, and a smart manager must learn when to stop perpetuating a culture that is unresponsive to the needs of business. In such circumstances Chief Executive may institute a change in overall organisational culture, which involves not merely structural and technological change, but also change in shared symbols, rituals and beliefs.

In this chapter, we have attempted to share some vital aspects of the organisation culture:

1. Importance of organisation culture as a technique in OD.
2. Characteristics of organisation culture.
3. Elements of organisation culture transmitted to employees.
4. How organisation culture starts in an organisation.
5. Socialisation process—familiarisation with organisation culture.
6. Maintaining organisation's culture.
7. Can organisation culture be altered or realigned?
8. Alternative approaches to creating culture change.
9. Is corporate culture now in crisis?
10. Steps for rebuilding organisation culture in highly turbulent competitive environment.

I. IMPORTANCE OF ORGANISATION CULTURE AS A TECHNIQUE IN OD

I. Background

In USA, during 1980s CEOs were successful in taking over a firm that had problems, by cutting the work force and rebuild organisation to be effective. However, during 1990s, much different approach has followed for survival a growth of an organisation:

(a) Create pride and enthusiasm in *the firm;*

(b) CEOs worked as *role models* to direct and work long hours to attain goals;

(c) Encouraging *positive way* how things can be done efficiently and differently;

(d) CEOs *shared* in meeting with managers to turn out best programme; and

(e) To *look after the best people* and place them best suited, jobs to so as encourage team work and creative ideas, etc.

Thus, various aspects which influenced culture were initiative, trust, support and innovation. *One culture is usually typified* by quality of excellence, high quality, openness in communication, participation in decision-making, high standard of safety, good corporate citizen, emphasis on new technology, modern management trends.

The other extreme type culture can be devoid of initiative and flexibility, lack of discipline, *chalta hai* mentality, mere conformity to rules rather than ends.

Thus, it came to realised that corporate culture is important to corporate growth, success, excellence and survival. It has motivating effect on employees. Culture influences an organisation's competitiveness over time. It can make organisation more effective. If developed to be a strategy for organisation effectiveness, which OD aims at. It has various advantages for the organisation such as:

(i) Organisation culture is necessary to adapt for changes arising due to competition.

(ii) Values and beliefs, provide a sense to common direction, energy and guidelines for day-to-day behaviour. Common bond promotes emotional and social cohesion and establishes sense of identity. Values provide a spirit and drive for achievement. Values also provide guidelines for employees for taking decisions.

(iii) It influences every one's perceptions of business and accepted ways of behaving.

(iv) Strong and positive culture give many benefits to companies. It leads to high morale, sense of commitment and organisation pride. Strong cultures are core values (shared by majority) are intensely held and widely shared.

(v) Variations in cultural values has significant impact on employee turnover and job performance.

Any organisation that wants a lead over its competitors, therefore, needs to have a clearly defined, commonly shared set of values which guide the stakeholders in all their actions and decisions. If these are not in place, the decentralised organisation may well become the disintegrated organisation.

2. CHARACTERISTICS OF ORGANISATION CULTURE

Stephen P. Robbins has stated that the following seven primary characteristics, capture the essence of an organisation culture:

(i) The degree to which employees are encouraged to be *innovative and risk taking.*

(ii) Degree of expected *precision and attention to detail.*

(iii) Degree to which management focuses on *result orientation* rather than techniques and processes.

(iv) Degree to which management has *people orientation*—its decisions effect of outcomes on employees.

(v) Degree to which activities are organised on *team work* rather than individuals.

(vi) Degree to which people are *competitive and aggressive* rather than people are easy going.

(vii) Degree to which organisation activities emphasise *on stability* (maintaining *status quo*) in contrast to growth.

These characteristics exists on a continuum from low to high. How things are done in organisation and the way members are supposed to behave.

How organisation culture effects the performance and satisfaction of employees? We have observed that seven characteristics highlighted by Stephen P. Robbins (Organisation Behaviour) are the essence of organisation culture. These characteristics exists on a continuum from low to high. If those characteristics are appraised as high by the employees then they perceive the organisation's culture as favourable. Their common perceptions then affect employees performance and satisfaction as high. This is depicted in Fig. 17.1.

FIG. 17.1

How Organisation Culture Effects Performance and Satisfaction

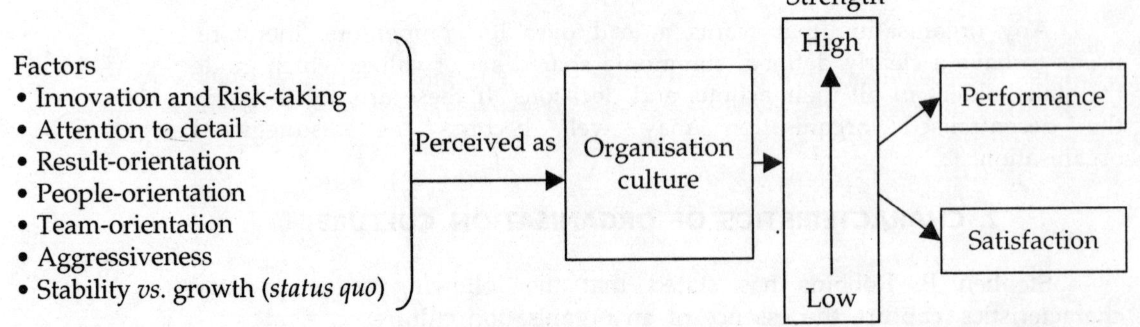

3. ELEMENTS OF ORGANISATION CULTURE TRANSMITTED TO EMPLOYEES

Employees learn organisation culture in number of forms, the most potent being values, rites and rituals, stories, heroes, etc.

1. Values

Values are core of the culture. Both values and beliefs provide guidelines for employees to follow in their work. Values provide sense of direction and shape behaviour. They indicate what matters are to be attended carefully.

Few examples of Credo's in organisations are: Cater Pillar, USA committed to customers "in 24 hours parts service anywhere in the world". Larson and Tubro (India)—"People are prime movers". Bill Gates (USA)—"Computer on every desk and every house." TERI (India)—"Faith in youth and tap the youth."

2. Heroes

Heroes personify these values. Manager's provide as role-models for employees. They set the standards of performance and dress norms as formal codes of behaviour.

3. Rites and Rituals

If culture and values are to thrive (and not die) these must be ritualised and celebrated repeatedly. These rituals may be of different types such as social rituals, work rituals, management rituals, recognition rituals, etc. For example, some companies celebrate their annual day function on regular basis and publicly recognise outstanding performers at these functions which serves as motivator.

4. Setting up of Cultural Network for Communication

These are story tellers, priests, gossips. This network reinforces the values of the organisation. Some jargon and jokes are only understood by insiders. These elements are manifestations of organisation culture and new people have to learn them. When employees interpret the meanings of these, their beliefs, perceptions, experiences constitute culture. During the days of Henry Ford II when he was Chairman of the Ford Motors Company, it was famous story reminding his executives. When one got too arrogant with the chairman, he would point that "It is my name that is on the building". The message was clear: Henry Ford ran the company!

4. HOW ORGANISATION CULTURE STARTS IN AN ORGANISATION

Some steps commonly adopted by organisations in starting and maintaining their culture are indicated in Fig. 17.2.

FIG. 17.2

Starting, Formation and Maintaining of Organisation Culture

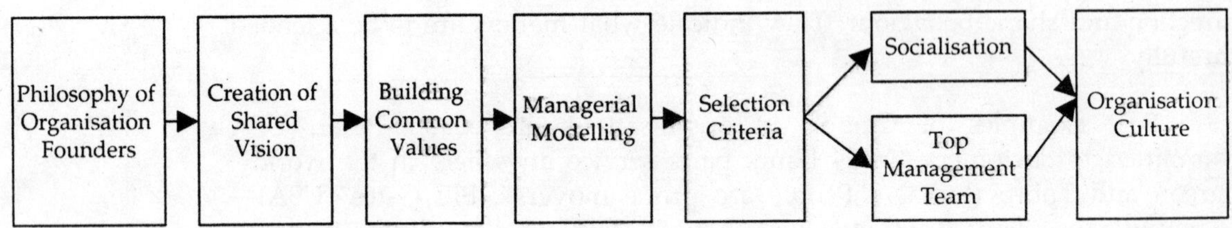

These steps are elaborated as under:

(i) Founder has an idea for new enterprise. Leadership behaviour sets the culture tone. *They formulate a statement of organisational philosophy* and communicate to employees. A particularly deep intervention is E. Schein's "*cultural analysis*". It probes deeply into the organisation:

(a) artifacts (such as symbols, modes of dress, office layout),

(b) Values behind artifacts, and

(c) Cultural assumptions in group meetings.

Some contemporary examples of founders who had an immeasurable impact on their organisational culture would include Bill Gates at Microsoft, Akio Moritra at Sony, David Packard at Hewlett Packard, Naraina Murty at Infosys and Azim Premji at WIPRO.

(ii) *Creation of a Vision*: Transformation leadership *creates a vision*. He provides *mission* and *mobilises commitment* and support.

(iii) Takes key people and creates a core group that *share a common vision*, mission, values, goals and strategies so that it is institutionalised and become reality.

(iv) Founding group *acts in concert* to create an organisation culture. They *adhere* faithfully to the values.

(v) Involving of others' employees and common values begin to be *built and solidify*. Organisation's values are in various areas such as—relationships to customers, social responsibility, managerial style are focused.

(vi) *Managerial modelling behaviour* strongly influences the employees.

5. SOCIALISATION PROCESS—FAMILIARISATION WITH ORGANISATION CULTURE

New employees are unfamiliar with the organisation culture. The new employees are thus potential who may disturb the beliefs and customs of a new place. The organisations, therefore, want to help new employees to *adapt to its culture.* This adaptation process is called *socialisation.*

The most critical socialisation stage is at the time of entry into the organisation. This is when organisation seeks to mold the outsider into an employee, i.e. its standards and norms. Socialisation can be conceptualised as a process made of three stages—*pre-arrival, encounter, metamorphosis.* (Maanen and Schein) (See Fig. 17.3).

FIG. 17.3

A Socialisation Model

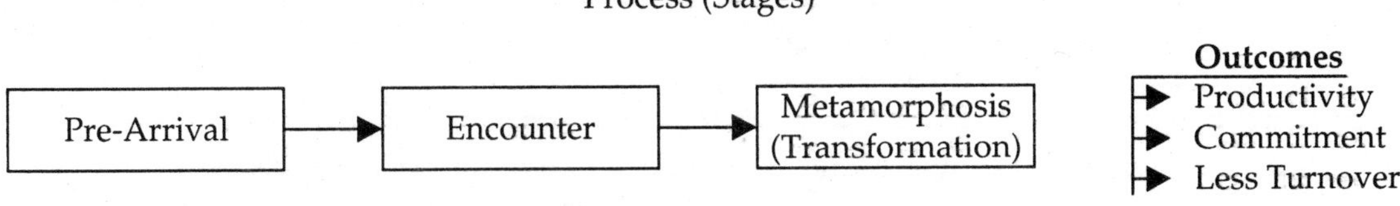

(i) Pre-Arrival Stage

It is process that occurs before new employee joins the organisation. The success depends on the degree *new candidate* has correctly *anticipated* the expectations and desires of selection members. Those type of people should be selected, who will fit into organisation culture.

One major purpose of a business school is to socialise business students to the attitudes and behaviours that business firms want. Management students should value the will to work, loyalty, desire to achieve and willingness to accept directions from superiors, then firms can hire executive from business schools, who have been pre-moulded in this pattern.

(ii) Encounter Stage

This is a stage in socialisation process in which new employee sees what the organisation is really like and *detach his previous assumptions* and replace them with another set that the organisation deems desirable.

(iii) Metamorphosis Stage

This is a process in which a new employee *adjusts* to his work group values and norms. He has become comfortable with the organisation and his job. He is now committed to the organisation and productivity increase.

6. MAINTAINING ORGANISATION'S CULTURE

Once organisation culture is build, various steps of socialisation are given below. These steps are also explained in Fig. 17.4.

FIG. 17.4

Steps in Socialisation of Organisation Culture

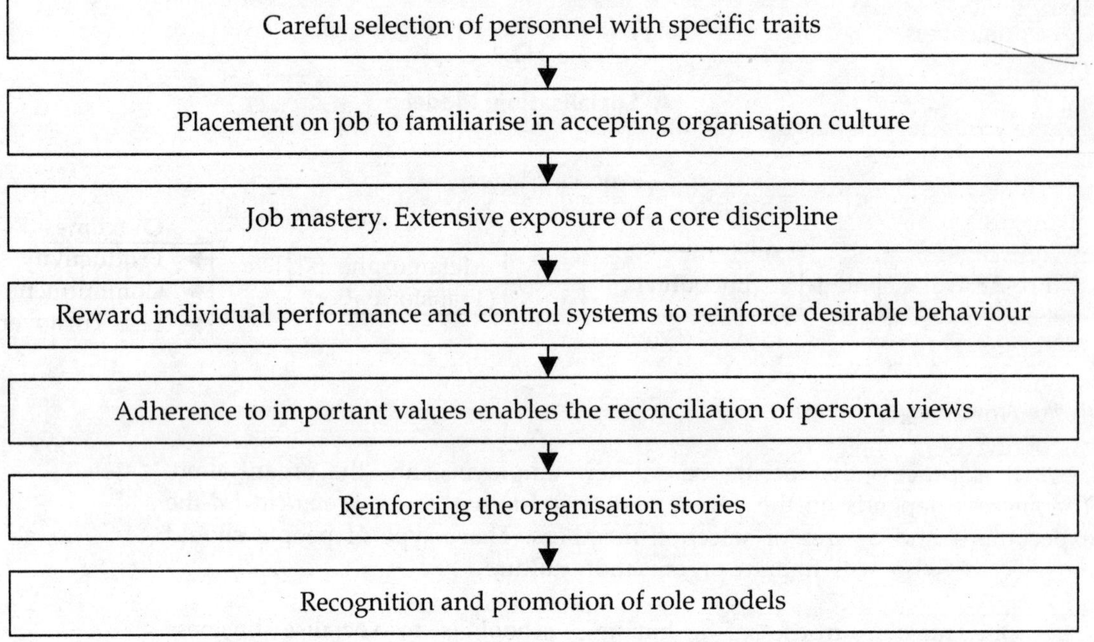

(a) *Selection Criteria*: *Selection of entry-level personnel.* Using standardised procedures and seeking specific traits that lead to effective performance and candidate will fit into the organisation's team-oriented culture.

(b) *Socialisation—the process that adapts employees to the organisation's culture: Placement on the Job itself.* Exposure to different experiences whose purpose is to cause them to question the organisation's norms and values and to decide whether or not they can accept them.

(c) *Job Mastery*: Once the initial "cultural shock" is over, the next step is mastery of one's job. This is done via extensive and carefully reinforced field experience.

(d) Measuring and rewarding individual performance and matching employee's values to those of the organisation. The actions of top management have a major impact on the organisation culture as to what actions will pay-off in terms of pay raises, promotions and other rewards.

7. CAN ORGANISATION CULTURE BE ALTERED OR REALIGNED?

Organisation culture can be altered. It can be managed and realigned to the strategic direction an organisation wishes to take. Bate (1995) argues that, within organisations, culture is a dynamic, continuously developing phenomenon. If managers can manage organisations' cultures they can change culture and also prevent its change as well as abandon or destroy it (Ogbonna, 1993). We explore possible frameworks for managing both gradual or developmental change and more radical or transformational change to a new culture.

Frameworks for Managing the Change

Lewis (1996) reviews a range of frameworks for managing cultural change. One of the most widely quoted of these is Lewin's (1952) three steps of unfreezing, moving and refreezing. Lewin's framework emphasises that before an organisation can be transformed to a completely new culture, the embedded culture must be unfrozen and made more susceptible to change. Subsequent to the change his framework highlights the importance of stabilising and institutionalising the new culture, in Lewin's words refreezing. As shown in Fig. 17.5, these features are common in frameworks involving both questions and steps which offer a process.

FIG. 17.5

Typical Frameworks for Managing Culture Change

Kilmann (1984, 1989)	*Wilkins and Patterson (1985)*
Five Steps: • surfacing actual norms (more or less equivalent to surfacing the culture) • articulating new directions • establishing new norms • identifying culture gaps • closing culture gaps	*Four Questions:* • where are we now as a culture? • where do we need to be going strategically as an organisation? • what are the gaps between where we are as a culture and where we should be? • what is our plan of action to close the gaps?

Cultural change will occur from and within an existing organisational culture and be influenced by wider societal and notional cultures. Strategies for cultural change can be either top-down or bottom-up approach. Change in organisation culture may take a form explained in Fig. 17.6.

FIG. 17.6

The New and Old Organisational Cultures (Developed from Hastings, 1993)

Old Culture	New Culture
• Hierarchies • Boundaries • Internal focus	• Teams • Connections • External focus
• Paternalistic • Second guessing • Controlling	• Empowerment • Trusting • Supportive
• Analysis • Risk aversion	• Action • Calculated risk-taking or innovation

8. ALTERNATIVE APPROACHES TO CREATING CULTURE CHANGE

Once a mindset is audited and gaps are identified, the mindset can be changed. Making a cultural change happen has become more practical in recent years as more organisations are undertaking variety of cultural change efforts.

Types of culture change efforts are explained in Fig. 17.7.

FIG. 17.7

I. Top-Down
(Directive Approach)

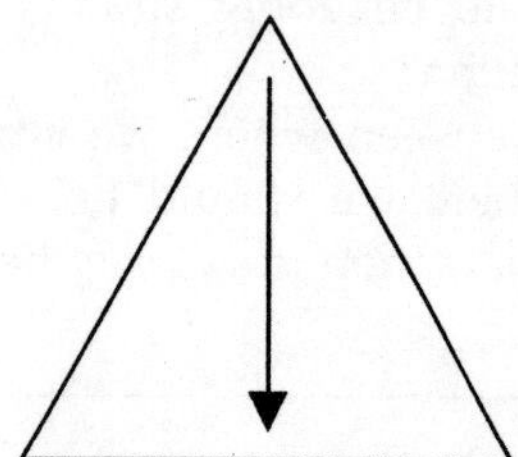

II. Side-to-Side
(Process Approach)
(Process Reengineering)

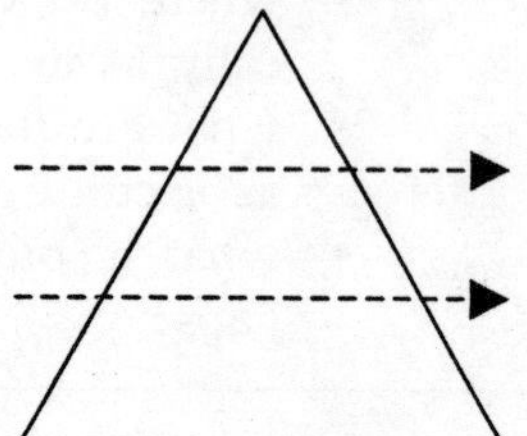

III. Bottom-Up
(Employee Empowerment)

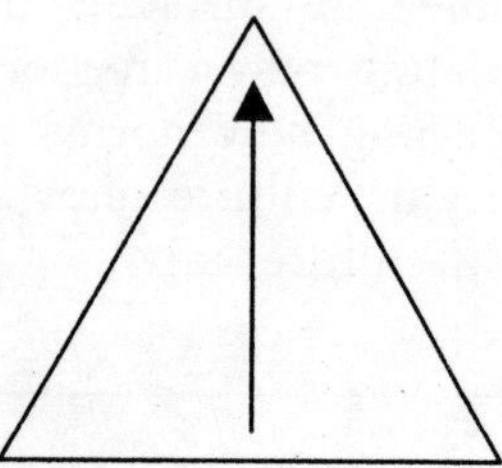

These types of cultural change efforts may be explained by simple metaphor. If you are going for walk and a mosquito lands on your arm, what would you do? There are three approaches:

First, *the top-down approach*—to making sure that mosquito did not attack, a government programme to train people to avoid mosquito infested areas, to wear long sleeves shirts, to study causes of the mosquito problem.

Second, *the process approach*—would be to reinvent and re-engineer efforts to draw the severage spray for mosquitoes so as to prevent mosquito attacks.

Third, *the empowerment approach*—would be to kill the mosquitoes when it lands on your arm. Employees jointly act and bring the change quickly (kill the mosquitoes). The third type bottom-up empowerment cultural change occurs when the desired culture is quickly translated into employee actions.

It may be mentioned that strategies for changing culture can adopt a range of approaches. These are often divided into *top-down* and *bottom-up* approaches have more chance of achieving cultural change because they start from concrete problems related to the organisation, whereas top-down approaches start with people's values. The choice of approach is, however, dependent upon what an organisation wishes to achieve and the time frame available. Both top-down and bottom-up approaches can be supported by a range of interventions. Interventions need to project the same values as the desired culture.

9. IS CORPORATE CULTURE NOW IN CRISIS?

Even in the beginning of new millennium the "corporate culture" had become widely accepted term in business.

Commonly shared values and assumptions are important, but are of no use, if they are just a set of phrases and sayings that are written down, but not actually practised, by each and every person in the organisation. In fact, when an organisation pays only lip service to its values, the management of organisation loses credibility and faith not only within, but also outside the organisation.

Terrence E. Deal and Alian A. Kennedy have now focussed that the *corporate culture landscape has shifted*. In some corporations traditional cultural pattern have seriously eroded, e.g. GM, GE, Kodak, IBM, Woolworth. It is not easy to maintain a cohesive culture in the face of external flux and economic ups and downs. It is *difficult to balance* the conflicting demands of customers, shareholders and employees. So managers are bereft of ideas for where to turn.

Factors Causing Crisis in Corporate Culture

According to them the corporate cultures are in crisis—due to following factors:

(i) *Shareholders' value* movement and the impact it has had on corporate decision-making.

(ii) Focus on *downsizing*, which has cut the soul of many corporations.

(iii) *Outsourcing* has emerged as new tool of cost-cutting when conventional cost-reduction approaches have begun to run out of steam.

(iv) How *corporate merger-mania* has forced the most—unlikely combinations on the work-forces which are still realising from waves of cost-cutting of early 1990s.

(v) How *computerisation* (potentially a tool for relieving employees from drudgery), has instead violated employees from one another and made them *servants to machines*.

(vi) How *narrowing boundaries* of the world have thrown peoples together in *global workplace*.

Combination of these factors have thrown traditional corporate cultures, replacing joy, commitment and loyalty with fear, alienation and self-interest.

Need for Building New Corporate Culture

So they have stressed the need for rebuilding new corporate culture. So task is to rebuild cohesive cultures:

(i) *Importance of leadership.* In an effort to rebuild the cultural cohesion of buisness leadership role is vital. They can add momentum to a culture re-building.

(ii) It is essential to rebuild the *social context of work,* if *people are to be motivated* to give their best efforts to their employers. This is the challenge of decade.

- ❑ Manager can begin the process of *redefining the workplace* as a meaningful *human environment* with high potential for top productivity.
- ❑ They can help to make work an attractive place to be.
- ❑ Managers can recapture the spirit of employees and channel this energy into furthering the goals of the business. But they can do so only if they recognise the *mutual dependencies* of

employees and employers and need to create a cultural milieu that benefits all. Managers who accept this challenge will become the business leaders of tomorrow.

10. STEPS FOR REBUILDING ORGANISATION CULTURE IN HIGHLY TURBULENT COMPETITIVE ENVIRONMENT

Terrence and Kennedy have suggested following steps are:

(i) Making people *want to go to work*, by providing good *favourable compensation* and remove pay as demotivating factor.

(ii) Reasonable level of *job security*. Employers have created the problem of rampant job insecurity by their own actions. Although the promise of a job security for two years is hardly enough to allow workers to feel secure, even such a limited guarantee can make a much difference. All it takes on the part an employer is a little foresight and a willingness to be *fair to employees*.

(iii) Focus on *job content and job satisfaction*. Decentralisation of work can help in this aspect.

(iv) A *socially rewarding environment*:

- the first crucial element is *respect* for employee and feeling that *he is valued*,
- building *happy and productive* employees through fun and adventure (full of challenge) at work, and
- *fellowship at work*. Teamwork with similar values.

(v) Physically comfortable work environment:

- cleanliness; and
- *informal place for interaction* and socially friendly working environment.

(vi) Preparing to *live in globalised world*, such as *cross-cultural differences* and preparing to learn from others:

- Develop potential synergies to be gained from *understanding and using other's values, knowledge and experience.*
- Not to undermine foreign cultures and team members to work together.

(vii) Building a *learning environment at work*, e.g.:

- creating a knowledge-based environment;
- steps for individual learning and organisation learning; and
- knowledge people as the basis of future business.

Terrence and Kennedy have concluded with the observations that *business inevitably moves in cycles*. Americans are optimistic enough to balance and shake-off some of the recent excesses. The rebalance of business interests is needed to help restore some semblance of sanity to the workplace. The ability to judiciously manage and balance the competing interests (of the stakeholders) is of vital importance. The need of any one particular stakeholder is best met by serving the needs of all the stakeholders. A study spanning 172 companies in 19 industries, conducted over 11 years by Kotter and Heskett shows that multi-stakeholder culture companies are far more successful than those with a narrow focus. For sustaining the culture, it is imperative that the movement is oriented to a higher good.

Long-term higher goals, by their very nature are unselfish. They focus on the good of many rather than advantage to a few. If we take a look at Japanese companies which have been storming the world with high quality, low price products, we will find that these organisations never have selfish or limited motives such as mere generation of profits as their long-term higher goal.

An example of such a company would be Sony. Co-founded by Akio Morita, the company was able to produce high quality products only because of the desire to provide good products to the people. It could have as well, made a quick buck by producing cheap products, but the higher goal guided it towards an unselfish, and in the long-run, a phenomenally successfully objective.

Reference

S.K. Bhatia, Management of Change and Organisation Development, Deep & Deep Publications Pvt. Ltd., New Delhi.

CHAPTER

18

Learning Organisation

The works of Peter Senge has stimulated considerable interest in the conditions under which individuals, teams and organisations learn. Senge (1990) writes about the importance of systems thinking ("The Fifth Discipline") in organisations and learning disabilities such as—focussing on one's job exclusively with little sense of responsibility for the collective product, another is blaming the "enemy out there" for things that are wrong, whether it is another department in the same organisation or a competitor overseas (W.L. French and C.H. Bell, Jr., "Organisation Development", Sixth edition, p. 47).

MEANING

Senge has characterised the learning organisation as the simpler *adaptive learning* and is the first stage of the learning organisation, i.e. adapting to environmental changes. *Generative learning* involves: (i) creativity and innovation to being ahead of, and (ii) anticipating change. The learning organisation ensures that change enhances its experience, and thus promotes learning.

Generative learning goes beyond merely *adapting to change;* instead, they *thrive to anticipate and learn from change.* Here emphasis is on continuous experimentation and feedback.

Let us understand certain aspects, such as—why need for learning organisation has arisen and what are common practices such organisations follow. These aspects are explained as under:

WHY NEED FOR LEARNING ORGANISATION?

With the fast changes due to advanced *information technology* and *total quality*, it has become important for organisations for entry into competition in global economy. To become successful and gain *competitive advantage*, organisations must become learning organisations.

To survive in tough business world, it is not important to *be the best*, but also to keep evolving to *stay the best*. This is the identity of learning organisations. It must open its eyes, ears, and mind to ground conditions and not miss the sights and sounds that can form the basis for its future. The philosophy of learning organisation is examining, enhancing and improving every business experience. Learning organisation ensures that change enhances its experience and thus promotes learning. Change is an input that leads to learning.

VALUES OF LEARNING ORGANISATION

Fred Luthans states that learning organisations are characterised by *human-oriented cultural values* such as these:

(a) *everyone can be source of useful ideas*, so personnel should have access to any information that can be of value to them;

(b) *the people closer to the problem* usually have the best ideas regarding how to solve it, so *empowerment* should be promoted;

(c) learning *flows up* and down the hierarchy;

(d) new ideas are important and should be *encouraged* and rewarded; and

(e) *mistakes should be* viewed as learning opportunities. This point of learning from failures is important for people in the learning organisation.

PRACTICES OF LEARNING ORGANISATION

Some common operational practices in learning organisations, particularly dealing with people are:

I. Openness

Managers must be *receptive to new ideas and overcome* the desire to *closely control* operations. Learning organisations break this mould and teach their people to look at things differently.

For example: Whirlpool Corporation in USA was concentrating for large share of the US market. However, economic analysis revealed future growth would be outside the USA. In order to teach its managers to change their thinking and begin focusing world-wide, the firm held a world-wide leadership conference in Europe and established cross-national and *cross-functional teams* to develop and implement plans of action.

People openly communicate with each other (across vertical and horizontal levels) without fear of criticism. It is team learning through dialogue and discussion. It is fostering learning in other teams in the organisation to think insightfully about complex issues.

2. Developing Systems Thinking

Senge calls systems thinking the fifth discipline because it integrates the other four disciplines. Systems is the discipline of treating organisations, issues and problems as a whole. Another way to operationalise the *learning process* in the organisation is to *develop systems thinking among managers.* This involves the ability to see connection between *issues, events and data* as a whole (inter-relationships) rather than series of unconnected parts. *Teaching* people to identify the sources of conflict they may have with other personnel, units and departments and to negotiate and make trade-offs skillfully. Use of inter-functional teams on projects, thus, removing artificial *barriers between functional areas* and between line and staff. People discard their old ways of thinking and doing jobs.

3. Development of Creativity

Another practice of learning organisation is to *develop creativity among personnel.* Creativity is the ability to formulate *unique approaches* to problem-solving and decision-making. Learning organisations focus on getting employees to break their habits and think "outside the box".

For example: We quote a contrast between the American and Japanese firms in radio industry. American firms felt in 1950s that radios would follow the natural growth curve, reaching maturity and then decline phase of product life. Japanese, on other hand, went "outside the box" of predictable thinking and looked at creative ways that the demand of radios could increase in future. So Sony created a product that focused the peoples' need—Sony Walkman.

4. Proactive Approach

Another practice is *proactive approach to problem-solving by managements.* They should solve the problems before critical situation develops.

5. Instill a Sense of Empathy and Sensitivity

Another practice in learning organisation is to instill a sense of *empathy* and *sensitivity towards others.* People to sort out misunderstandings through discussion, mutual problem-solving, maintain confidence and trust in the other party. This encourages team working.

6. Institutionalise Learning

Organisation to build not only individual knowledge, but also *institutionalise knowledge and values* so that these are transferred when some one leaves the scene. The culture retains the knowledge and values. One way to launch learning organisation is to create *teaching organisation* where people teach, what they learn, to others.

7. Leadership

(a) Leadership in the organisation to develop a culture of *strategic thinking* so as to completely overhaul the organisation.

(b) They should build *shared vision* for the organisation. A shared vision provides focus and energy for learning and bringing about change. It was a shared vision of freedom from colonial domination that lead the Indian people to rally behind Mahatma Gandhi.

(c) They also define the *core values* around which organisation will operate.

8. Fostering Positive Mental Mindset (Mental Models)

Learning organisations foster *the right mental model* among employees for meeting all situations. Organisation has ability to challenge existing dogmas, values and practices, in order to learn or unlearn from business situation. Organisation has to *learn for the future.*

9. Learning from Mistakes

Teams to review experiences after completion of a project and do self-reflection. They should have an honest assessment of success and failure experiences of the project.

10. Risk Taking

Management to encourage employees to take calculated risks in business operations, which will increase opportunities. Managements to have quick response to market forces.

Senge summarises the differences between learning organisations and traditional organisations in Table 18.1.

TABLE 18.1

Traditional *Versus* Learning Organisations

Function	*Traditional Organisations*	*Learning Organisations*
Determination of overall direction	Vision is provided by *top management.*	There is a *shared vision* that can emerge from many places, but top management is responsible for ensuring that this vision exists and is nurtured.
Formulation of implementation of ideas	*Top management* decides what is to be done, and the rest of the organisation acts on these ideas.	Formulation and implementation of ideas take place *at all levels* of the organizations.
Nature of organisational thinking	Each person is responsible for his or her own job responsibilities, and the focus is on developing *individual* competence.	Personnel understand their own jobs as well as the way in which their own work *interrelates* the influences that of other personnel.
Conflict resolution	Conflicts are resolved through the use of *power* and hierarchical influence.	Conflicts are resolved through the use of *collaborative* learning and the integration of diverse viewpoints of personnel throughout the organisation.
Leadership and motivation	The role of the leader is to establish the organisation's vision, provide rewards and punishments as appropriate, and maintain *overall control* of employee activities.	The role of the leader is to build a shared vision, empower the personnel, inspire commitment, and encourage effective decision-making throughout the enterprise through the use of *empowerment* and charismatic leadership.

It may be mentioned that the book called "The Fifth Discipline: The Art a Science of the Learning Organisation" by Peter M. Senge (1990) has left a major impact on managers and practitioners around the world. In this book, Senge emphasises that five components *together* can promote learning in an organisation. These are:

(i) systems thinking,

(ii) personal mastery by continual learning mode,

(iii) mental modes—positive mindset,

(iv) building shared vision, and

(v) team learning.

Over a period of time lot of books have been written elaborating concept of learning organisation.

TO SUM UP

Some of the common operational practices in learning organisations dealing with people are *openness, systemic thinking,* creativity, proactive approach in problem-solving, empathy and sensitivity, risk-taking growth.

To be effective and to have a competitive edge, the organisation must be an *applied learning organisation,* which means it would *have processes* which are totally *aligned with organisation objectives.* Learning organisations constitute the future environment for the study and application of organisation behaviour.

Reference

S.K. Bhatia, Management of Change and Organisation Development, Deep & Deep Publications Pvt. Ltd., New Delhi.

UNIT IV

EXECUTIVE DEVELOPMENT: PERSPECTIVES

CHAPTER

19

Executive Development: Concept

Managers are a vital link in the success of any organisation. No organisation can hold place of prominence without competent executive reservoir. Thus, most organisations spend lavishly on executive development.

We shall discuss this important concept under following heads:

(i) The concept

(ii) Objectives of management development programmes

(iii) Need of executive development

(iv) Methods of executive development

(v) Steps in organisation of management development

(vi) Suitability of executive development techniques

(I) THE CONCEPT

Executive or management development consists of activities by which executives *learn* to improve their *behaviour* and *performance*. It is to improve the effectiveness of managers in their *present jobs* and prepare them for *higher jobs* in future.

Management development is a systematic process of growth and development of managers abilities to manage. It is through participation in *formal courses* and also by *job experience*.

(II) OBJECTIVES OF MANAGEMENT DEVELOPMENT PROGRAMMES

Some objectives are as under:

1. To increase *overall knowledge* and *conceptual* and *decision-making* skills.
2. To improve *performance* in their present positions and future needs. It is to make them more versatile.
3. To *introduce change* in the organisation by developing executives as change agents or facilitators. They are able to *influence behaviour* of workers.
4. To *update* their knowledge, skills, analytical abilities in respective fields.
5. To provide opportunities to managers for *career advancement* and management succession.
6. To stimulate creative thinking.
7. To give the specialists an overall view of functions of an organisation and equip them to coordinate efforts effectively.

(III) NEED OF EXECUTIVE DEVELOPMENT

(a) Due to rapid pace of *technological change* require managers working knowledge of new technologies.

(b) Tough *competition* in the market require managers to meet needs of consumers.

(c) Increased recognition of *social responsibility* of modern business requires manager's awareness of these.

(d) *Socio-cultural* environment is changing, so it requires to understand behaviour of people.

(e) Frequent *labour-management conflicts* need trained managers to bring industrial peace. As workers want participation in management and motivation, manager have to develop professionalism.

(f) To impart latest management concepts, techniques and practices.

(IV) METHODS OF EXECUTIVE DEVELOPMENT

Executive Development Methods

In view of fast technological, social and environment changes executives need following categories of executive development methods:

(i) Common methods which improve *decision-making* skills of executives:

- Case study method
- Incident method

(ii) Common methods which improve *interpersonal competence* and team work of executives:

- Sensitivity training
- Passive, aggressive and assertiveness (PAS)
- Role play
- Transactional analysis
- The Johari Windows

According to P.C. Tripathi (HRD): Inter-personal competence of an individual refers to the degree to which he is accurately aware of his impact on others and of the impact of others on him. So he must know himself more accurately relating to his interpersonal behaviour. Schutz W.C. (Firo) explains that there are three interpersonal needs that cause one establish and maintain relations with others. These are given below:

- Inclusion—the need for interaction and association.
- Control—the need for Control and Power.
- Affection—the need for love and affection.

It may, however, be pointed out that sometimes a person takes the initiative to include, influence and express affection and at some other time he expects others to include, influence, and recognise him. In this way we have six types of needs that cause him to develop interpersonal relationships.

A knowledge about an individual's needs can be acquired by administering to him a cross-culturally valid instrument called FIRO-B (Fundamental Interpersonal Relationship Orientation of Behaviour) designed by Schutz in 1958. This instrument has fifty-four questions each of which can be answered in six different ways.

(iii) Common methods which improve executive knowledge:

- Conference
- Self-learning
- Job rotation
- Under-study
- Multiple management

- Lecture

(iv) Various methods of executive development are summarised in Fig. 19.1.

FIG. 19.1

Methods of Executive Development

Purpose	*Methods of Skills and Knowledge*
1. Job knowledge	(a) On-the-job experience (b) Coaching (c) Understudy (d) Conferences (e) Self-learning (f) Lecture (g) Job rotation
2. Decision-making skills	(a) Business games (b) Case study (c) In-basket exercises (d) Incident method
3. Inter-personal skills	(a) Role play (b) Sensitivity training (c) PAS (d) TA (e) Johari Window (f) FIRO
4. Organisational knowledge	(a) Job rotation (b) Multiple management (advisory committee of managers)
5. General knowledge	(a) Special courses (b) Special meetings (c) Specific readings

(V) STEPS IN MANAGEMENT DEVELOPMENT IN THE ORGANISATION

Steps in management development are as follows:

1. Analysis of organisational *developmental needs* which should cover present and future developmental needs of the organisation.
2. Preparation of *inventory* of management talents—with information of each executive in each position.
3. *Appraisal of talents so that manager's* strengths and weaknesses met future needs of the organisation. (Refer Fig. 19.1)
4. *Planning development programmes for individuals*—these may include assignment of special projects, committee assignments or specific readings.

5. *Establishing development programmes* for identified managers like on leadership courses, management games, conference training, etc.
6. *Evaluation of executive development programmes* through opinion surveys and judging effectiveness of these through changes in productivity, quality and cost, etc.

(VI) SUITABILITY OF EXECUTIVE DEVELOPMENT TECHNIQUES

The success of any management development programme depends on selection of method of training. No single technique may prove to be adequate, but only a suitable combination of techniques may yield results. Technique-based suitability are mentioned in Fig. 19.2.

FIG. 19.2

Techniques and Suitability

Technique	*Suitability*
Job rotation	To develop *diversified skills* and broaden outlook.
Under-study	To aid *succession planning* by developing skill of juniors.
Multiple management	To assist managers in expanding the knowledge in various *functional areas.*
Case study	To develop *analytical, reasoning* and *problem-solving skills.*
Role playing	• To translate theoretical knowledge into action plans • To promote human relations skills
In-basket exercise	To promote situational judgement and social sensitivity
Business games	To develop smart thinking, quick reactions, initiative, organising and leadership skills.
Sensitivity training	To promote *self-awareness* and its *impact on others.*
Conference	To expand knowledge, attitudes and develop inter-personal skills.
Lecture	To impart conceptual knowledge to large audiance within short time.

CHAPTER

20

Developing People: Some Lessons

The best managers pay careful attention to developing their people and creating their loyalty and dedication. Some lessons in developing people are:

- Hold senior people accountable for how well they are developing the careers of those who work for them.
- Be rigorous about "on time" performance reviews.
- Encourage others to take over your projects (i.e., delegate).
- Encourage people at all levels to do more and more as time goes on.
- Encourage your employees to be involved at all levels of decision-making.
- Have a variety of forums for the employees to approach management.
- Encourage your people to be fearless in speaking their mind on business or personal issues.
- Ensure lots of risk-taking. Always push the people.
- Ensure people realize that if they reach out for responsibility, they can create the environment they want. Give people flexibility, encouragement, ownership and the opportunity to get things done.
- Give people the ability to do their own thing, and if you don't agree, give them the right to discuss.

- Have a commitment to the performance review process. Establish a two-way review system in which both the evaluator and the person being evaluated fill out the same questionnaire.
- Help people understand what is needed and how to grow. Don't assume they know.
- Hold people accountable for fulfilling their responsibilities. Allow nothing to fester.
- Invite junior people into monitor a conference call that someone a level above is having, so that they can see and learn directly how a situation is handled.
- Let people define their own work and build their own roles.
- Make public commitments about initiatives and actions; keep people informed in real time.
- Move people from team to ream.
- Once a year have a formal sit-down with each person and talk about what he or she likes to do and what he or she wants to work on. Work hard to find out what people like and try to accommodate them.
- Ensure people know where they stand on a daily basis and nor just at evaluation time.
- Be very willing to give people another chance. (Some people who look as if they are not succeeding just aren't in the right spot or role.)
- Actively work at helping people "dream," and make it fun.
- Understand that employees are looking for help from managers in growing their career.
- Use your own client work as a chance for one-on-one coaching.
- Ensure that all managers are "boosters," people who will say, "You can do it, you can do it!"

CREATING AN ENERGIZING WORKPLACE

Another hallmark of successful managers is their ability to create the energy and enthusiasm for work that clearly accounted for their financial success. Here are some suggestions for creating an energetic (and energizing) workplace:

- Allow employees more control over their lives.
- Measure (and react to) employee attitudes and concerns on a regular basis.

- Allow employees to explain where they want to be, and try to accommodate them.
- Ask each person, "Where do you want to go next? What are the resources that you need?"
- Encourage everyone to grow with the job.
- Encourage those who have left and returned to talk about their outside experiences.
- Ensure everyone is going to do 100 percent. Don't tolerate less.
- Ensure people have a sense of where they are going.
- Allow middle-level managers the freedom to do what they have to do in order to improve morale.
- Stroke each other, and challenge each other.
- Be willing to give up ownership of an idea.
- Challenge conventional wisdom in every facet of the business.
- Be creative in allowing work patterns outside the traditional tracks.
- Celebrate success and teamwork, and don't bear down on failures.
- Watch closely for people who may be getting bored, and re-assign them.
- Avoid telling people how to do things, unless absolutely necessary. As long as the "outcome" gets done, allow people as much freedom as possible to do it their way.
- Don't focus on job descriptions and formal policy and procedures.
- Eliminate non-productive things like too many meetings and complicated procedures.
- Ensure everyone knows that the firm will support them.
- Have disrespect for titles and hierarchy.
- Have it understood that no matter what they come to you with, your people will receive an honest answer and it will go no further if they don't want it to.
- If someone goes on vacation, remember where he or she went and make it your business to come by and inquire about it.
- If someone makes an error, don't jump on him or her.
- Adopt the attitude: "You will not get penalized for doing something, only for doing nothing."

- If you lose a person, rather than rush to fill the slot quickly, reassign work to give more responsibility to those who did not have it.
- Let your people be the best judge of their own priorities.
- Let your people manage their own time; try new things; have a long rope; do their own thinking; run their business.
- Make people superworkers by helping them do the kind of work they want to do.
- Make sure it is an intense work experience at your firm.
- Motivate by enthusiasm and energy, not by telling people "you need to be energized."
- No spoon-feeding. Expect people to step up to the plate and fix their problems without waiting for someone to tell them to do it.
- Challenge people but do not subject them to excessive demands.
- Send handwritten notes to everyone on their anniversary with the firm.
- Give people honest explanations of everything that is happening. (They are always curious about anything going on.)
- Loosen up. Don't stay in your role all the time.
- Give people ongoing feedback along with more in-depth guidance to develop.
- Allow people to grow at their own pace and feel comfortable with what they are assigned/told/asked to do.
- Overhaul your firm's performance appraisal scheme to reflect balanced scorecard principles.
- Try to do personal things for your people.
- Regularly ask your employees which one person is the magnet for them to stay.
- Promote managers from within.
- Make sure people know where they stand in performance.
- Provide flexibility about what people want to work on and what their personal issues are.
- Provide opportunities to move ahead rapidly.
- Push to be on a leading edge, always trying to do something different and better.
- Put people in new situations and work roles.

- Put people together from different disciplines.
- Recognize achievement immediately.
- Recognize that work life and home life need to balance.
- Regularly interview people at all levels in the organization.
- Sometimes, drop by just to see people. No reason. Just to find out how they are.
- Speak freely to allow people to relax and feel comfortable to do their jobs.
- Speak regularly with everyone individually about his or her pay and performance.

  Take a moment and say "we need a time out." People need to have some fun.
- Emphasize the positives of each person.
- Prove that management cares, that the staff are people and not just bodies to be burned out.
- Run a relaxed atmosphere (and be relaxed yourself) to let people feel empowered and not under the gun.
- When a subordinate's recommendation or request is turned down, always explain why.
- Work hard to give everyone a fair chance.

APPRECIATION AND OTHER NON-FINANCIAL REWARDS

- Managers can create feeling that people efforts were appreciated some ways are.
- Be willing to give time-off if it is needed for personal reasons or for a job well done.
- Consistently thank people for a job well done and give them a pat on the back.
- Express appreciation on an informal, continuous basis.
- Give "Thank you's" every day.
- Give people an extra week-off when they get married.
- Have a leave programme for everyone, when people can do whatever they want.
- If someone comes up with a good idea that gets used, give him or her a gift certificate.

- Reward people with more diversified work by giving them more stimulating work and with different opportunities.
- Show appreciation for even small accomplishments, as soon as they happen.
- If a client has positive things to say, share them immediately via e-mails.
- Ensure that compliments from clients get transmitted to everyone in the firm, so everyone knows when a client has praised an individual.
- Show appreciation, not just with money but in small ways like sharing between teams and e-mail "thank you's."
- Worry about outcomes, not process.

CREATING FUN

Many of the firms are engaged in events like parties, days out and other similar activities that the workplace can be fun? Is fun really incompatible with hard work, or does it facilitate it? Here are some suggestions:

- Arrange a series of group days out of the office.
- Constantly merchandise the firm to their people.
- Create "Moments of Fun."
- Eat lunch together every day as a group.
- Have a charity day where the firm pledges one day of volunteer work per employee to a group of local charities.
- Have a high-profile internal creative award, the winners chosen by expert external judges.
- Have a self-deprecating, satirical, fun firm magazine.
- Have *ad-hoc* events like firmwide parties and open days.
- Keep doing things that surprise people.
- Laugh at their mistakes and kid each other.
- Offer free massages, book clubs, exercise classes, language lessons, surprise ice cream sundaes, gifts on Mother's Day, and so on.
- Arrange office outings to film premiers and shows.
- Announce promotions in song.
- Announce the top ten mistakes of the year.

- Provide a budget to decorate meeting rooms for regular office meetings.
- Hold a parents' day: Let people bring their kids to work.
- Fund client entertainment liberally.
- Make work as pleasant as possible because that is where you spend the most time!
- Regularly throw a good party! This can retain people and increase bill ability by 15 percent!
- Work hard with their people and play hard. People like and need a release.

References

S.K. Bhatia, Management of Change and Organisation Development, Deep & Deep Publications Pvt. Ltd., New Delhi.

CHAPTER

21

Career Planning and Management: Two-Way Process

To motivate employees, career planning has been emphasised as an important instrument. It is considered as an effective channel for development of employees so that they are able to give their best.

Career management is an important activity that provides benefits to both organisation and individuals. The benefits include better use of human resources, more satisfied and productive employees and more personally fulfilling careers. Some other beneficial outcomes are, reduced turnover and absenteeism, improved morale amongst the employees. It provides greater self-awareness and career awareness to employees about one's skills, abilities, weaknesses, needs and goals.

In this chapter, an attempt is made to discuss few important questions: (1) What is meaning and purpose of career planning? (2) Who is responsible for career planning and management? (3) What are organisation career development programmes? (4) What should individual do to plan his career? (5) What makes career planning successful? These are dealt with seriatum.

I. MEANING AND PURPOSE OF CAREER PLANNING

(a) Career planning essentially *means* helping the employees plan his career in terms of his capabilities within the context of organisational needs. Career planning implies planning of specific career paths of the employees in the foreseeable further in the organisation. It may be useful to workout career path charts for incumbents of different job cluster.

It does not mean predicting or envisaging what higher jobs will available for each employee. Career planning also need not imply any specific commitment on the part of the management to promote an employee. It only implies that an individual after becoming aware of some of its capabilities and career opportunities and development opportunities, chooses to develop himself in a direction that improves his chances of being able to handle new responsibilities. Identification of career opportunities becomes easier once the future manpower needs, rate of mobility, etc., are known. The reporting officer or officers at two or three levels above the employee are in a better position because of their experience and insights, to counsel the employee on his career development.

(b) As regards the *purpose* of career planning, it may be mentioned that an employee values most his career and his growth upwards within the organisation, as it gives him money, prestige and status on an increasing scale. It provides an employee with opportunities to achieve his ambition and at the same time enables him towards achievement of organisation goals. Through career planning management can work out broad schemes and plans to suit mutual goals. Career planning provides a reasonable level of satisfaction for its employees and helps in a systematic growth of the enterprise. In this connection it may be pertinent to mention that the future of an employee or his growth has a direct, one to one relationship with the growth of the company. The career planning directly flows from the overall corporate plan of the company. Career planning is, as such, an important tool in the hand of the management for developing talents of its employees.

(c) There are basically two aspects of a career plan: (a) Professional career plan; (b) Monetary compensation career plan. In order to have a successful and effective career plan in the above areas, there are certain basic ingredients, which an enlightened management, interested in effective performance of its company, can look into.

2. CAREER PLANNING AND MANAGEMENT—WHOSE RESPONSIBILITY

(i) Until recently, an individual's career was decided by the organisation. If the organisation needs some one in another location, some one was transferred. The success of one's career was often indicated by the number of moves that were made, since these moves were generally rewarded by promotions to more important and better-paying jobs. The organisation was rarely concerned with whether the new job was really what the individual wanted, and the individual had very limited control over his career.

(ii) Organisations have recently become involved in career management activities. Now, organisations are becoming concerned about whether an individual's abilities and needs are really matched to the job. Previously, organisations were concerned only with the matching an employee's abilities to the demands of the job. Now they are also concerned with matching an employee's needs to the rewards of the job. For example, organisations are beginning to accept the fact that not all people want to be promoted or can be promoted. As a result, it has become more legitimate to have a successful career without climbing to the top of the organisation.

(iii) There are two components of career planning and development. One is development programmes that an organisation can provide its employees in order to help match employee's needs, goals and abilities with organisational job demands (current or future opportunities and challenges). In other words, the purpose of career development programme is to increase the employee's likelihood of achieving personal fulfilment and to ensure that the organisation places the right people in the right place at the right time. Career development programmes are, therefore, aimed at satisfying the two matches, the match between individual ability and job demands and the match between individual needs and job rewards. These development programmes help improve overall performance and contribution of individuals. Career development programmes make an organisation more attractive to stay in.

The second component is Career Planning Activities. Although organisations may offer career planning activities, one can engage for himself to help ensure his own career success, job security, self-esteem, growth and comfort. Career planning programmes help an organisation obtain and retain the right people.

(iv) Having these two components planning and development, thus underlines the need and importance for the individual as well as the organisation to be involved in career management. One has therefore to be aware what organisation can do for his career and what he can do for his career. It is a two-way process. Organisation can be most effective in helping and encouraging them to do their own career planning.

3. ORGANISATION CAREER DEVELOPMENT PROGRAMME

Taking the second question, it may be mentioned that career development programmes are offered by organisations to assist employees in career planning and development. Few are mentioned below and these illustrate the diversity of needs that are filled by these programmes in the career management.

3.1 To Develop Career Paths

Career pathing programmes consist of two major activities:

(a) One is career planning which is offered by the organisation and is directly related to it and its specific jobs. Career planning essentially means helping the employees plan their career in terms of their capabilities within the context of organisation needs. Career path charts are worked out for incumbents of difficult job clusters. Career profile or career ladder or career map outlines the hierarchical progression of fresh entrants at induction level in different functions. It is natural the young management trainees would like to know about their prospects 8-10 years after recruitment. Really good men want to seek a career rather than short period job. In this employee is also helped in the personal appraisal activity. It implies that an individual after becoming aware of some of his capabilities and career opportunities, chooses to develop himself in a direction that improves his chances of being able to handle new responsibilities.

(b) The second is job progression programmes. It provides a set of experiences that helps an employee: (i) satisfy some of those values, goals; (ii) utilise sole of those strengths and abilities; and (iii) improve upon some of these weaknesses identified in career planning activity. It serves the practical needs of the employees and the organisation. Here the focus is on the job as the vehicle for career development. This is due to the reason that most important influences occur of the job and different jobs demand the development of different skills. Different jobs require three basic dimensions: know-how, problem-solving, and accountability. These dimensions require different employee skills. A rational sequence of job assignments for an employee's career development would consist of jobs with different dimensions. Such a job progression programme can be very helpful in opening up career opportunities.

3.2 Develop Performance Appraisal

Performance Appraisal is an important part of a career development system, since it identifies how well employee's performance. The information can be used to plan that employee's career path.

Develop Training and Development Programmes

These are quite complementary to career planning and management and rather are part of it. These are most useful where it is intended to focus on a specific skill to be taught in order to improve an employee's performance in the short-term.

3.3 Redefine, Measure of Success in the Short-Term

Many organisations are experiencing slow growth and less ability to offer unlimited advancement. This, combined with the bulge of 35 to 58 age group in the 1980's and 1990's will really limit, for many employees, the traditional route to success—the promotion. Organisations are responding to this potential crisis by redefining the essence of success, that is, by reducing the level of importance of promotion in the definition of success. One way they are doing this is through cross-functional lateral transfers, where once employees avoided lateral transfers, they are beginning to value them. The benefits go to both the organisation and the individual. The job rotation programme opens up promotion opportunities that were previously blocked to a person because he lacked the necessary experience. Thus, though promotion time may be slowed down with lateral transfer programmes, they help ensure an employee that there will be promotion opportunities down the career.

3.4 Career Stress Management

Many employees experience stress at work that is just as damaging to an individual's career as it is to be organisation. Not all employees experience career stress or blocked in the job. Such symptoms include apathy, withdrawal, dissatisfaction, irritability, absenteeism, ulcers, hypertension, increased likelihood of heart disease and accident proneness. In order to help alleviate or reduce the occurrence of these stress symptoms, it is important to know two of the major reasons in career stress in organisations. One is uncertainty because when one feels blockage of career. The other is lack of control when one feels that he is on way out. It is out of his control.

As a consequence of these two reasons for stress, organisation can offer career stress management programmes to help individuals get back in control and to clarify uncertainties. One way of clarifying uncertainties or reduce stress associated with job responsibilities is through performance appraisal. To help the individuals get back in control there are various ways. For example, by implementing a programme to increase the level of employee participation in decisions that most clearly affect how and when one does a job. Other steps could be such as: (a) structure one's time stringently. To make a list of activities every day and force oneself to do that; (b) marshal one's social support system by using every friend and family member that one can count on to give a boost when one's spirits are sagging; (c) find one's most effective and constructive escape routes such as to do more than regular amount of exercise. Reading habit may feel one positive and motivate. Negative escapes such as TV, over-eating, drinking can be avoided by positive persists; (d) balancing work and leisure and also reward oneself when one finishes a task; (e) doing every thing one can to activate his own motivation. It is to be remembered that no one can care and it is the individual has to do himself.

4. INDIVIDUAL'S CAREER PLANNING ACTIVITIES

It is also important for any employee to remain attractive to the organisation. People should, therefore, definitely assume some responsibility for their own careers. Although organisations may offer career planning activities, one can engage in oneself. This helps him to attain for himself—job security, career success, high self-esteem, growth, comfort and peace. It is also accepted fact that without conscious planning, one is less likely to attain those career purposes. Some of the steps are:

4.1 Personal Appraisal and Career Thinking

Personal appraisal is critical for one's personal success. So one should identify—values, goals, skills, strengths, weaknesses and objectives.

4.2 Know the Realities of Organisation Life

Two realities of organisation life are: (a) organisation expectations, and (b) organisation disappointments. Organisation expectations are competence to get a job done, ability to generate and sell ideas, loyalty and commitment, high personal integrity and strength, capacity to grow, ability to accept organisational realities. Organisational disappointments: What organisations do or do not do bring employees disappointments (reality shock). Here are several likely reasons: (i) providing low initial job challenge to new employees as they are perceived as novice; (ii) New comers have unrealistically high aspirations; (iii) Inability of the employee to create his own challenge out of unstructured situation; (iv) Inability to determine the real criteria for performance appraisal and complaining about non-feedback, although their supervisors may claim the opposite; (v) Another area of reality shock is the amount of conflict and uncertainty in the organisation. Employees think that rules and procedures, directions, and communications will be clear. The reality is that many situations are just the opposite.

4.3 Becoming Useful to Organisation

In order to manage one's career effectively, *one has to do well* so that one can get one wants from the organisation. It may mean getting promoted by becoming *valuable and useful to the organisation*. As such one must know: (i) dealing with his boss through an outstanding performance. It pays to work for a good boss who has something to teach, who is on the move and who is capable of taking others along. People are less dependent and uncertain if they are allied with bosses who are strong leaders; (ii) one must know how to get promoted. For this one has to acquire certain qualities such as: (a) developing credibility with senior managers, for having ability to produce results and take risks; (b) to have reputation of being an expert and innovative; (c) another important way is to know how to unstop a career bottleneck. To avoid getting stuck in a job that no longer provides growth or promotional opportunities, one has to investigate the possibility of a lateral move. If that does not work, one has to make out ways to increase job responsibilities and if that fails to work, consider changing the organisation.

5. MAKING CAREER PLANNING SUCCESSFUL

For making the career plan work as an effective instrument for development of men there are two important aspects that have to be accepted. Firstly, a commitment on the part of the supervisor that his men and their growth are his primary responsibility and that his success should be judged in terms of men's career he has held to build by his contribution and assistance. Secondly, the management as a whole should be committed to help the employees attain their full potential by training, job rotation and acceptance and greater challenges and responsibilities. This calls for imaginative planning and involvement of management at various levels. Personnel policies are to be tailored to fit the needs of the organisation and employees so that motivation is kept in a dynamic form.

6. TO CONCLUDE

Career management has numerous benefits for the organisation and employees. Organisations can help employees by offering career development programmes and encouraging them to do their own career planning. Employees have to definitely assume some responsibility for their own careers. As such they should identify their own goals, strengths and weaknesses. They should also prepare for the realities of organisational life, and do well so that they are useful to the organisation. Career planning is an important instrument for motivation and development of employees in an organisation.

Reference

S.K. Bhatia, Principles of Human Resource Management, Deep & Deep Publications Pvt. Ltd., New Delhi.

CHAPTER

22

Promotion: Individual's Role

To survive in this tough competitive environment in the world, it is not important to be the best, but also to keep evolving to say the best. We have to form the basis for our future.

Career management is important activity that provides benefits to both organisation and individuals. The benefits include more fulfilling careers for progression and experiences that help employees to utilise strengths and abilities. So organisations provide two components—(a) career planning, and (b) development programmes. The *career development* activities are aimed at satisfying the two matches, the match between individual ability and job demands and the match between individual needs and job rewards. Career development programmes make an organisation more attractive to stay in for employees.

These two components—career planning, and development, underline the need and importance for the individual as well as the organisation to be involved in career management. One has therefore to be aware what organisation can do for his career and what he can do for his career. It is *two-way process.* Organisation can be most effective in helping and encouraging employees to do their own career planning to be ahead in the race for future opportunities. While organisation provides various *career planning and development programmes*, such as, career profiles/paths, job progression programmes, develops performance and appraisal systems, career stress management for employees.

In tomorrow's highly competitive and dynamic world, one thing will be constant—customer is important. To attract and retain customers you not only anticipate and satisfying customer's needs, but also delight. In this way you will be considered innovatively contributing on continuous basis to the organisation.

PROMOTION—THE INDIVIDUAL'S ROLE

Let us start with an obvious question: Can one plan his own promotion? The simple answer is 'yes'. It may be difficult and like other plans may go wrong. Nonetheless, we have a better chance if we plan than if we do not. Individuals need to plan their own careers and their own promotion with just as much care as a successful company planning its operations.

Planning is not just a matter of deciding you'd like to become managing director by writing a few notes on a piece of paper. It is a process that requires a considerable amount of time and thought. A plan, once made, should be subject to continual review and revision to take account of new opportunities or obstacles. The point we would like to make here is that it does take time. It does not seem unreasonable to devote 5 per cent of one's time to furthering one's own career. At times you will spend a much high proportion of your time, for instance, when you are on a training course. But week in, week out, you can probably use two hours in a week to planning and developing your career. Some essential considerations in the planning process are:

1. KEEP YOUR OPTIONS OPEN AND MAKE YOUR OWN OPPORTUNITIES

In any case, it is a fairly sound rule to keep your options open as long as possible. In the course of a lifetime there are many opportunities you can take or miss. Some people say that it is a matter of luck as to what opportunities come your way. Others say that the lucky ones make their own opportunities. Either way the ambitious man should examine developments, not just in his own department but in the wider context of the organisation he works for and world outside it. One should know how to overcome a career bottleneck. Each development should be considered to see whether any opportunity can be identified for one's own personal advancement. You have to plan your opportunities; you have to create them and be ready to take them.

2. DOES YOUR CONTRIBUTION HELP?

It may help to illustrate this point with the contribution of two young men towards their job. Rahul was a pleasant steady young man. He worked normal office hours and did what he was told to do, no more and no less. At the end of an assignment he got a small rise.

Another youngman Vivek joined the organisation because of his specialist knowledge. He was better educated than rest of the group. He worked extremely hard, was full of *ideas and contributed* significantly to the projects entrusted to him. He made use of this knowledge to good effect. He made positive suggestions to improve the work and took pains to understand the work being done by the rest of the team and to learn something about their special knowledge and techniques. He has moved upwards steadily in the organisation.

It illustrates a number of points related to promotion. While doing the bare minimum job and keeping one's nose clean, as Rahul did, may ensure a rise through one or two levels in a service type organisation, it is disastrous in any more dynamic organisation.

The successful pattern is seen in Vivek. He went *out of his way to do everything* he could to make projects a success. His promotion has continued in the subsequent years. This is because he brings his mind with him to the job and makes *a positive contribution* to any organisation he works for.

3. YOU ARE MASTER OF YOUR OWN DESTINY

When an organisation enters a new project, it plans the project carefully. It sets out its objectives, evaluates the risks, counts the costs and estimates the rewards. The individual must do the same in planning his career. It is, however, important to keep one's career in perspective. The man of average intelligence, who has sufficient determination, can reach the top of most pyramids. To make your way up the promotion ladder, both *determination and planning* are needed. Take care to get what you like or you will be forced to like, what you get. You need to clear your own mind about what you want. Remember also that work and promotion are not the whole thing in life. You must decide what part you want them to play in your own life.

4. THE GOLDEN RULES

A few golden rules to guide you along your promotion path are outlined below:

4.1 Know Yourself and Your Job

The first step in making the plan for your own promotion—your life career plan—is to collect the relevant information. The most relevant information is information about yourself. Knowing yourself is the essential prerequisite to developing your full potential. An assessment by individual of his abilities, interests and career goals is vital.

(a) Exploit your Strengths

Individual has to assume responsibility and has to make conscious efforts. One has to carry out his personal appraisal and what is termed as strengths and weaknesses balance sheet (SWBS). We all have strengths and weaknesses. It is generally more profitable to make an effort to exploit your strengths than cover your weaknesses. Protect yourself from your weaknesses either by avoiding unsuitable jobs or by covering your weakness with staff who do not share your weaknesses. Remember that *you will be promoted for your particular strength*. If you are strong enough in one thing you will be promoted for this strength in spite of your weaknesses. An established principle of war is 'Reinforce Success'. In the same way as you build on your strengths, so should you also build on your interests.

(b) Become a Jack of All Trades and Master of One

Mastery of one skill or specialisation or core competency brings you initial promotions. As you move higher up the ladder, particularly if you move into general management, a very broad interest and knowledge of the business and competitive environmental challenges is clearly an essential. Too narrow a specialisation limits promotion prospects in the long-run. In the competitive era, we have to learn new competencies so as to be ever preferred person with customer orientation attitude.

(c) Develop your Independence

No one can be independent if he is up to his ears in debt or if he is tied to one organisation. There are two aspects of independence you should give your mind to if you are *ambitious*. The first is to develop a degree of financial independence, so that you can afford to take up opportunities when they occur. It also enables you to stick to your views on what is right without that awful worrying feelings about what will happen to you and your family if you lose your job. The second is to develop and *keep up-to-date* in your own particular skill and profession. A justified belief in your own ability to do a particular *job better than most* and the knowledge that you can move almost at will into a similar job elsewhere is the best guarantee of real independence.

(d) Be Prepared to take Risks

By this we do not suggest that one should become a gambler. Risks should be carefully evaluated and you should try to arrange things so that you stand to gain the greatest reward from the lowest possible risk. If you are to get on in life you will have to take some risks to catch opportunities.

(e) Understand Realities of Organisation Life

Organisation has expectations and organisation disappointments. These expectations from individual are—competence, commitment, integrity and capacity to grow in the organisation. While some disappointments are—unstructured situations, conflict and uncertainty and politics in organisation. We have to deliver results in times of discontinuity.

4.2 Know Your Boss

(a) Perhaps the single most important factor affecting your promotion, outside yourself, is your boss and your relationship with him. You may think that your boss will have less influence over your future as you move up a hierarchy; this is not so. The higher up you move, the more critical your relationship with your boss becomes. It is important to know your boss or even to like and to respect him. You must know what makes him tick; what his prejudices and hates are. The first thing is to establish to your own satisfaction that you are reasonably compatible. Try to paint a picture in your own mind of *what he expects from you.*

(b) Cherish your Boss

Your future is bound up with him. You can learn a lot from your boss—whether he is a good or bad one. If he does well, he can help you. If he goes steadily to the top, he can take you with him. In formal appraisal or annual review system, it is your boss who will review you. What he writes about you will remain on your performance appraisal record, while you remain with the organisation. If he is successful, he has a better chance of securing privileges, and promotion for his staff. There is a very noticeable difference in your working conditions and prospects if you *work for a successful boss* as compared with one who is struggling.

(c) Never Stab your Boss in the Back

It doesn't pay. Your boss is the man who should be your first champion and advocate in the organisation. If you try but fail to move him, you will have to move yourself or life will become very uncomfortable. If you succeed you will not necessarily get his job and his successor may be worse. If you get a *reputation for treachery,* no one will want to have you on their staff. Even the man who encourages you to do the deed will probably disown you.

(d) Help your Boss

The first and most important way in which you can help your boss is to refrain from wasting his time. Do not disturb your bóss unless you need to. If you need to do so, try to do it at a time which is convenient to him rather than at the time it is easiest for you. More important, *be prepared* when you do go to see him. Have a clear idea in your own mind what you want from your discussion with the boss. It is still best to go to the boss with the problem and with a suggested solution. Another way you can help your boss is to be prepared to do that *little extra*. Some awkward or difficult jobs crop up in any department. Be prepared to do it. If your boss develops a picture of you as *keen and willing*, it is likely to be to your advantage. There is one major way in which you can do a little extra to help your boss. Accept delegation of some of his work. Let him see that you regard the work he delegates to you as opportunity, not an imposition. We have to develop our potential for accepting challenges and shoulder higher responsibilities. We have to depict our qualitative difference.

4.3 Plan Your Development

(a) Increase your Effectiveness

If you hope for promotion, one essential is to increase your effectiveness and work just smarter. The key is learning how to use your time effectively. Your time is perhaps the most important resource you have. It is also a finite resource. It pays you to find out whether you use your time towards achieving objectives of your real job. The first principle to improve effectiveness is to cut out unnecessary work and concentrate on your real work. One method to save time and to make sure you use your time effectively is to keep action lists. Sit down quietly for a quarter of an hour and list out all the things you ought to do with dates by which these are to be done. Besides, you should be careful and thorough in your preparation for the meetings and know what you want to achieve from them. The *more you know* about the individuals you are going to meet, the more effective the meeting is likely to be. It must be realised that it is a mistake to work long hours regularly. The secret is not to work longer hours, but to work smartly and more effectively. Further, if you want to be effective, learn not to take things at face value. Look below the surface to find out the reason. And be an achiever and peak performer. Develop a reputation of being innovative and creditability for ability to produce results which contribute to organisation goals and values. One should also grow by acquiring wider experience and maturity.

(b) Be Positive and Determined

Be clear about your own plans and objectives. Do not approach them half-heartedly. Be determined to achieve what you set out to. Doubts and feelings that it is probably worth a try are a recipe for disaster. If you have realistically appraised a situation and decided on a plan and on your objectives, go firmly forward to success and do not allow yourself to be discouraged or diverted. *Self-discipline* is perhaps the essential key to advancement in any field.

(c) Be Resilient

Always take a positive attitude to your work and your own promotion plans. When you suffer a setback, as you will, plan and fight your way through. Having learnt the lessons, overhaul your plan, set your new objectives and set out with a firm determination to achieve them. Many people in their 40s and 50s feel that a serious setback means the end of their career. It is too late; they feel too old. By contrast, some refuse to accept defeat. Perhaps, in the end, only one person can defeat you and that is yourself. Never give up your determination, work again with passion towards your goal confidently and innovative way.

4.4 Improve Your Basic Skills

(a) Stay Learner

Certainly in your early and middle years part of your time must be set aside for self-improvement. Time must be spent in developing your own talents and skills as well as your own knowledge of the industry and firm for which you work. Fast reading, good memory, public speaking, simple and clear writing are essential for business communication. It takes time and trouble to develop these skills. They are, however, basic.

(b) Never Demand as a Right, What you can ask for Favour

No one likes to face demands. This is particularly true if they know they have to do what is demanded. With no option, the matter and your manner will rankle. On the other hand, if you ask politely for a favour it makes the person granting it feel good. He will often feel almost grateful to you and may even come to regard you as a friend.

(c) Speak no Evil

In any organisation, there is a lot of gossip. It is easy enough to speak away at other people's reputation with your tongue. The normal reaction of someone who hears that you have been making slanderous comments about him is that he will reply in kind. Whether his comments are true or not, some of the mud is likely to stick. It is better to keep your views on other people to yourself and to accept them as they are.

(d) Write no Evil

You may sometimes in the course of your work feel that someone has been unhelpful, obstructive or behaved just as a fool. It is a mistake to write and tell him so. It is even more unwise to express your views in a clever, witty or sarcastic way. Every time he turns up that memo on the file; his resentment will be rekindled. Unpleasant things are sometimes said just to relieve one's own feelings and frustrations. This is a mistake. It is much better not to write but to say the things face to face. It is not always easy to do so, but you make your point with less danger of long-run resentment and enmity.

4.5 Look After Your People

A manager is dependent on the people who work for him. To do well he has to *collect a team* who are knowledgeable and can do their job. Has to motivate them to do a good job and to meet their objectives. He is likely to do this most successfully if he looks after them, make sure that they get the benefits they are entitled to, and ensure they have good working conditions. If they are worth promoting try to see they get it. Don't hang on to them to block their career. Your strongest allies in any organisation should be the people you have developed, coached and helped for promotion.

Do unto others as you would be done by. When you do anything try to put yourself in the other person's position. Try to get into his shoes and see things from his point of view. If you take action that affects someone else, consider how you would feel if it were done to you. If you would feel that it was unfair then refrain from doing it to someone else. Inter-personal relations which are congenial and collaborative with pears are key to success. Nurture them.

There are some who hold the theory that productive results only come from abrasive relationships, i.e. by threatening or abusing them. Everyone has their good points and most people will produce their best in an environment in which they *feel trusted and feel that the value of their work is recognised.* In the long-run, you will move further up the promotion ladder if you can carry other people with you—the people who work for you, your colleagues at all levels in other departments. The central factor in management is people. The men who work for you may be the ones you most need to influence.

Management process is increasingly becoming cross-cultural with the globalisation. It become necessary to have an understanding of various cultures for achieving competitive advantage. We cannot remove differences in cultures, but manager's should respond to individual expectations valuing differences to bring out best in the team. This change in mindset is important in multi-cultural environment.

4.6 Build Your Home Base

(a) Keep Healthy

If you are in poor health it will affect your performance. Good health is not just a matter of luck. Admittedly you can be unlucky and suffer a serious accident or disease. Much more ill-health, particularly among the middle aged arises from lack of care. Moderation in smoking, drinking and eating are likely to contribute greatly to your good health. So too is regular exercise, even if it is only a daily walk or swim. Your health is one of your prime assets—cultivate it.

(b) Be lucky in your choice of Life Partner and take the time and trouble to establish and maintain a firm home base

A secure, tension-free home provides a good starting point for any manager. So too, does the right spouse, who can cope with the many exigencies of the promotion path. Coping with an adversity is much easier for the person with a happy spouse and home.

(c) Recognise your own Motives

When you decide on a certain course of action, be clear about your own motive and intentions. It is not proper to conceal them from yourself. Recognise your own greed and ambition. You do not have to say good-bye to your principles and ideals if you set out to climb the promotion ladder. Indeed you will probably find it easier to live with yourself if you stick to your principles and ethical values. One has to develop one's character, integrity and Dharma.

To include, you can to a great extent, plan your own promotion by identifying various opportunities, evaluating risk and by making significant contribution to your job. Both determination and planning play a great role in this direction. All successful inter-human relationships depend on creative imagination and also on capacity for imaginative sympathy you have for others. The guidelines mentioned above are of paramount importance in your advancement path. Such career awareness about one's skills, abilities, competencies, weaknesses and strengths, needs and goals leads to self-development process. It will be appropriate to conclude with the views of Dr. P.N. Singh that it is important to prepare a career growth plan. This plan should be reviewed for implementation at regular intervals. The competition in the new millennium will be much more intense. The preparation for facing that competition through continuous value addition must start without any delay. Continue developing new ideas and objectives.

References

Dr. P.N. Singh, "Continuous Value Addition is the Key to Success", in *Training and Management*, November 2002.

S.K. Bhatia, "Human Resource Management", 2nd Revised Edition, Deep & Deep Publications Pvt. Ltd., New Delhi.

UNIT V

EMERGING DEVELOPMENTS IN TRAINING

CHAPTER

23

Fashioning a Coherent Training Strategy

In this chapter we shall attempt to cover as under:

(i) Training strategy
(ii) The training policy
(iii) The role of training function
(iv) Tasks of training function
(v) Modalities of training
(vi) One to one training model *vis-a-vis* increased effectiveness model
(vii) Qualities of trainers
(viii) How to show your commitment to training

(I) TRAINING STRATEGY

The training strategy is to be based on "performance management":

- The task of producing training strategy, which *reflects business strategy,* is made easier, if the organisation is undertaking a *major cultural change* programme. A training initiative is to be key component of this programme.
- Organisation performance can be improved by following business goals. Then developing people to meet these goals.
- Training needs should be regularly reviewed against business objectives.
- Then there should be skills audit with a clear business focus.

Thus, training manager must accept responsibility for translating business strategy and/or objectives first into human resource terms and then into training terms. For training manager, it is necessary to *maintain close relationship* with business planning group and use "investor in people" or "performance management" as a model.

(II) THE TRAINING POLICY

The inter-relationship between the *training department* and its *organisational context* is often incorporated in the training policy. This can improve training department's contribution to *maintenance of skills* and the *preparation for future challenges* of the organisation. Linking corporate mission and corporate objectives with training policy is explained in Fig. 23.1.

FIG. 23.1

Linking Missions and Objectives/Policy

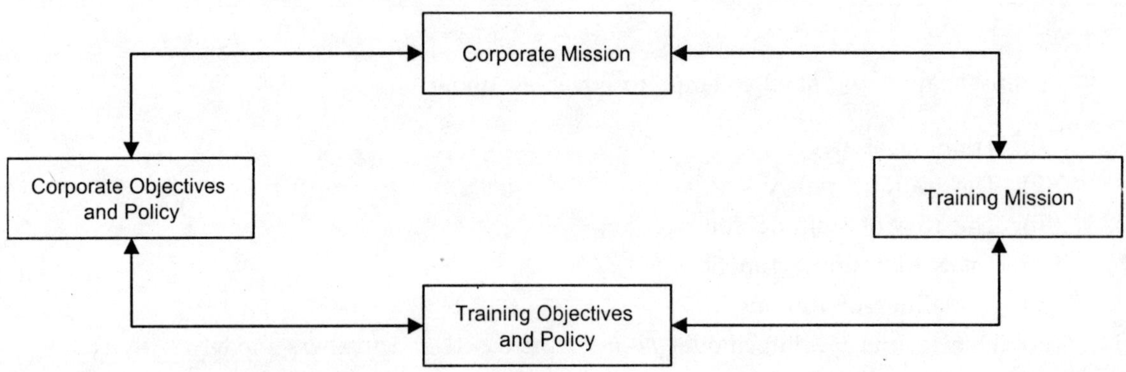

Statement of Training Policy

A sample of training policy of ABC Co. Ltd. is given below. The elements of training policy are:

(i) The *training plan* will be established by reference to the requirements of *company's business plan. Unit objectives* will be agreed with *managers* concerned and *individual targets* derived from these objectives and *agreed with employees.* A performance review system will be adopted training.

(ii) *Training needs* will be identified through *performance review* system, or in special cases when there are changes in internal policies or systems or external factors such as government legislation.

(iii) Establishing *organisation set-up* of training department.

(iv) *Training programmes* will be carried out by training or line manager or by external consultant to be determined by training department.

(v) All new employees will be given *induction training* which will comprise familiarisation with the business as well as initial job training so that they feel part of company and settle down early.

(vi) In approved cases employees will be given assistance to pursue further education. They may be provided cost of training and books, etc.

(vii) Training equipment will be procured and conference room set-up.

In summary, a training department strategy should embody:

(a) An overall sense of direction,

(b) An assessment of environmental challenges, and

(c) Proactive role as catalyst in areas involving changing organisation culture.

(III) THE ROLE OF TRAINING FUNCTION

The training function shall be contributing to the *organisational goals* by increasing the effectiveness of the work being carried out *in particular parts* of the organisation. The role of *training function* is explained in Fig. 23.2.

Fig. 23.2

The Training Function

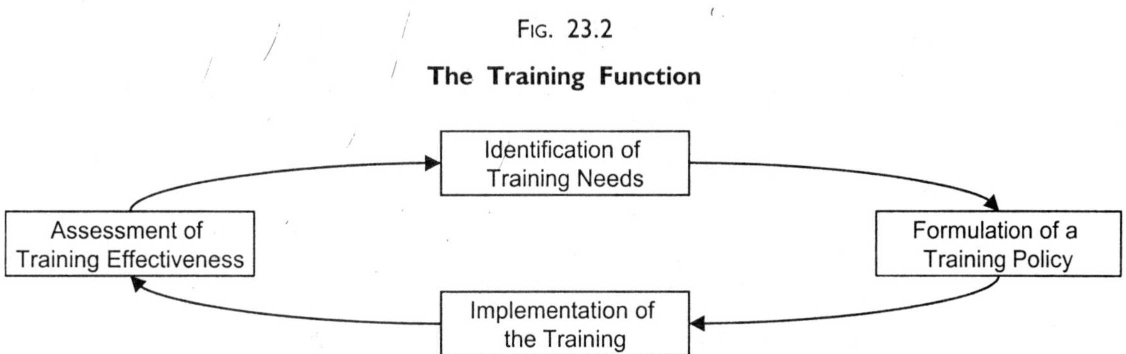

This contribution can be seen to have two main aspects:

(a) *Maintaining the present skills pool.* This can be done by provision of induction and initial training, and

(b) *Preparing employees for new challenges.* The training function should be *drawing up plans* for the development of management and workforce to enable the organisation to change in the desired directions. Training should contribute to the process and should be integrated into corporate planning.

According to A. Bannerjee, "Training unit should understand the organisation's strategic direction and can design and implement a creative way of moving people in that direction. Many organisations have already shifted their thinking about the training function. They have seen for themselves that training is where skills are developed, attitudes are changed, ideas evolve and the organisation is reinvented. In the course of learning the skills that will increase sales, build effective teams, improve quality standards or meet a wide range of other objectives, employees create a new organisational culture."

Essentially, training department becomes internal consultants, as well as maintaining the more traditional role.

The *traditional role* involves training needs analysis at the job and individual levels, and development and running of courses. It is a role of responding to be quest and it is a fairly stable function.

The *proactive role* involves individual and group counselling. It is largely a role of *catalyst and coordinator* of management workshops and problem-solving groups. Its primary focus is on developing HR skills, particularly where this involves *changing the culture*.

Training manager will be unable to do this alone, and team of specialists will be needed to carry through organisational changes.

(IV) TASKS OF THE TRAINING FUNCTION

The tasks can be classified in many ways. They can be grouped under the essential functions as follows:

1. Building and Maintaining Support

The first strategy objectives for building support is to involve all levels and parts of the organizations that are prospective users of the outputs.

Building continued mutuality into all relationships is particularly important for maintaining support; all partners need to gain and also feel that they are gaining.

2. Building Training Competencies and Overall Training Capacity

At the system level, overall training, consulting, organising, and administrative functions, it involves, recruiting and building trainers into a coherent staff and making additional trainers available through networks of resources. The training system's credibility rests largely on its displaying the capabilities to manage itself well within its own boundaries. Increasing competence in training organization and programme implementation, in turn, builds the staffs confidence in their system which raises competencies further.

3. Developing Training Materials

This task supports competency building and also reflects it. The most useful materials are developed from within the work settings in which training is needed.

4. Strategic Planning

Strategic Planning starts with using projections of training needs for mapping the system required for meeting these needs. It is useful to go down the list of a components inside a system, its relevant environment and map what would be needed by each. A systematic training cycle is described in Fig. 23.3 on next page.

5. Networking Training Resources

The important components of this task include—improved information gathering and management, the development of resource pools of trainers and materials at various levels of the system and ready access mechanism.

6. Monitoring and Evaluation

Each task to be performed by a training function has a purpose, and its performance can be assessed in terms of both outcomes and the processes by which they were attained. Regular monitoring yields the data and system needs to improve its immediate functioning, structure, and looking forward further development. This task is important to carry out for all tasks, also addresses the often intricate inter-relationship between particular tasks and the performance of the system as a whole.

(V) MODALITIES IN TRAINING

Modality is a broader concept than the training method; several methods can be used for implementing one modality. Training modalities can be distinguished into three types:

(i) Direct Contact and Distance Training

In contact training programmes trainers and learners are face to face. This limits the number of participants in a programme. Distance training can respond more readily to the need to train large numbers and, with the introduction of new technologies, is becoming increasingly important.

FIG. 23.3

A Systematic Training Cycle

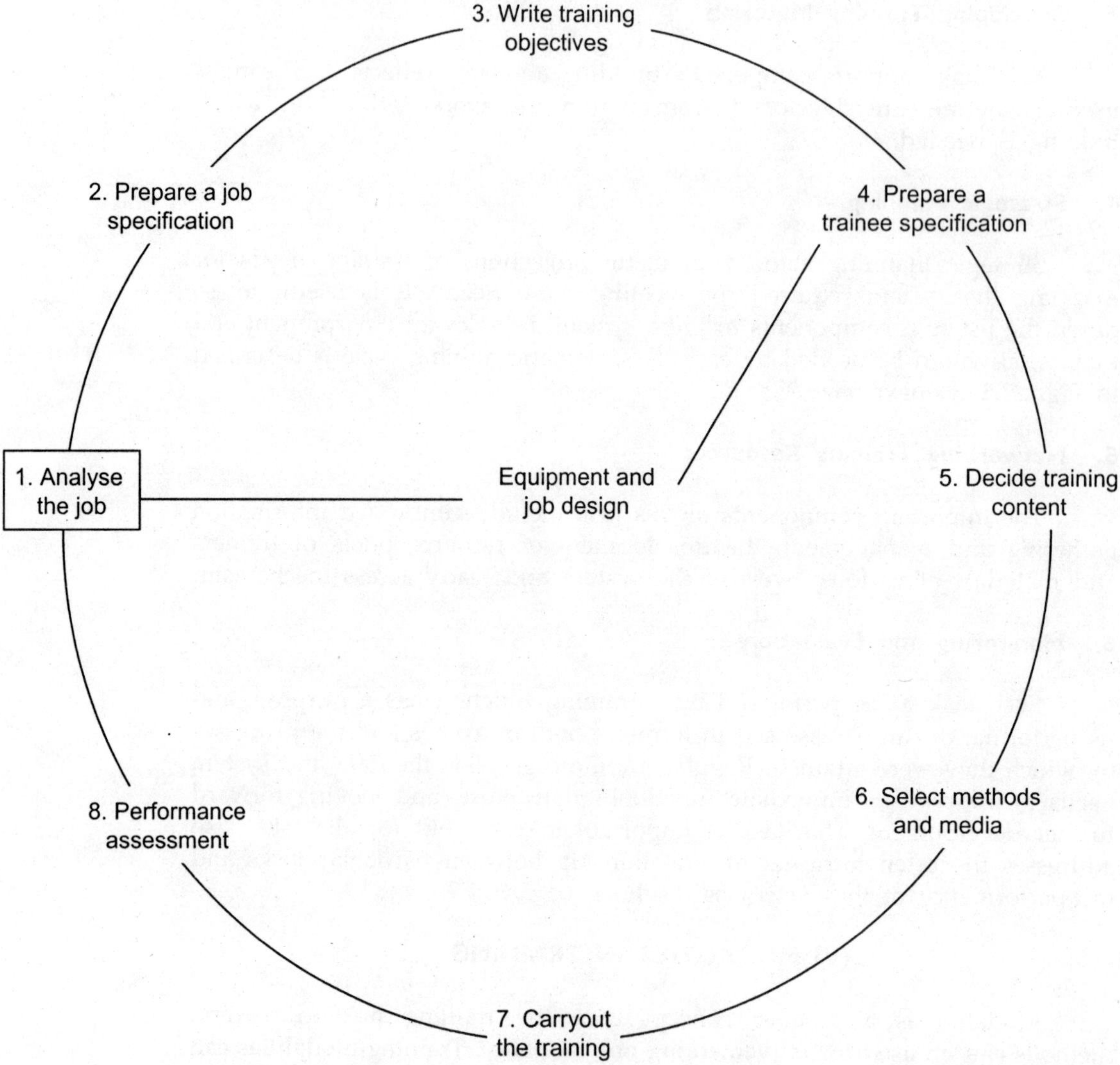

(ii) Formal and Non-formal Training

Training in *formal programmes* conducted at a particular place with a fixed syllabus. Training can be planned and conducted through various *"non-formal" modalities*. Participant can learn many things in a planned way. Here the emphasis is on conscious, guided experiences.

(iii) Centralized and Dispersed Organization of Training

Training modalities can also be differentiated along organizational lines. In a simple centralized model, central institute initiates, guides and supports all aspects of training, and other subsidiary units carry out its plans. At the other extreme are networks of largely autonomous training unit each responsible for its own training plans and programmes as needed or desired.

Mixed models are increasingly becoming common in which a central institute sets frames of training. Subsidiary units do the detailed planning staffing and management.

(VI) ONE TO ONE TRAINING MODEL VIS-A-VIS INCREASED EFFECTIVENESS MODEL

(a) The training programme described by Sykes was planned using an individual in Fig. 23.4

FIG. 23.4

One-to-One Training Model

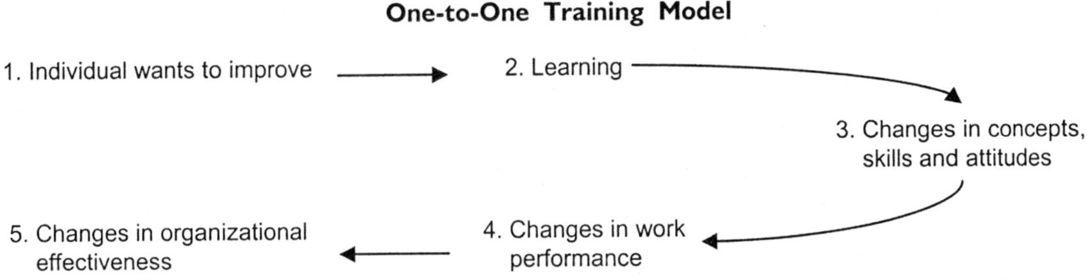

(b) In one-to-one training model, the focus is on individuals and the process includes imparting skills to learn something set to be simulated and then expecting them to find uses for the task.

(c) An approach in which organisation must be first subjected to change the organisation. This is described in Fig. 23.5. (next page)

(d) Feedback, with or without training on topics such as joint target setting, listening or holding team meetings, could help change the management style in the organization to a more participative one.

(VII) ASPECTS OF ORGANISATIONAL EFFECTIVENESS

It is necessary to identify various aspects of organisational effectiveness in leadership, policy and strategy, people management, resources, processes, customer satisfaction, people satisfaction, impact on society, business results in relation to planned performance. Details of aspects of organisation

FIG. 23.5

Increased Effectiveness Model

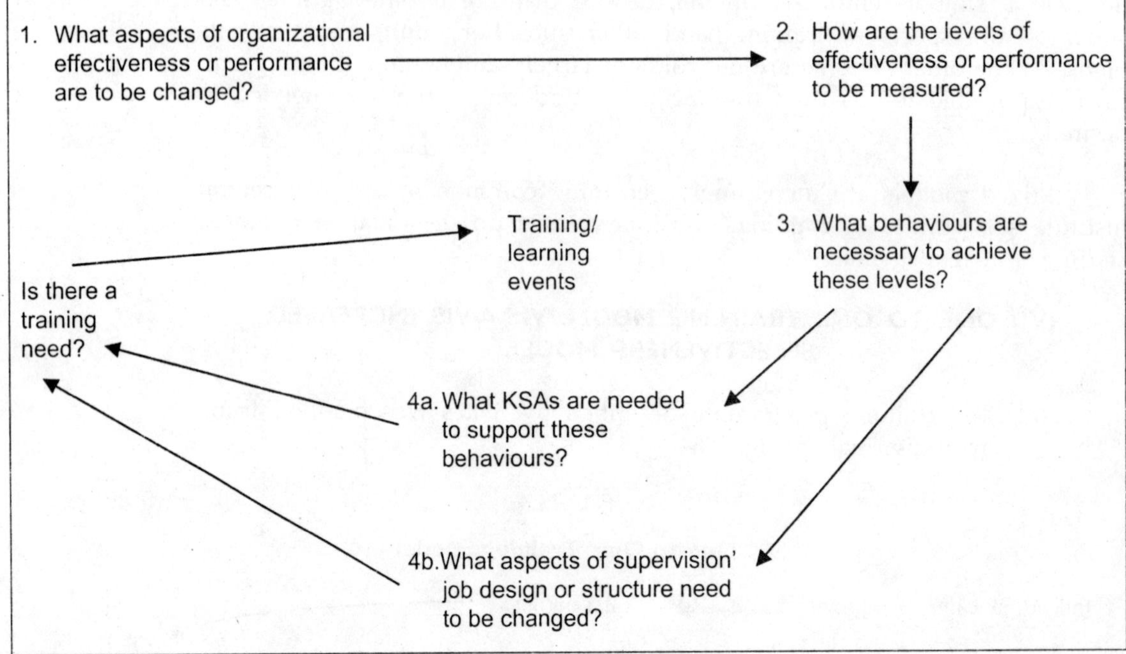

effectiveness are described in Fig. 23.6. One way of identifying training requirements in the organisational context is by defining aspects of organisation effectiveness.

FIG. 23.6

Aspects of Organisational Effectiveness

Achieving goals of:
- product or service quality
- output productivity

Increasing resourcefulness by
- increasing share of the market
- increasing employee versatility
- moving into new markets

Satisfying customers by
- improving organisational (or functional image)
- reducing complaints/returned material
- increasing proportion of on-time deliveries

Improving internal processes by
- increasing group cohesiveness
- improving quality of supervision
- helping to resolve departmental boundary problems
- increasing managers' ability to set realistic and tangible objectives for their departments.

(VIII) QUALITIES OF TRAINERS

(a) Some Basic Qualities of Trainers

There are some inherent skills and some acquired skills that qualify a person to become a trainer. Inherently he needs to be compassionate, communicative and humorous, and the skills to be acquired would include the ability to influence and the use of different training and facilitation techniques of behaviours. Listening actively is the best guide. Watching signs of fatigue of participants.

(b) Types of Trainer's and their Focus

There are two types of trainers. First are those who *solely motivate*; who simply enhance the willingness of people. However, willingness cannot be sustained unless 'ability' exists.

Then the second kind of trainers would be those who not only *motivate, but also improve the abilities of people*. These are the ones who are able to touch and transform; they not only influence the cause, but also the function. (Training and Management, Oct. 2003).

(c) Abilities to Establish Relationship

Abilities of internal resource trainers could be assessed and developed particularly about establishing and maintaining a productive relationship that will achieve goals.

(d) Obtaining Feedback

Ensuring new ideas are understood by participants and trainers can use some tactics:

- Evaluating the part of the programme.
- Short application tests to encourage, listen and motivate.
- Asking participants to summarise key concepts, action plans, etc.
- Encouraging note taking of new material.
- Acronyms. First letters of a list of concepts are arranged to form of meaningful word, so that ideas can be easier to remember.

(e) Ways to Motivate Learning by Trainers

- Talking one-on-one with resistant or negative trainees before the programme by explaining contents of the programme so that it is relevant to his job.

- Asking experienced participants to share their experiences and ideas at key points in the programme.
- Asking experienced employees for input on programme content.
- At the conclusion of each session, asking participant to summarise what he learnt.

(f) Focus on Skill Applicable for Global Market

In globalisation, corporates need employees with skills that translate well to the international arena and focus on these for motivation of participants.

(g) Improving Impact of Training

For improving impact of training programme following areas need attention:

- An effective introduction of programme or session covering objectives/expectations, benefits, relevant, audience centered, fun/humorous.
- An effective conclusion to contain: summary, benefits, link with the introduction, plan of implementation, motivational, polished, personal and power-packed.

(h) Trainer's Statements having Direct and Indirect Influence

The statements that characterise direct and indirect influence of trainers on participants is given in Fig. 23.7.

FIG. 23.7

Comparison of Kinds of Statements by Trainers which have Direct and Indirect Influence

Statements of direct influence are those in which trainers:	Statements of indirect influence are those in which trainers:
• Express or lecture about ideas or knowledge • Give directions or orders • Critize or deprecate participants' behaviour with intent to change it • Justify their own position or authority	• Accept, clarify and support the ideas and feelings of participants • Praise and encourage • Ask questions to stimulate participation in decision-making • Ask questions to orient participants to the task or to the topic of discussion

What studies show is that a *below-average proportion of direct to indirect influence* over an extended period of time will establish more desirable participant attitudes and superior patterns of work.

(i) Trainer as Resource Person

Trainer's image to be a *resource person* (rather than traditional authoritarian image). The new approach demands from the trainer's great acumen, sensitivity and adaptability, and continuous application.

(j) Trainer's Hidden Roles

Trainer's three functions: These are hidden functions in trainer's role in addition to the well-recognised one of conducting training sessions:

(i) Providing *guidance and support* to individual participants—mentoring. Here both parties, mentor as well as participant, can benefit from this special relationship.

(ii) *Intervention* means designing and helping to implement organisational change strategies. To ensure that newly gained competencies will be effectively used by the participants in their work organisation. Such interventions will be critical for success of trainers in present context.

(iii) The third function is a *managerial function*, i.e. preparing (plan and organise) and running effectively entire training programme, i.e. staff, materials, facilities, participants have to come together on schedule, house-keeping and within budget limits.

(k) Trainer's Style

(i) Effective trainers are *flexible* and able to vary their roles and methods to suit changing needs. They are 'business like', they vary beahviour to suit different situations. This contingency approach to their matter of appropriateness.

(ii) *Adaptability* as trainers have a variety of tools—concepts and skills in their experience and can move between them to suit the fluid situation in session as well as differing needs of individual participant.

(iii) Trainer to maintain training environment which is *supportive*. Participants will feel certain of a genuine response, and see the effects of their new behaviour.

This is the direction of effective training for development (Ned A. Flanders, "Teacher Influence, Pupil Attitudes and Achievement", *Training for Development*, University of Minnesota).

(IX) HOW TO SHOW YOUR COMMITMENT TO TRAINING

- Begin the process of becoming an employer of choice in your industry. Gather information on what is needed and sell it to top management.
- Give bonuses to those who take the time to improve themselves.
- Have a tuition assistance programme available for all employees. Make sure the CEO and other top managers show support by attending various training programmes.
- Ensure managers teach classes to other employees.
- Measure how many hours each employee spends in training each year.
- Provide just-in-time training to employees. If they know they will immediately be able to use new skills, they'll be more motivated to learn.
- Each meeting should begin with the question, "what new thing have we learned recently?"
- Focus on improving individuals' weaknesses and their strengths a well.
- Identify organizational core competencies and provide necessary training.
- Allow younger members of the workforce to train older employees.
- Eliminate training programmes that are obsolete or no longer needed.
- Have the training department identify new training requirements

CHAPTER

24

New Concepts of Training

It is desirable for trainer to remember new concepts of training developed by Lynton and Pareek to make training efforts effective and useful to the organisation.

Assumptions

Prevailing Concepts	*New Concepts*
1. Acquition of *knowledge* by participants leads *to action.*	1. *Motivation* and *skills* leads to action. Skills are acquired through practice.
2. *Participants* learns what *trainer* teaches. Learning is *capacity* of participant to learn and ability of trainer to each.	2. Learning is a complex function of *motivation* and *capacity of participant, norms of training group, training methods,* and *behaviour of trainers,* plus *general climate* of work organisation.
3. *Individual action* leads to improvement on job.	3. Improvement on the job is complex function of *individual learning norms of work group* and general climate of organisation.
4. Training is responsibility of training department. It begins and ends with course.	4. Training is responsibility of three: (i) The participants, (ii) His organisation, and (iii) Training institution. It has a preparatory stage, training and-subsequent post-training phase. All are important for success of training.

SHIFT IN FOCUS IN TRAINING

Some focus areas are as under:

	From	*To*
Emphasis in training programmes	On methods and technologies	Emphasis on: attitudes, approaches, philosophies of the organisation development and effectiveness, and goals.
Training intervention and input	In general	Precise and specific where necessary and where it would be most useful. Organisation goal-oriented.
Training in culture	Administrative and supervision	• Managerial, entre-preneurial, company culture, commitment and behavioural. • Effective work habits. • Professionalism.
In organisation structure	Hierarchical	Flatter organisation.
Strategy in Training	Individual basic skills, e.g. teach selling skills, etc.	• Aims to build team work skills and more closely linked to business strategy. • To influence critical aspects of business. • Participation, mutual goalsetting.
Training beneficiaries	Internal customers, i.e. managers, supervisors and employees	Also external customers, i.e. users of product and service. All the beneficaries.
Focus on	Average and weak employees	On all, even on most successful so that they can identify reasons of their success.
Goal	A happy employee considered as productive employee	Happiness is relative and it is function of fulfilment.

In nutshell, training as a *limited skill-drill exercise,* or a *mere efficiency-generation process* is totally inadequate to handle the present situation. Training has to change its character—as a tool of "Education for Cultivation" to prepare for future.

There has to be focus on *total man* (not compartmental) and training has to be a holistic.

Traditional focus of training on "skill generation" had lately been reinforced by "attitudinal transformation" and there it ended. Training should now cover wider area to be effective in emerging challenges of change. Like "single window" or "composite counter" concept, an employee must be a "multipleman" and training must cater to this "multiplicity role" requirement.

CHAPTER

25

Evolving Training Strategy: A Case Study

Enormous amount of efforts have been put in training and development of managers in the last three decades and the companies have benefited a great deal. In the current stage of development, however our focus is on making training more meaningful and effective. In this direction the real problem emerges of lack or inadequacy of objective where we intend the organisation to reach, in terms of human asset development. Further, it may also be due to inadequacy to identify the gap between the individual's aspiration and the organisation growth. As such an objective has to be spelt out so as to have a specific goal to achieve in the training effort.

In this chapter we propose to share a study undertaken in a large engineering organisation to evolve a training strategy. Methodology adopted in this direction was to carry out a survey feedback project so as to determine the gaps in training needs. The survey feedback presents a picture of the style of management being practised in the organisation and also what the respondents consider as a desirable managerial style for the future. Accordingly, as a next step, to bring about an organisational change from the present style to the desirable style training and development approach has been utilised. The strategic objective is to sensitise managers for change in their style through innovative management development programmes.

THE STUDY

The study seeks to understand the present status of the managerial style. In addition, it also tries to identify a desirable managerial style for being projected in the future. To measure where the organisation stands with respect to this basic objective, Rensis Likert in his studies found that the prevailing management styles of organisation can be depicted on a continuum from system 1 through system 4. The instrument on Management System developed by Rensis Likert has certain advantages. The variables listed are easily understandable; they describe the behaviour and attitudes in direct, simple terms. They are exhaustive, consisting 51 variables under eight broad categories viz., (i) Leadership, (ii) Motivation, (iii) Communication, (iv) Interaction-Influence, (v) Decision-Making, (vi) Goal-setting, (vii) Control Process, (viii) Performance goals and training. Against each variable descriptive statements of how behaviour and attitudes get manifested in the four systems are furnished. These statements are in a graded form one extreme to the other. The four systems are designated as:

1. Exploitative authoritarian,
2. Benevolent authoritarian,
3. Consultative, and
4. Participative.

System 1 is a task-oriented, highly structured authoritarian management style, while system 4 is relationship-oriented management style based on team work, mutual trust and confidence. Systems 2 and 3 are intermediate stages.

To measure where the organisation stands with respect to this basic objective, it was decided to use the Rensis Likert model for this study. The questionnaire was administered to 275 managers and 141 (51%) responded. The respondents preferred to stay anonymous

SURVEY FINDINGS

The data relating to responses was tabulated under the different variables of managerial style as mentioned above. In summary, the overall organisational scenario in terms of eight variables of managerial style are seen to be around systems 2 and 3, i.e., Benevolent Authoritarian and Consultative styles. But between 75 per cent to 83 per cent of the respondents have desired the organisational change towards system 4 which is participative style. This is shown in Exhibit 25.1.

TRAINING PLAN

Based on the gap under various variables of managerial style to be filled, a comprehensive training process involving the managers has been prepared. For this purpose, a check list of five types of training programmes

EXHIBIT 25.1

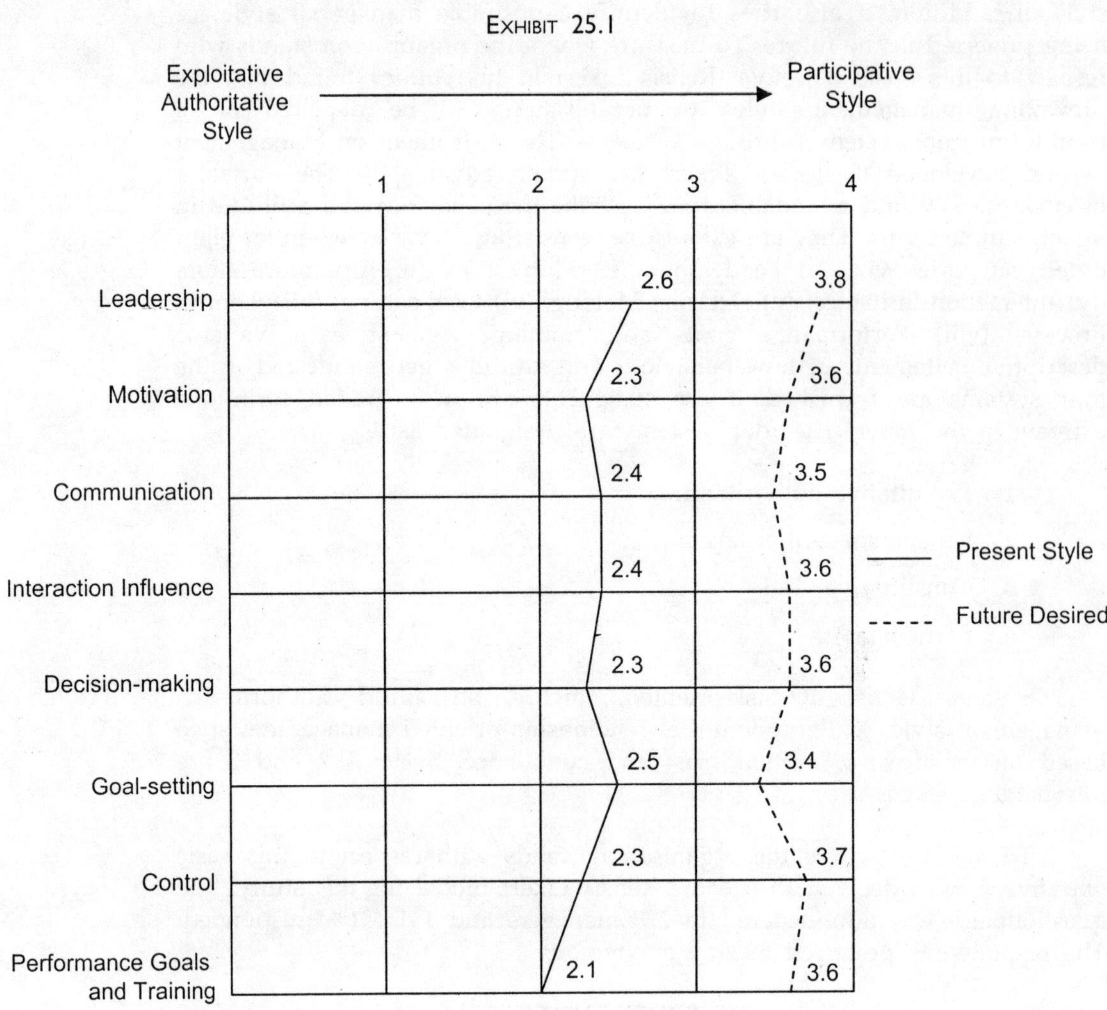

specially designed to meet the requirement of charge towards system 4 (Participative style) was circulated to departmental heads. A list of objectives for each programme were prepared to give idea of the contents of the programmes.

Departmental heads nominated the participants for each course from amongst the managers reporting to them. Number of managers nominated for each course and the number of programmes planned are given below. A programme schedule for couple of years has been drawn up to cover all the nominees.

To sum up, in this chapter an attempt has been made to share the methodology adopted to determine the training gaps in managerial cadre of

Course	*Nominated Number*	*No. of Programmes*
Leadership	135	6
Motivation	123	6
Communication	107	5
Decision-making	132	6
Control process	112	5

the organisation. Based on this tailor-made training courses have been developed. It is hoped that this goal-oriented training package will certainly make learning process more effective. This will also enable us to give a deliberate thrust to the organisation towards the direction managers want to take it.

Reference

S.K. Bhatia, "Human Resource Management", 2nd Revised Edition, Deep & Deep Publications Pvt. Ltd., New Delhi.

CHAPTER

26

Mentoring

Workers and managers alike *develop* themselves by interacting with those they admire and by building *trusting relationships* with people who nurture, support, and guide them. It focuses on establishing mutual *understanding and its confidentiality.*

When young people join organizations, they need guidance and support from experienced people whom they admire, can confide in, and receive advice from them. Such a relationship is called mentoring, and the senior person is called a *mentor*. The concept of *mentoring* centres around the emotional support and guidance given by an older, more experienced person to a younger, less experienced person called a *protege.* Mentors need not be, and preferably should not be, the protege's supervisor.

However, employees also need to develop trusting and supportive relationships with their supervisors, who can set challenging work goals, provide support to achieve them, help analyse barriers to higher performance, and plan goals for the future. This process is called *coaching,* defined as the help supervisors provide to their subordinates by analyzing and guiding on-the-job performance. While mentoring centres around general development and psychological well-being, coaching is linked to the analysis of job performance and identification of training needs.

Mentoring affords an opportunity for individuals to *share their concerns* and receive moral support and guidance for their development. Mentoring begins when a trusting relationship is established Mentor's model behavioural norms for their proteges. They also listen to their proteges' personal and job concerns, help them search for solutions to problems, share relevant experiences, respond to their emotional needs without making them dependent on the mentors, and cultivate long-lasting yet informal personal relationships.

Mentoring involves support offered to a person by someone who is senior in competence experience expertise, or position. Three processes are central to successful coaching and mentoring: communication, empowering and helping.

Enlightened organisational leaders are now paying more attention to mentoring. Generally, high potentional young managers are assigned to mentors, who are senior in position and age and occupy senior positions. Mentors are selected from any department and have their interest, availability and 'mentoring competence'. One mentor may have more than one proteges. The ultimate goal of both coaching and mentoring is to help employees attain psychological maturity and effectiveness as observed by Prof. Udai Pareek.

Reference

S.K. Bhatia, "Boost Your Professional Career", Deep & Deep Publications Pvt. Ltd., New Delhi.

CHAPTER

27

Assessment and Development Centre

If organisations want to remain dynamic and growth-oriented, they must possess competent people. To cope with their present assignments, but also to face future challenges effectively, the competencies of managers have to be managed and developed strategically, as competencies add value to the organisation success. The assessment centres as tools of evaluation for selection of candidates or identification of competencies have not yet become popular in India. Whereas assessment centres are significantly being used by organisations in USA and European countries. Very little literature or experiences are available except in form of small paragraphs in some text books.

The American Society for Training and Development has defined—an assessment centre is a multiple assessment of several individuals performed simultaneously by a group of trained evaluators using a variety of group and individual exercises.

I. Thus Minimum Requirements of Assessment Centre to be Considered as an Assessment Centre are:

(i) It must measure multiple qualities or competencies.

(ii) Multiple assessment techniques must be used, at least one of these techniques must be a simulation.

(iii) Multiple assessors must be used and are trained.

(iv) Judgements resulting in an outcome (i.e., recommendations for selection, development, promotion, training) must be based on pooling information from assessors.

(v) An overall evaluation of behaviour must be made by assessors.

(vi) Qualities or attributes evaluated are determined by an analysis of relevant job behaviours.

2. Following Activities are not an Assessment Centre

(a) Panel interviews,

(b) Reliance on a specific technique,

(c) Single assessor assessment using variety of techniques, and

(d) Psychometric test batteries.

3. History

Assessment centre was started in Bell Telephone Company, USA in 1958, and then in AT&T, IBM, GE, Standard Oil by 1972. The number swelled to over 100 centres in USA. In Europe, it was adopted by Shell, Philips and Siemens and others. In India, the Defence Services Selections Boards (SSBs), follow a discreet three-phase system of an interview, a battery of psychological tests (mostly projective), and group outdoor exercises. The evaluation is done individually and integration takes place only at the very end, at a conference of all the assessors from the various techniques. Assessment Centre is becoming a significant method of evaluation and development of employees.

4. How do Assessment Centres Work?

The procedure adopted at the assessment centres is as under:

A more elaborate set of performance simulation tests, specifically designed to evaluate a candidate's managerial potential, is administered at the assessment centre—

(i) A small group of employees/applicants come to the assessment centre.

(ii) The assessment centre has about 6-8 assessors.

(iii) For about 2 to 4 days, the assessors are asked to participate in exercises such as:

(a) An interview,

(b) In-basket exercise, where applicants solve day-to-day problems, that managers find in the in-basket,

(c) A case exercise,

(d) A group discussion,
(e) A business game,
(f) A set of projective personality tests, and
(g) A set of general ability tests.

(iv) Assessors, in pairs, observe and record the behaviour of applicants.

(v) Each assessee is rated in 20 to 25 characteristics (i.e., organisation planning, decision-making, creativity, resistance to stress and oral communication skills).

(vi) Judgement is made about assessee's potential for meeting the job requirement.

Radha R. Sharma has highlighted step involved and factors in the assessment process as under:

In planning the assessment process, three factors merit consideration:

(a) list of competencies or other qualities to be assessed and the procedure for scoring and rating,

(b) the weightage to be assigned to each element and exercise, and

(c) the various forms of assessments for a competency to ensure consistency of judgement and prevention of any bias.

The various steps involved in Assessment! Development Centre have been presented diagrammatically. (Fig. 27.1)

FIG. 27.1

Steps Involved in Assessment/Development Centre: Sharma, Radha R., 2002.

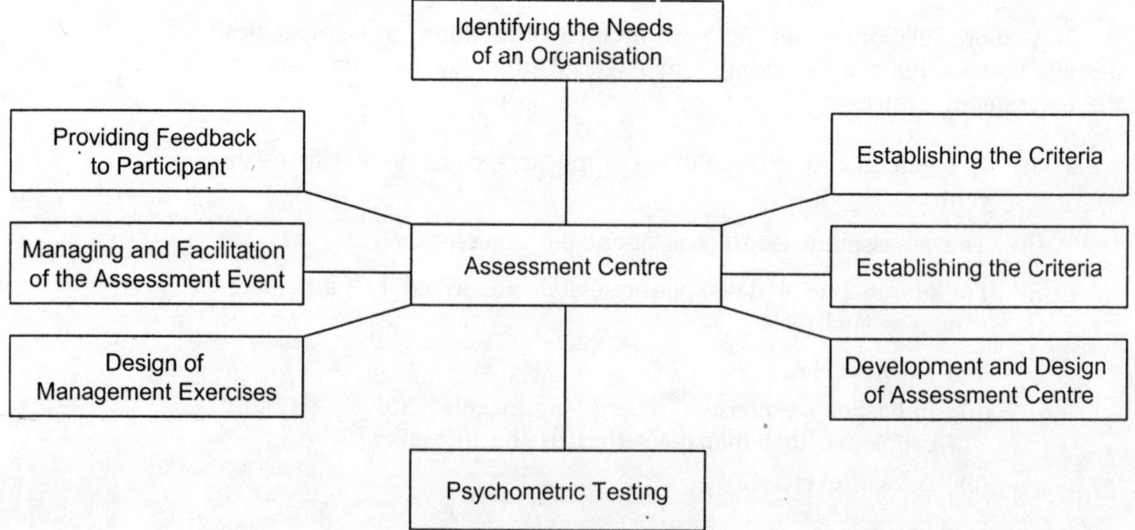

Having identified the need for having an assessment centre and also establishing criteria of competencies, weights need to be assigned for various parameters. One can give even equal weight to all.

Some organisations include psychometric testing as an integral part of an assessment centre. Psychological assessment of participants through standardized psychometric tests can effectively supplement the assessment ratings provided the tests have high reliability and validity and meet the requirements of the competencies and the participants. The most important aspect of psychometric testing is the knowledge, expertise and familiarity of the psychologist with test. Psychometric tests and questionnaires provide useful information about range of competencies of an individual and proves as a scientific aid in selection, potential appraisal, promotion, training and development of an individual or a group of individuals.

Radha R. Sharma adds that in India a number of progressive companies now make use· of psychometric tests not only for assessment centre but also for recruitment, potential appraisal, promotion and training and development.

5. Difference between Assessment Centres and Development Centres

(a) Assessment Centres

Assessment Centres are one of the most accurate methods of measurement of individuals. Common uses of assessment centres are:

- Selection of employees.
- Placements.
- Potential appraisal.
- Promotion.
- Career and succession planning.
- Development of employees.
- Estimation of training needs of the organisation.

The transparent and introspective nature of assessment centres leads to credibility within the participants and this adds to the belief in the integrity of the system.

(b) Development Centres

Assessment centres lend themselves very easily to the development function because of their essentially introspective nature. During the course of an assessment centre, each participant gets the opportunity to see himself performing the same tasks as his peers in exactly the same circumstances.

This enables him to see the effectiveness or otherwise of his own approach *vis-a-vis* his peers and leads to an insight, which is seldom available elsewhere in the workplace. Thus, assessment centres which are used for development (hence called development centres) form the ideal platform to base a management development programme.

Development centres are further bolstered by a separate feedback session at the very end of the programme, wherein, the data elicited during the development centre is fed back to each participant. This is the approach which has caught on with industry, using it to bolster their HR strategy in the long-term. More and more organisations are beginning to see competency as a path to develop their employees with their direct participation.

Assessment Centre vs. Development Centre

There are a number of differences between Assessment and Development Centre. The basic difference is that assessment centre is geared towards evaluation of a candidate against a predetermined criteria for selection or promotion. The assessors act as a judge and focus on what a candidate can do now.

Development Centre uses the techniques of assessment centre to assist individuals in their self-development and career planning, in other words, their present and future roles. The focus of development centre is not on assessment but on observation in order to provide feedback to the person about his/her strengths and weaknesses against relevant competencies. The competencies assessed during development centre are larger in number, than those in assessment centre. Development Centre can be a great learning experience enabling a person to focus on feedback received and charting out a path through the development centre for self development based on the feedback. (Fig. 27.2)

6. Benefits of Assessment Centres

Assessment centres results normally predict later job performance in managerial positions and training gaps for development of competencies. The greatest benefits accrue to the organisation, such as—appraisal of performance selection of candidates, for promotion and also numerous benefits to participants and internal assessors.

Benefits for the Participants

In addition to the more obvious benefits like getting a clear idea of the competency disparity between the present level of competency and the required level of competency the participants in an assessment centre have some added benefits such as—

FIG. 27.2

Comparison Between Assessment and Development Centre

Assessment Centre	*Development Centre*
Have pass/fail criteria	Do not have a pass/fail criteria
Are geared towards filling a job vacancy	Are geared towards developing the individual
Address an immediate organisational need	Address a longer term need
Have fewer assessors and more participants	Have 1:1 ratio of assessor to participant
Involve line managers as assessors	Do not have line managers as assessors
Have less emphasis placed on self-assessment	Have a greater emphasis placed on self-assessment
Focus on what the candidate can do now	Focus on potential
Are geared to meet the needs of the organisation	Are geared to meet of the individual as well as the organisation
Assign the role of judge to assessors	Assign the role of facilitator to assessors
Place emphasis on selection with little or developmental feedback and follow-up	Place emphasis on development feedback and follow-up with little or no selection function
Give feedback at a later date	Give feedback immediately
Involve the organisation having control over the information obtained	Involve the individual having control over information obtained
Have very little pre-centre briefing	Have a substantial pre-centre briefing
Tend to be used with external candidates	Tend to be used with internal candidates

Source: Psychometrics Co., UK, from an article by Dr. Radha R. Sharma, *IJTP Journal*, Jan.-June 2003.

(i) Discovering how 'I' behave across group situations.

(ii) Developing awareness of influences on their own behaviour and its implications.

(iii) Recognising gaps between thinking and action.

(iv) Opportunity to experiment with untried behaviours/approaches without fears of failure that dogs him in organisational life.

Benefits to the Internal Assessors are such as:

- The internal assessors are more committed to the process of selection and the methods used for that.
- The assessors develop new insights into behaviour through observation of the behaviour of the participants.
- The assessors improve their managerial skills through working with cases, in-basket exercises and other such exercises related to their organisation.
- The communication skills of the assessors improve substantially due to the experience in listening and in briefing the participants.
- Their observation skills improve considerably and they learn of focus on behaviour without judging.
- They learn an entirely new, more precise vocabulary of behavioural terms.
- They also learn to write reports in an objective and balanced manner.
- They learn interviewing skills through the various interviews conducted as part of the assessment centre process.
- They also learn to give and receive feedback as a part of assessment centre process.

7. Assessment Centre: Future Perspective

According to Radha R. Sharma, the assessment centres have been found to add value to the organisation and are proliferating the world over. Despite being time-consuming and expensive, the 'Assessment Centre' is presently the strongest predictor of future job performance if designed and implemented properly. It presents a comprehensive picture of each participant's professional skills required in a job and thereby helps him gain self-knowledge. Experiences of organisations indicate that having gone through assessment centre, participants feel that they have been fairly assessed. When it is employed for recruitment, candidates give a positive feedback which sends out favourable image about the organisation's professionalism. When it is used for development, participants develop valuable insights into their strengths and areas of improvement.

It is desirable that Assessment/Development Centre follows skill audit which could be carried out for measuring and recording skills of an individual or a group required for various job positions in an organisation. It will not only save time but will also facilitate running of an assessment/development centre.

Considering the trends, assessment and development centre have a bright future as in the globally competitive environment, the competitive edge of an organisation will depend on competency edge of its people.

IN SUM

The competence of the employees decides the competitive edge of the organisations in their struggle for survival and success.

References

Nitin Sawardekar, *Assessment Centres*, Response Books, New Delhi.

Radha R. Sharma, Assessment and Development Centre as Tools for Competency Development, IJTD Journal, January-June, 2003.

S.K. Bhatia, "Boost Your Professional Career", Deep & Deep Publications Pvt. Ltd., New Delhi.

CHAPTER

28

Competency Development

We shall understand following aspects relating to competency and core-competency in organisation setting:

(i) What is competency?
(ii) Characteristics of competencies.
(iii) Some common competencies in organisations.
(iv) Methods of identifying competencies.

These aspects are discussed as under for easy understanding:

(I) WHAT IS COMPETENCY?

What is a competency? Assessment centres are basically measuring tools. The specifications most commonly measured by assessment centres are called competencies. There is difference between *competence* and *competency*. These terms though quite distinct are sometimes used interchangeably. Accordingly, the difference between them is as follows:

- *Competence* refers to abilities based on work tasks or job responsibilities.
- *Competency* refers to abilities based on behaviour. These are the characteristics of the persons who are doing the job. For example, a competency that would be relevant to any managerial function in any organisation could be decision-making. The associated behaviours for this competency could be 'uses all available information in making decisions'.

In effect, *competence* concerns the job and *competency* concern the person. A very relevant definition of competency by Hogg B. is:

> "Competencies are the characteristics of a manager that lead to the demonstration of skills and abilities, which result in effective performance within an occupational area. Competency also embodies the capacity to transfer skills and abilities from one area to another."

(II) SOME CHARACTERISTICS OF COMPETENCIES

An analysis of this definition reveals the following aspects:

(a) Competencies are the characteristics of a manager. Competency is a characteristic of a person.

(b) Competencies lead to the demonstration of skills and abilities. These must be observable.

(c) Competencies must lead to effective performance. Competency thus refers to behaviour, differentiating success from merely doing the job. It must be clear and easy to understand. The competencies must be relevant to the organisation to which they are associated. The people in the organisation must be able to relate to the behavioural indicators as something which they do on a daily basis. It must be discrete.

(d) Competency also embodies the capacity to transfer skills and abilities from one area to another. This is best exemplified by the salesman who may be able to deliver his sales pitch flawlessly but may be tongue-tied elsewhere. He lacks the competency of 'communication'. Thus, competencies cannot be restricted to a single job alone but the person must be able to carry them along.

(III) SOME COMMON COMPETENCIES IN ORGANISATIONS

Each organisation has its own and distinctive style of business which it holds prime, and thus each organisation should require different competencies for its people to be successful in that organisation. These may need to change from time to time as the organisation evolves. Hence, the competencies in an organisation are characteristic to the organisation and dynamic, since they may change with time and with organisational development. However, some commonly occurring competencies in business organisations are. (see Fig. 28.1)

As assessment centre evaluations are competency-based assessment of a candidate's performance.

FIG. 28.1

Some Common Competencies in Organisations

(a) *Intellectual*
Comprehension
Analytical Ability
Innovation Lateral Training
Decision-Making—Problem-Solving
Planning and Organising
Strategic Perspective Thinking

(b) *Interpersonal*
Communication
Adaptability
Interpersonal Skills and Relationship-Building
Ability to Influence Others
Leadership
Teamwork

(c) *Dynamic*
Initiative
Drive
Resilience
Stress Resistance
Result Orientation

(d) *Business Related*
Business Understanding
Customer Focus

Competencies are the underlying characteristics of an individual—knowledge, skills, attitudes, values, self-concepts, traits and motives that have causal relationship with effective/and or superior performance in a job situation. Competencies may be classified as:

(1) Central and Surface Competencies

It may be mentioned that competencies exist at surface as also at core personality level. The surface level competencies of knowledge and skills are visible in behaviour or performance and can be developed with appropriate training and development. However, the core motives and trait competencies reside deep within and are difficult to understand measure and develop.

(2) Threshold and Differentiating Competencies

Threshold competencies are characteristics required by a job-holder to perform a job effectively whereas differentiating competencies are those characteristics which differentiate superior performers from average performers.

(IV) METHODS OF IDENTIFYING COMPETENCIES

There are a very large number of methods for competency analysis. Some of them have been used for job analysis over the ages. There are also a great number of proprietary methods. The more popular methods are the *Repertory Grid* method as developed by George Kelly, for the identification of personal constructs. There are also the common methods of job analysis like the *Critical Incident* method as well as the *Behavioural Event Interview (BEI)* as developed by the consulting organisation Hay McBer. All these methods have their own pros and cons and each produces results in its own mode. However, there is no single way that produces consistently perfect results. A flexible solution, which reacts to the requirements of the situation, is probably the one that works best. It is necessary to get to the basic behaviours exhibited respondents in the job analysis. One method—which we have used successfully—is a modified version of the BEI.

Competencies

A competency may be described as characteristic of an individual that can be shown to predict outstanding performance in a job. These, typically, are characteristics that enable top performers to demonstrate critical behaviour more often, in more situations and with better results. The key drivers in determining competencies are strategic requirements, work culture and role requirements. Since, usually, there is a broad variety of strategic requirements and work cultures in current-day organizations, the primary driver of competencies become role requirements. These role requirements normally operate on an increasing scale of scope and complexity ranging from executor, through specialist, to a leader.

However, just being different is not enough. With competition rising up we have no choice but to execute our development strategies better and faster than the competition. In fact, one can list many organisations that share the honours for creating amazing strategies. A few are however credited with flawlessly executing them. Outstanding organisations achieve great things with generally available talent and resources. This is possible only by effective execution. And this is one competency that is evergreen and always in demand. It has indeed become a metacompetency.

Metacompetencies

Competencies are a collective expression of effective preparation and execution of learned skills and behaviour. Generally, this is a linear programme. For example, let us look at the process of product development. Inputs are required from marketing, which in turn, would get it from customer services. This is passed on to the designers and then on to production. Almost like passing the parcei it happens like a relay.

Metacompetencies, on the other hand, are neither linear in acquisition nor in execution. The product development professionals will need to work upfront.

While competency-based development goes a long way, certain frameworks also propose "learnability" as one of the much-required behavioural traits in an organisation. This primarily links business objectives with process objectives, help execute full circles, e.g., close sales cycles with not just registered nominations but collected dues as well, as so on and so forth. Subsequently, organisations would need to identify their key thrust roles and match them with the key competencies identified. This could then be sustained and enhanced through coaching and mentoring.

Organisations may collaborate in such metacompetency environment to achieve goals and then delink again making for yet another breakthrough! These ideas, integrated, provide the design of how successful organisations world-wide tend to enhance organisational, individual, and group competencies that lead to world class performance. Systems and processes simply serve the purpose of channelising employee performance. They act as the guiding beacon.

From an OD point of view, organisations will continue to refine and enhance five key metacompetencies: strategic business planning, process orientation, performance management, knowledge management and enterprise leadership.

Organisations undertake competency development to constantly enhance their capabilities to be able to effectively perform their tasks and responsibilities. The majority of competency development occurs through practical hands-on experience in the form of variety of assignments.

According to Radha R. Sharma, "Identification of competencies and development a competency model is a specialized task. The best way to identify a competency/competencies is through behavioural event interviews (BEI) which is a form of structured interview focused on the individual and their competencies rather than on the task. Through this method data is collected on sample behaviour leading to success in a role or behaviour during events of frustration when a person failed to achieve what one wanted to. Expertise in using BEI is needed which focuses on thoughts, feelings, behaviour and outcomes to identify patterns of intentional behaviour leading to star performance. A comparison of the two extreme group-star performers and average performers throws up the data on how the two groups differ on performance criteria in a particular job/role in a particular organisation.

Identification of competencies for various job positions can be done

FIG. 28.2

Metacompetency Cluster

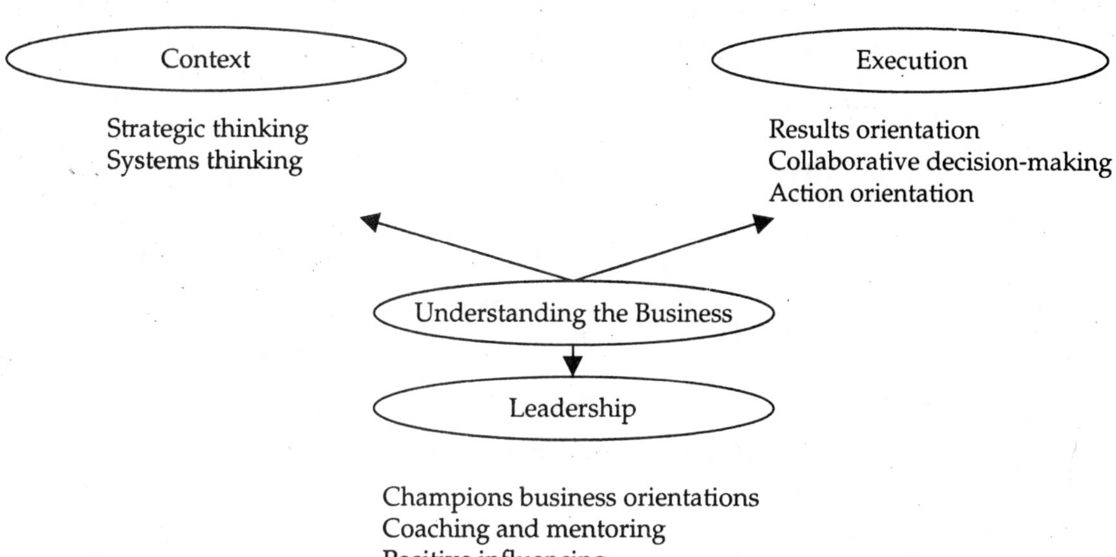

with the help of 360 degree feedback in which the employee, his supervisor, subordinates and peers can help identify competencies which differentiate star performers from average performers. Their ratings on a 5 or 7 point scale can be assigned weightages and these weightages can be multiplied with the scores given by them to get the final score for a competency. Similarly, data would be collected on other competencies required for the job position. Based on these scores competencies could be ranked in order of importance for a particular job position. However, if an organisation is aware of its competency requirements for various level jobs, it can straightaway go for assessment centre approach."

The competency-based assessment can be carried out for any of the following objectives:

- individual and organisational growth,
- strategic alignment of competencies with business growth, .
- selection for job or culture fit,
- career planning of succession planning, and
- training and development.

In competency-based assessment, assessment of an individual's knowledge and skills is based on demonstration of these in the workplace or other relevant contexts. The process begins with self-assessment against the competency standard. The person also collects evidence in the form of certificates, letters and reference to demonstrate the competence. This is followed by workplace assessment by an assessor who reviews individual's self-assessment and the evidence produced by him. This is further followed by interview and observation of the skills performed by the individual in the specified job?

Where focus is on development, the assessors provides feedback to the individual. The assessor keeps a note of areas requiring development. With the help of this, a development plan for the individual is prepared. Companies differ in approach for competency-based assessment and it is linked to the objective of assessment. However, the approach revolves around the following process model:

FIG. 28.3

Process of Competency-based Assessment

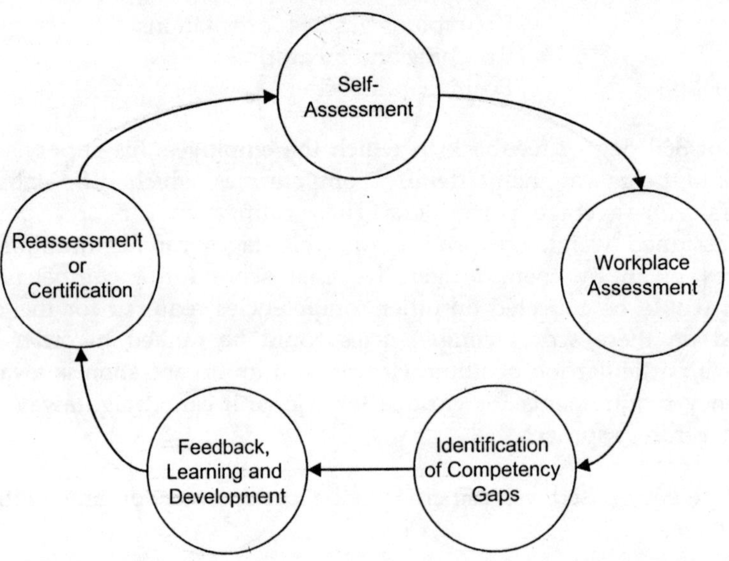

Competencies can be developed through various methods including—(a) Open learning through any source, i.e. books, journals, CD-ROM, internet, (b) Action learning through real life work-projects, (c) Accelerated learning through situation handling, and (d) Distance learning from universities, etc. Individual has to identify his own competency *needs.* More enlighrened organisations will, of course, provide resources such as finance, time and programmes.

References

Nitin Sawardekar, Assessment Centres, Response Books, New Delhi.

Human Capital, New Delhi, 2002.

Radha R. Sharma, Assessment and Development Centre as Tools for Competency Development, *IJTD* Journal, January-June, 2003.

CHAPTER

29

Developing Potential

I. NEED FOR POTENTIAL APPRAISAL

The measurement of an individual's potential to *determine to day* what *he could accomplish tomorrow* is gaining importance. Companies want to *evaluate and reward managerial potential* in addition to present performance.

People are like Iceberg. What you see above the surface (performance) is only a small part. A large part of *attributes* needed to perform excellently in a *future job,* which is called potential is not immediately visible. It is hidden below the surface. (See Fig. 29.1)

FIG. 29.1

Individual Like Iceberg

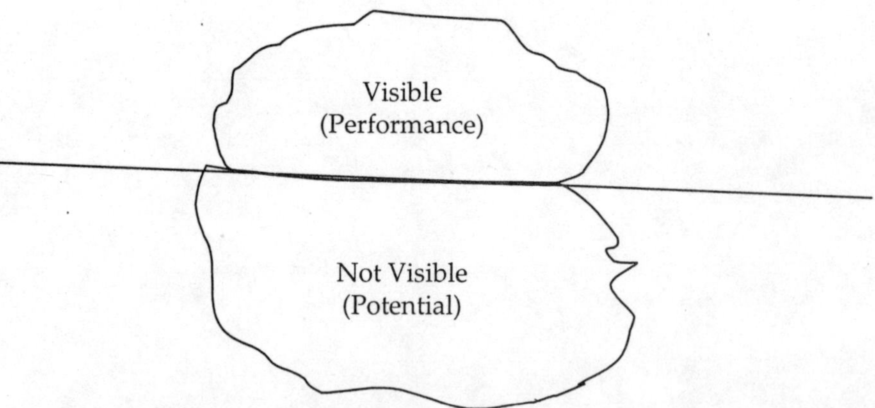

Although it is difficult to uncover the Iceberg, it is prerequisite to *organisation survival*. The task also helps in *identifying highfliers* early for career planning.

Potential is an important area as people have to be prepared to *take up higher responsibility*.

It is because of these strategic importance of potential that Indian companies have redesigned performance appraisal system to shift from simple performance orientation to *potential-cum-performance-based appraisal system*. Cadbury, Sandoz, Philips, Glaxo, P&G, etc. have long ago made this change.

2. For measurement of potential different practices are followed by companies:

(a) Philips India—Provides for evaluation of four qualities on five point scale:

I. Conceptual effectiveness:
- Vision
- Business-orientation
- Entrepreneurial-orientation
- Sense of reality

II. Organisational effectiveness:
- Result-orientation
- Risk-taking
- Control
- Individual effectiveness

III. Inter-personal effectiveness:
- Networking (relations)
- Negotiating power
- Personal influence
- Verbal behaviour

IV. Achievement motivation:
- Drive
- Professional ambition
- Innovativeness
- Stability

Companies use potential appraisal system as an integral part of management development process and also use for career planning of top positions.

(b) Glaxo India uses certain psychometric tests developed abroad to capture abilities on several areas, e.g. apptitude, deduction, inference, logic, etc.

Observations on situations such as—who is utilised by other departments? Whom functional heads refuse to release? Who is consulted by head of the department for problems. In Glaxo, they have adopted assessment—centre approach.

(c) Some organisations are assessing potential by inserting general criteria such as:

- His promptability. Is he fit for shouldering higher responsibilities?
- His capability for transfer to other units of the organisation.
- Will he be able to have functional mobility?
- Areas where he has done exceptionally well:
  - o Managerial,
  - o Technical/functional, etc.

CHAPTER

30

Learning in Fifth Generation Management: Knowledge Management

The *evolution of computers* offers an interesting parallel to what we are being challenged to do organisationally.

What are five generations of computer technology. These are explained in Fig. 30.1.

FIG. 30.1

Generations of Computer Technology

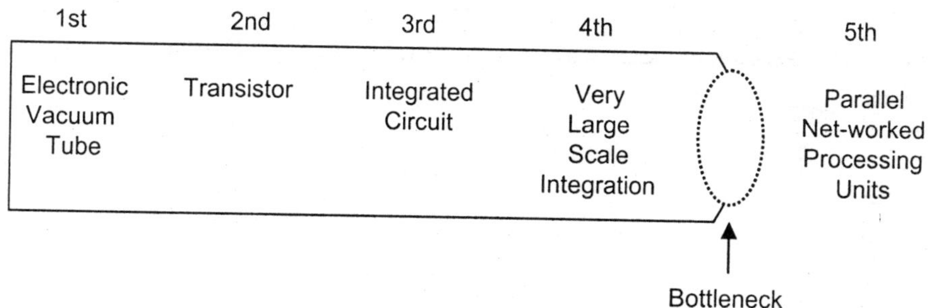

Computers of the first four generations pass all information through single CPU. It use binary numbers, operate electronically, and perform its operations one at a time or sequentially.

The key to the *fifth generation computer*, parallel processing, is in the *networking of multiple processing units*. Parallel processing has advantage of speed and we can develop more effective user interfaces, *common windowing* interfaces to interact with several different applications concurrently such as designs, process plans and marketing strategy in an interactive manner. The bottleneck has been overcome.

Fifth generation computing and networking make it possible new ways of working together but *organisation assumptions* (hierarchy, etc.) often block effective use of this technology. We are wedded to organisational forms that were evolved to the needs of industrial revolution.

GENERATIONS OF MANAGEMENT

The generations of management (organisation) and sources of wealth are explained in Figs. 30.2 and 30.3.

FIG. 30.2

Sources of Wealth and Types of Management/Organisation

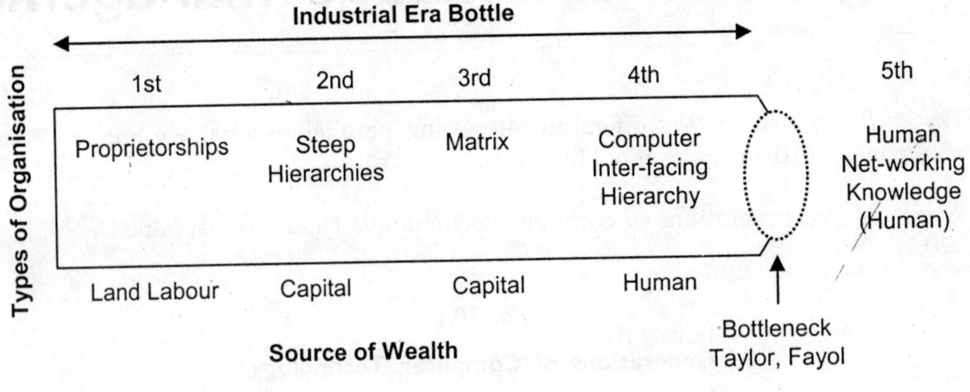

FIG. 30.3

Hierarchy and Calculus of Importance of People

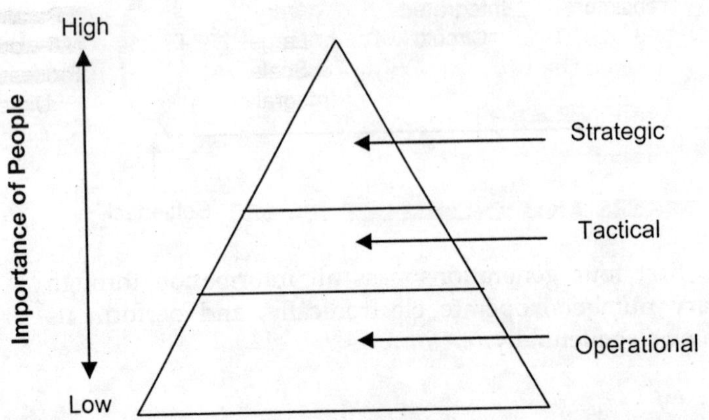

The first four generations of management are a creation of industrial era. Only as we get beyond them can we expect to tap the fuller potential of *both our people* and computer-based systems.

Knowledging (the basis of wealth in the knowledge era), is a dynamic and ongoing process that involves our human capabilities to see existing patterns and at the same time envision new patterns.

In industrial era, we have assumed that it is possible to plan everything ahead of time, divide the work among various functions, then monitor and control what is done so it meets expected outcome.

This model is out of synchronisation with changing expectations of market. Instead of large ocean-liners, or companies, we need swift run-abouts that can customise solution to particular needs. Our knowledge and capabilities to see patterns becomes the key asset of the enterprise.

The *industrial era defined fixed resources,* the *knowledge era* needs to draw upon *variable or virtual* resources to meet unique market and customer demands in a timely manner by configuring and reconfiguring the appropriate cross-functional teams.

It is clear that real knowledge needed to run an enterprise resides in the heads of those working there. The task is now of *networking the right people* to handle task-focused assignments.

In addition, *multiple teams must* be networked in order to achieve team work of teams. This suggests a whole *new vision* of what might be possible *outside the industrial era bottle.*

IN SUM

- The proprietorship form represents *first* generation management.
- Bureaucracy (or steep hierarchy), is *second* generation management.
- *Third* generation matrix organisation and *fourth* generation interface hierarchies, are simply super imposed on steep hierarchy.
- The *fifth* generation networked organisation requires *fifth* generation management.

KNOWLEDGE WORKERS AND KNOWLEDGE MANAGEMENT

Meaning

"Knowledge is the only *meaningful* resource today" asserts

management guru Peter Drucker. What the assembly line was to 20th century manufacturing, knowledge is proving to be just that the 21st century business. Knowledge people (professionals) are representatives of new global economy.

I. Some Feature of Knowledge People

(a) Knowledge is Superior Resource

Human being is self-conscious. He is aware of himself, and aware of others. He has a mind and a heart. He wants to know. He has power to think. He can have creative and innovative mind. He can be self-motivated to manage himself also. All these make knowledge people *more superior than any other resource* (such as technology, capital, information, etc. which are available to all companies). Knowledge people generate ideas which are now valued. Knowledge is actually a combination of know-what, know-why and know-how which is possessed by human beings who have great potential.

(b) Knowledge can Provide Competitive Edge

A company can attain edge over its rivals in a global market due to knowledge workers. These knowledge employees provide three abilities:

(i) Innovation in the market,

(ii) Originality of service, and

(iii) Deep understanding of customer needs which market surveys yield.

Increasingly, the real value addition is knowledge. Knowledge is core competence for coping with change. The importance of knowledge workers is also due to their scarcity.

(c) Knowledge People are Necessary for every Operation in a Company

Due to their creativity and innovation, such as for product design, excellence in product to service, team work, total quality, global competition as environment is fast changing. Inspiring, and motivation of potential energy of knowledge workers is critical. So individual knowledge is the starting point of organisational knowledge. Only knowledge people can spread/share knowledge across the company. So management must create favourable climate in the organisation. Organisation needs knowledge to leverage all organisational capabilities. Knowledge people can be the most important asset of the organisation. We are in the era of brain-power industries such as—computer, software, telecommunication, semi-conductor chips, internet, knowledge people are core-workers.

(d) Learning is an Ongoing Process of Acquiring Knowledge by Individuals

Innovative patterns of learning individually or collectively lead to success in global market. The new people management philosophy, i.e. learning organisation can be created by:

- Keep the company in a state of *constant change,* from vertical (hierarchical) to one that will operate horizontally and collaboratively across organisational borders.
- Practicing to unlearn old and obsolete knowledge and acquiring knowledge by sharing or creating network world-wide for interaction.
- *Innovative culture,* i.e. recognition of ideas, values or emotions for conceptualisation.
- *Creating conditions* under which individuals, teams and organisations learn. Peter Senge calls it systems learning ("The Fifth Discipline") or generative learning.
- To anticipate and learn from change through experimentation and feedback. This means to *practice proactive approach* to problems by the management.
- To *institutionalise knowledge* and values so that these are transferred when individual leaves.
- Fostering *positive mental mindset* among employees for their ability to meeting all future solutions.
- *Learning from mistakes* and taking calculated risks in business for increasing opportunities.
- Employees must learn *system thinking* (Holistic approach) which means to understand the forces, inter-connections and inter-relationships that shapes the behaviour of systems. This calls for coordination, integration and synthesis of all components for having harmony in the working of the organisation.
- Learning organisation constitute the future environment. Learning organisation brings the people closer to the problem, who have knowledge and ideas. It is an age of knowledge capital. The owners of knowledge and wisdom, i.e. people are real assets of the company in 21st century.

2. Background

We are in knowledge era. Alvin and H. Toffler, the grand masters of future thinking, had predicted long ago in terms of transformational change, a few true turning points in history, each associated with the emergence of different systems of wealth creation.

First Wave: The invention of agriculture provided the human race with a new way to convert the earth's resources into wealth, and almost everywhere launched a 'First Wave' of change in civilization that gave rise to *peasant-centered* economies as means of human subsistence.

Second Wave: Similarly, the *Industrial Revolution* triggered a 'Second Wave' of change that gave us a factory-based system for wealth creation. In turn, this led to mass production, the drive for larger and larger markets, and the need for bigger, ever more bureaucratic business organizations. Until very recently, most of what was taught in management texts and in schools of business reflected 'Second Wave' thinking.

Third Wave: Today's *knowledge revolution*, having launched a gigantic 'Third Wave' of economic, technical and social change, is forcing businesses to operate in radically new, continually shifting ways that stand 'Second Wave' notions on their head. The industrial faith in such things as vertical integration, synergy, economies of scale and hierarchical, command-and-control organization is giving way to a fresh appreciation of outsourcing, minimization of scale, profit centers, networks and other diverse forms of organization. Every shred of industrial-era thinking is now being rescrutinized and brilliantly reformulated.

In knowlege era, the primary factor of production is knowledge, for wealth creation. Knowledge is a dynamic and ongoing process that involves our human capabilities to see existing patterns and at the same time envision new patterns. We expect to tap the fuller potential of both our people and computer-based systems. So now there is much need for synergy of technological and human capabilities. An increasing amount of work is being done by consulting firms on questions of knowledge management—the assessment of knowledge assets. New approaches to organisational and in individual learning, attempt to create a metric for dealing with knowledge.

3. What is Knowledge Management?

Knowledge Management (KM) is the process through which organizations *generate-value* from their intellectual and knowledge-based assets. Most often, generating value from such assets *involves sharing* them among employees, departments and even with other companies in an effort to devise best practices. It's important to note that the definition says nothing about technology; while KM is often facilitated by IT, technology by itself is not KM. The key to KM is *achieving better business results,* which could come from improved organisational learning. So, KM is *about learning,* learning is the process by which we get knowledge. It helps us to apply knowledge. From the business point, learning is important.

4. What Constitutes Intellectual or Knowledge-Based Assets

Not all information is valuable. Therefore, it's up to individual companies to determine what information qualifies as intellectual and knowledge-based assets. In general, however, intellectual and knowledge-based assets fall into one of two categories: *explicit or tacit.* Included among the former, i.e. *explicit* are assets such as patents, trademarks, business plans, marketing research and customer lists. As a general rule of thumb, *explicit knowledge* consists of anything that can be documented, archived and codified, often with the help of IT. Much harder to grasp is the concept of *tacit knowledge,* or the know-how contained in people's heads. The challenge inherent with *tacit knowledge* is figuring out how to recognize, generate, share and manage it. While IT in the form of e-mail, groupware, instant messaging and related technologies can help facilitate the dissemination of· tacit knowledge; *identifying tacit knowledge* in the first place is a major hurdle for most organizations.

5. K.M. has now made any Information Accessible at a Click

When L&T's engineering and construction (E&C) business division executed turnkey projects in various corners of the country, problems at the site would mean a flurry of phone calls to locate experts within the company who might be able to solve it. In the process, time, a crucial element in completing projects, would be at a premium. Obviously, communication costs mounted. Not surprising, therefore, that the E&C business division was the first in L&T to embrace knowledge management with its portal KnowNet in late 2000.

Currently, KnowNet helps L&T to not just solve niggling problems at project sites, but also to identify alternative cost-effective solutions on the use of raw materials. Example: While executing a project for a public sector refinery in South India, L&T's engineers felt that the specified material of construction was of a higher grade than required. The result would be higher cost and a longer lead time because the material was more difficult to source. By delving into the learnings of KnowNet, L&T engineers discovered that in three similar projects in the past, a more cost-effective grade of material had been used without any problem. This was double-checked with other contractors who had executed similar projects. As a result of its KnowNet learnings, L&T was able to save nearly Rs. 1 crore on the project. Says K. Venkataramanan, president (operations) of L&T: "KM goes beyond storing information. We are trying to leverage tacit knowledge, which lies in the skill of our people, to deliver results."

Just as L&T uses KM to roll out real-world construction projects at lower cost, infotech major Infosys Technologies, which executes software projects both onshore and offshore, is another pioneer in the use of KM in India. Reason: projects heads and staff tend to be mobile in software. Unless the *learnings from* one project are captured and templated permanently, the speed and quality of execution may suffer. This is simply unaffordable in an era where software vendors are being squeezed on margins by cost-conscious customers.

6. Driving Forces for KM

There are actually two drivers behind the new-found enthusiasm. One is competition, and the other is IT. At a fundamental level, companies know that in a *super competitive marketplace* the right knowledge at the right time makes all the difference to performance. With products and services getting commoditised, it is speed and customer and market knowledge, among other things, that gives the edge. It is not enough to have this information in your database somewhere; you need this at the point—and at the instant—when your customer makes a call to the call centre to make a complaint. Companies that can bring deep customer knowledge out of the can and into the heart of day to-day decision-making cannot do so without adopting KM.

The second *driver for KM is IT push.* Today there is not a single major international software vendor without a KM-related offering: IBM, Microsoft, Oracle, Siebel, SAP, the works. Not to speak of a whole range of smaller software companies focusing on niche KM areas. From "brainstorming" and collaborative tools to content and document management, from data mining to expert and decision-support systems, from indexing and search engine tools to intelligent agents, every segment in the knowledge management chain has vendor selling solutions or prices of it.

To be sure, KM is not about IT. It is about *creating, recognising, accumulating, sharing and using knowledge to add value to organisations.* When it comes to adding value to corporates, it is organisational knowledge—and not individual knowledge—that matters. This has led to a more formal approach towards managing knowledge, by not just pre-serving information but analysing it and presenting it in a access-friendly format on company intranets.

7. Companies are Encouraging their Employees to Share Knowledge

Many recent entrants are devising ways and means of encouraging their employees to share knowledge. Because employees will only visit the knowledge portal if the information they are looking for is available. In the case of ad agency Lowe, it offers K-Points to employees who contribute to the portal. To encourage usage of the portal, employees who access the information also get points.

8. How to Build Human Networking into Enterprise?

Some steps are as under for sharing KM:

- Working together in *virtual task-focusing teams,* i.e. human networking enterprises.
- Developing *visionary capabilities about the challenges* in our enterprises, through networking or knowledge. Developing data integration strategy and also grow the knowledge base.
- *Encountering blockades* in transition process by listening and learning from one another.
- Extend virtual task-focusing teams which can *include* suppliers, partners, distributors and customers.
- To practise of *continual learning* and work more in parallel.
- We can share learning to enhance our capabilities in an ongoing process approach advanced by Petersenge. He has suggested five human values of learning organisations:
  - (i) Personal mastery (competencies and skills);
  - (ii) Spiritual growth—mental models of values and principles;
  - (iii) Shared vision;
  - (iv) Team learning and unlearning; and
  - (v) Systems thinking.

Thus, we can use the new source of "wealth-creation."

9. Process of Implementing Knowledge Management

Knowledge management is as much *an activity* ("something you do") as it is a *type of system* or technology. That's why it's worthwhile to explore what's involved in implementing KM, or to put it more formally, in *capturing* existing knowledge within an organization, and then *adapting* that knowledge while capturing new knowledge going forward. Once such knowledge is captured, KM professionals can apply *the processes* of analysis, organization, assigning relationships and priority rankings between questions and answers.

(a) Document knowledge

Analyze all possible sources of organizational knowledge to build a taxonomy-of-knowledge-types, and to decide what attributes and values should be associated with each type (let's call an instance of some knowledge type—a specific item of knowledge—a knowledge element). Next, examine all possible sources to uncover existing knowledge elements, and make it possible to discover new knowledge elements.

(b) Share Knowledge

Start by recording all known knowledge elements from documents, communications, and subject matter expert interviews. At each step along the way, include input forms to elicit feedback from KM system users about knowledge elements, element organization, element search and retrieval, and element relevancy.

(c) Apply Knowledge

This is where *customers and support staff interact with* the knowledge base to locate and use relevant knowledge. At this stage it is essential to refine the contents of knowledge elements and to adapt the structure of the knowledge base in response to such interaction. The ability to make and suggest useful relationships between problems and solutions is powerful enough to enlist a strong buy-in from support staff and knowledge management professionals when they see that a dynamic system can improve search results, agent productivity and customer satisfaction. In general, and within the context of customer service systems based on customer contact centers, KM encompasses the broad range of capabilities needed to logically capture, organize, share and use knowledge elements in order to recognize problems and suggest possible solutions to customer service queries.

10. Benefits of an effective KM Programme should help a company do one or more of the following:

- *Foster innovation* by encouraging the free flow of ideas.
- *Improve customer service* by streamlining response time.
- *Boost revenues* by getting products and services to market faster.
- Enhance *employee retention* rates by recognizing the value of employees' knowledge and rewarding them for it.
- *Streamline operations* and reduce costs by eliminating redundant or unnecessary processes.

These are the most examples of strategic benefits. A creative approach to KM can result in improved efficiency, higher productivity and increased revenues in practically any business function. KM to deliver business results.

11. Must have a Specific Business Goal

A KM programme should not be divorced from a business goal. While sharing best practices is a commendable idea, there must be an underlying business reason to do so. Without a solid business case, KM is a futile exercise.

12. KM is not Static

As with many physical assets, the value of knowledge can erode over time. Since knowledge can get stale fast, the content in a KM programme should be constantly updated, amended and deleted. What's more, the relevance of knowledge at any given time changes, as do the skills of employees. Therefore, there is no endpoint to a KM.

To Conclude: Think!

"What is greater than knowledge?" asked the mind.

"A heart that can see and care", whispered the soul.

References

Charles M. Savage, "Fifth Generation Management", Knowledge Management, Digital Press, Digital Equipment Corporation, USA.

Thirumoothy Paramasivan, "Knowledge Management Your Key to Develop Competitive Advantage", Jims 8M, Oct.-Dec. 2003.

Prasad Sangrameshwaran, "Knowledge Management Initiatives", *Indian Management*, May 2003.

Bhatia, S.K., "Knowledge Organisation", *Management of Change and Organisation Development*, Deep & Deep Publications Pvt. Ltd., New Delhi.

CHAPTER

31

Process of Knowledge Management

1. The new millennium has dawned new era marked by, technological, political and economic changes, that demand a new human, resources for the new century. The rules of conducting business and running organisations are changing and HR management has to gear itself to face the emerging challenges. There is going to be fundamental shift in the traditional employer/employee relationship and this shift presents a unique opportunity to HR professionals to develop a vision global in perspective.

2. Let us see what are the mega trends in people services. Schools from George Washington university have forecast emerging technologies during the next 3 decades as under:

MEGA TREND-I: TECHNOLOGY DEVELOPMENT PREDICTIONS (2001-2030)

(a) Growing use of manpower from all over the world at work place. The multimedia inter-connectivity allows people to easily interact. In a global market, "BEST and THE BRIGHT" workers will develop organisations that will employ citizens from every country. This has positive and negative concerns, due to overseas competition and use of foreign employees.

(b) Expert systems, computer models that stimulate human thinking, may see routine use and this will replace human labour.

(c) Hot new jobs and opportunities will be in the service sector.

The service sector, particularly the offshore remote processing services have thrown up whole range of new jobs, which were unheard. Some of these coveted hot jobs are for:

- Web site services
- Translation, transcription
- Animation
- Remote customer interaction services
- HR services
- Finance and Accounting services
- Data search, integration and analysis
- Engineering and design services
- Remote Education
- Market research

Employment target for these jobs projected is so high that one needs to develop a long term strategy to provide assured career paths and continuing education for employees.

MEGA TREND-2: INDIVIDUAL RESPONSIBILITY

For the career development, health care and retirement security, the employees are on their own and are not in service.

They have to continuously restructure their careers in the global economy.

Decentralisation of decisions empowerment and autonomy encourages employees to think independently.

MEGA TREND-3: IN THE KNOWLEDGE MANAGEMENT ECONOMY BRAIN POWER/SKILLS WILL DIFFERENTIATE EMPLOYEES

People will be the only competitive advantage organisations will have.

MEGA TREND-4: CONTINGENT WORK ENCOURAGES INDIVIDUALISM

Present trend is towards outsourcing, contracting will create vast army of individuals/consultants.

Human resource professionals shall have to recognise that these mega trends create a need for innovative HR management solutions.

3. We shall discuss how the HR professionals will face these new

challenges to manage the knowledge employees.

Harness new individualism amongst employees by working together for common objectives

Employees are now on their own and are growing self-reliant. The 21st century strategic HR professionals will need to get people working together for common objectives which are not clear as old theories won't work. None of the old models for manager-employee relations fit the new employment paradigm. Employers can harness the new individualism amongst employees in following manners:

(i) Provide for work-life balance and offer flexibility for Quality of life

Quality of life will become the controlling issue of the 21st century-much more important than income, new generation needs, time-flexible scheduling, Virtual Office, Telecommuting, Childcare.

(ii) Encourage and create participatory culture

HR professionals to encourage and create participatory culture among managers, so that employees are heard and can contribute new ideas at the workplace self-reliant employees crave for dialogue. HR professional to listen to their employees and adopt open communication policy for giving right information.

(iii) Reward individuals based on performance and contribution

Recent employee surveys show growing unhappiness with today's compensation systems. Companies are responding to pay for performance expectations, cash incentives and stock options.

(iv) Invest in human capital by providing continuing education

In a fast lane economy skills obsolescence is the new concern. Career security demands, lifelong learning, and employees expect employers to share the responsibility for continuing education not only by investing in training but actively encouraging it. Motorola is leading today's education and training revolution. Every employee, including the CEO, is required to complete at least 40 hours of training a year.

Hewlett-Packard (HP) hosts open houses inside learning centres and sends direct mail to employees home. Most important, HP recognises managers whose employees attend training classes.

Fluor Daniel India Pvt. Ltd., US based MNC in India encourages its executives to complete web-based training programmes for enhancing their management, technical and software skills.

(v) Create a sense of ownership in business through self-directed employee Involvement teams

Yesterdays middle management cadre bridged employees and senior management with flat structures. Today it is a missing link. Self-directed employee involvement teams offer great promise to connect employees to the companies larger vision and create a sense of community.

(vi) Provide people opportunities to excel

The way most people view work has changed. Employees are not merely looking for a job, they are looking for opportunities which will enhance their skill and knowledge and add value to the organisation. In workplace, highly skilled employees will only stay where HR professionals will provide employees the chance to excel and create a competitive advantage for the organisation.

(vii) International Human Resource Management will Gain Importance for Managing Diversified Cultures and Manpower

(viii) Practice Holistic HR Management to get Most of the Employees

Do not focus on the small picture. Holistic means helping and supporting employees so that they can be the best people in all facets of their lives We will ensure that our people, at the end of the day, still have the energy to be parents, family members and spouses. HR professionals help change work environment which has a positive impact on the company and family life of the employees. A healthy and happy workforce is a productive workforce.

Holistic approach again comes from leadership role that HR professionals need to take within their organisations at all levels.

(ix) Strategic alignment of business with potential

HR professionals must cease to assume that their role is confined within specific functional boundaries. They have to explore linkage between business interests of the organisation and the underlying knowledge potential of employees. In this way organisation develop its core competence.

(x) HR to have customer focus of internal customers

The employees return will give the best quality work and service to external customer.

(xi) HR professionals to create an atmosphere conducive to change in organisation transformation

They will have to take initiative to motivate others to build an atmosphere of trust and goodwill which is also conducive to the constant ongoing phenomenon of change.

(xii) HR professionals to use technology to gain more time for their fundamental strategic planning and interaction with the employees

HR professional to use automation tools to streamline administrative process and eliminate paper intensive work.

(xiii) HR personnel to play leadership role by influencing common vision and have multi-disciplinary exposure

Finally, the main concern of HR professionals in the coming years is on the shortage of leadership, i.e. about using influencing skills. Business are built upon networks. Leaders must not only have vision, but also be able to influence others in the network to see that vision. Managers have to learn to work on multiple projects and team cultures.

To conclude, the new millennium envisages an entirely new role for HR professionals, who have to force new strategies and practices to recruit, train, develop and retain the human resources, so that they are vibrant, responsive, adaptive, innovative and above all, content with their growth in the organisation.

CHAPTER

32

Factors to Improve Effectiveness of Training

1. THE EMERGING CHALLENGES IN TRAINING

- Make learning one of the fundamental values of the company.
- Commit major resources and adequate time to training.
- Use training to bridge the gap with the external world.
- Integrate training into initiatives for change management.
- Use training as a developmental tool for individuals.
- Link organisational, operational, and individual training needs.
- Install training systems that substitute work experience.
- Ensure that training allows the soft skills to bloom.
- Use retraining to continuously upgrade employees' skills.
- Create a system to evaluate the effectiveness of training.

(*Source*: *Business Today*, January 7-21, 185, 1996.)

2. FACTORS TO IMPROVE EFFECTIVENESS OF TRAINING

In the light of importance and the challenges in training R.S. Dwivedi has highlighted ten steps to maximise the effectiveness of training as under:

(i) Training-needs Identification

An effective system of training-needs-identification ensures that the employee is needed getting training in the area needed by him. This ensures that genuine needs are addressed via training and that the trainee could truly benefit from this training.

(ii) Pre-training Activities

Every superior is expected to explain to his subordinate the rationale benefits of nominating him for the training.

(iii) Planning and Organising the Programme

This is yet another crucial area towards training effectiveness. Factors such location, facilities at the training venue and duration have a significant impact learning.

(iv) Designing the Module

This is the most crucial aspect contributing to programme effectiveness. The training manager or coordinator should make it a point to discuss the module with the faculty (internal or external). The training manager has to ensure that he gets the "right" faculty and not necessarily the "best".

(v) Feedback on the Faculty

There should be well-designed feedback systems to evaluate the course and the faculty to check if the trainees are filling it up seriously enough. The forms are duly filled *immediately after the training* programme and collected by the training coordinator. Further the training coordinator or company official should conduct a course evaluation discussion upon completion of the programme. This could be preferably done after bidding good-bye to the external faculty so that the feedback is genuine and candid. This also ensures that trainees take up the task of course evaluation more seriously. Feedback can help the faculty to fine tune his programme and provide value addition to the training process.

(vi) Feedback from the Faculty

It is advisable to seek feedback from the faculty on the following areas:

(a) participation level of the trainees,

(b) training infrastructure existing in the company, and

(c) training support received from the company.

The above data if collected and compiled periodically would be very useful for the company is an effort to improve the training effectiveness. This also provides feedback to the company about seriousness of the trainee.

(vii) Training Plan and Budgets

It is necessary that every organisation plans its training activities on an annual basis, training calendar could be a tremendous focus to the entire training function. Some companies are even trying to look at the training function as an independent profit centre. Thus, each user department pays for the service that it avails from the training department. Further, the training department of the company by virtue of its profit centre concept also leases its services to other organisations.

(viii) Development of In-House Faculty

To suit the needs of the company an approach is becoming increasingly popular, i.e. developing in-house faculty. Managers are picked up who show the inclination towards training. They are further groomed, and training skills are imparted to them. This also brings about a job enrichment for the manager, as he sees a new satisfying role as a trainer or facilitator.

(ix) Nomination to External Seminars and Training Programmes

Training coordinators to study the brochures, look at the organisational needs and then nominate trainees. In order to ensure that trainees do not perceive this as a paid holiday in four-star comforts, suitable programmes need to be identified. Further, every such trainee who attends such programmes should be asked to make a presentation of about an hour or so about his learnings on the external seminar. This would also ensure that what is learned is shared with peers, subordinates and superiors.

(x) Quality Training Focus

We need to ensure that quality of training is the overriding factor over quantity of training. TQM which is the current fad in the management circuit should also be applicable to the training function. The top management of companies should ensure that training programmes should be of the highest quality where managers are nominated.

In conclusion, there is an ever-increasing awareness about the need and importance of training of the highest quality companies to look at people as assets and training and development activities as an investment for the future and not an expenditure.

References

R.S. Dwivedi: Managing Human Resources in Indian Enterprises, Galgotia Publishing Company, New Delhi.

Armstrong, M.: A Handbook of Personnel Management Practice, London: Kogan Page Ltd., 1995, 508.

Cascio, W.F.: Managing Human Resources, New York: McGraw-Hill; Inc.; 1995, 245.

Drucker, P.F.: Managing for the Future, New Delhi: Tata McGraw-Hill; 1992, 333.

Pedler, M.: Boydell, T., Burgoyne, J.: Towards the Learning Company, *Management Education and Development*, 1989, 20(1): 1-8.

Garvin, D.A.: Building a Learning Organization, *Harvard Business Review*, 1993, 78-91.

Burgoyne, J.: Cited in Personnel Management, *Plus*, 1994, 7.

Senge, P.M.: The Fifth Discipline: The Art and Practice of the Learning Organisations, New York: Doubleday, 1991.

Senge, P.M.: Transforming the Practice of Management, *Human Resource Development Quarterly*, Spring 1993, 9.

CHAPTER

33

Factors for Success of Training Activity

What makes a training function successful? Some of the ingredients for success of training activity are enumerated here:

1. Top Management Support and Commitment

The training function must be *supported with commitment* from those who are running the organisation. Indeed, it needs to be an integral part of the running of the business, since training is a major factor in establishing the levels of effectiveness of component parts of the system, its people. If those who wield power in an organisation do not recognise the value of training and consequently fail to give it the support it needs, it has little future. It is unable to demonstrate whether or not it can achieve success.

2. Build Team Work

Training is only partly concerned with optimising the effectiveness of its employees as individuals. The success of many organisations can be *attributed to team work,* not only at the top, but throughout the undertaking. Those firms which are able to operate as teams, rather than as conglomerations of individuals, are usually better able to agree their objectives and pursue them successfully than those whose members are steering their own courses in different directions. Normal conflict or disagreement may prove ultimately constructive: unrestrained obstinacy and inflexibility can frequently be highly destructive. The training manager who is able to achieve a team spirit throughout his organisation can make a positive contribution to its fortunes.

3. High Level of Professionalism as Trainer

Success breeds success, and it is therefore important for the *training function to make an early impact* in an organisation. It is mare difficult to establish credibility after a period of mediocre performance than it is to create a favourable image from the start. Once having gained a poor reputation, it is not at all easy to convince people that one is capable of better things. Often the more one tries the more difficult it becomes, because one's motives may be misinterpreted. The person in charge of the training function needs to demonstrate a *high level of professionalism* from the beginning and so instil confidence throughout the concern.

4. Good Knowledge of the Organisation

In addition to the practical training skills that the training manager has to possess to enable him to carry out his *training role effectively,* he needs to have a good *knowledge of the organisation.* Tact and diplomacy are called for in overcoming such difficulties and it is helpful to have warning of the problems in advance.

5. High Standard Work

Professionalism is not only required of the head of the department of training. *High standards are expected of everyone who works in the training department.* The penalty for not insisting on them is lack of credibility with adverse effects on the impact of the function on business performance.

6. Foresee Emerging Changes in Work Practices and Initiate Change

Being able to respond to the need for change is a matter of some consequence to training staff. Organisational performance can often be improved by adopting new methods and techniques. Changes in the law may affect the way in which managers and supervisors operate. Internal regulations, systems, work practices, etc. may have to be modified from time to time. Training departments have a responsibility to monitor these and other developments in order to capitalize on *new approaches to the conduct of business* and to ensure that the introduction of changes in work practices can be efficiently carried out, causing the minimum of disruption.

7. Regular Feed-back of Training Activities

Effective evaluation of training performance is itself one of the criteria for success. If it reveals weaknesses in the training carried out, it provides the *trigger for remedial action* which will bring the activity back on course. Conversely, confirmation that the training is adequately satisfying the needs gives the department confidence in its ability to meet its targets.

8. Effectively Meet Organisation Needs

The training department is required in influencing and *developing employees' behaviour* by appropriate means in any or all of the key areas of knowledge, skills and attitudes. The means will vary considerably according to the task and will be either instructional or experiential. The methods chosen must be appropriate to the particular task; the wrong methods may produce inadequate and sometimes damaging results. Measuring the results of training is vital in order to ensure that what is being done is effective and is meeting the organisational needs.

9. The factors which contribute to training success may thus be summarized as follows:

- top management support and commitment, preferably direct involvement;
- the encouragement of team work, i.e. work achievement by co-operative effort towards defined goals;
- high standards of professionalism, sound knowledge of training principles and methods and an intimate knowledge of the organisation and how it operates; a reputation establishment by a good track record in identifying and satisfying needs;
- skill in recognising the necessity for change and being able to handle it efficiently;
- adaptability in responding to varying individual and group characteristics;
- evaluation procedures which enable training activities to be monitored and if necessary modified; and
- recognition that training should be cost effective.

Reference

S.K. Bhatia, Principles and Techniques of Personnel Management/HRM, Deep & Deep Publications Pvt. Ltd., New Delhi.

CHAPTER

34

Management Training in the Future

In this chapter an attempt has been made to project a future scenario in the management training and development function. Such an attempt can suggest directional approach to be followed so as to improve management training in the companies. This chapter describes trends under different headings such as—(i) What are changes in role of training specialist?, (ii) How are training needs established?, (iii) What are training designs?, (iv) How to measure the results of training?, and (v) What are major problems? As a concluding part some of the future perspectives are summarised.

(I) CHANGING ROLE OF THE TRAINING SPECIALIST

They will need to totally understand the business. The role of training will change because the managers are better educated and work with more sophisticated business systems. They have been around the world, many of them work in multinational companies, and their expectations are high. Training managers will take moves to make the function more directly relevant to the business.

Training function will use a wider variety of methods, with trainers more like line managers or consultants and with training activities as much concerned with *solving business problems* as with imparting knowledge. The movement towards action learning, project work and solving critical work problems with teams of managers will accelerate. Managers will be trained in teams and will be developed more horizontally by job rotation and temporary assignments. More emphasis will be placed on how managers operate in their work teams than as individuals. Organisation Development has appeared on the organisation charts of training functions.

Training will be integrated with *management development*. There will be a swing of the pendulum towards development. More effort will be put into identifying potential managers and in helping them to develop. There will be more succession planning and career planning. There will be more effort behind moving managers in the company, exposing them to different functions and experiences to stretch the intellect, than on managers staying in current jobs. Management development will take place earlier in a person's career. The notion of self-improvement will be more of an essential tenet of work than of present.

Trainers will need to totally *understand the business*. They will have more working contact with senior management and will grasp opportunities from the total business environment and from business changes. Trainers will be a great deal more professional than at present.

There will be a fundamental re-thinking about the relationship between work and people. *A participative, consultative approach to solving problems will be accepted*. Training will be expected to change management styles to a more open, communicative, consultative approach. The generation of key managers now aged 4 will command the company in future and will have different values from the current directors.

There will be more training in advanced technology so that managers do not become technically obsolete or the company taken by surprise. Managers will need to understand the implications of improvements in technology and to grasp the opportunities they other. They will need to understand the spin-off effects, their effect on people and on other parts of the organisation. Managers will be trained more as generalists than as managers of specialist functions. There will be a broadening of management minds to encompass wide international themes.

The role of the training specialist is changing. He is no longer solely a tutor, except in a management education centre. Now, he is variously described as a *facilitator, a business analyst, an identifier of training needs, a specialist in training methods and a process consultant*. He does much of his work away from the training centre with managers in their departments.

Outside consultants are used when new concepts or ideas are required at senior level or when internal resources are not available. They are particularly useful for dealing with sensitive issues where opposition might be expected.

(II) ESTABLISHING TRAINING NEEDS

Training which reacts to changes in business situation:

Companies are basing training more and more on business plans and company problems rather than just a repetition of last years' training courses.

Categories of Training Need

Two distinct categories emerge:

(1) Knowledge and skills to do the management job; and

(2) Responses to business situations.

The second group reflects a newer type of training which is growing. It takes *training into the business situation* and is the more attacking approach. In addition, one new type of training emerges, reflecting increased interest companies are taking in the environment and local community.

Identifying Training Needs

Companies use a mixture of approaches. The use of a number of methods increases the chances of indentifying the real training needs.

The most common ways of indentifying needs continue to be by:

(i) *Performance appraisals.*

(ii) *Working contact with managers.*

(iii) *Support for established courses.*

(iv) *The fastest growing method is training which reacts to changes business situations*: Trainers are becoming more and more aware that changes in organisation or process or methods, or almost any business change, creates training needs. In addition, this type of involvement takes training into the mainstream of management which training courses can never do.

Also increasing are the needs based on company plans and objectives. Training managers are being taken into the confidence of directors and being involved in discussions about business strategies. Training needs are also established during team development and organisation development when managers and staff in teams identify and solve working problems under the direction of a trainer/consultant. Often part of the solution lies with training.

The use of research methods to establish training needs is developing. The methods most in evidence are:

(v) *Knowledge and Skill Surveys*: Questionnaires and interviews at various levels of middle and senior management to establish the knowledge and skills content of management jobs.

(vi) *Activity Analysis*: An analysis of what successful managers actually do, particularly what makes them successful.

(vii) *Management Assessment Questionnaire*: Completed by participants, their manager and several subordinates before the course. This assesses the strengths and weaknesses of participants for examination and improvement during the course.

(III) TRAINING DESIGNS

Integration of Training with Management Development

In most companies, Management Training and Management Development are integrated at the level of personnel director and are separated below this level. This is likely to change in the future. Most training managers forecast a single integrated function to which will be added the more recent innovations of Assessment Centres and Organisation Development.

The term Management Development is understood to include the activities of manpower planning, career planning, performance appraisals, identifying potential promoters, arranging developmental job assignments. The two functions work closely together in most companies, particularly on the joint identification of training needs. Management Development Officers take part in training programmes. Training Staff participate in conducting Assessment Centres and check training needs identified through the performance appraisal system. Often there is an interchange staff.

Nearly all training managers feel that management development is an essential function which is seriously neglected. The neglect is especially apparent in the conduct of performance appraisal interviews and in career planning. Although personnel directors intellectually understand the need, it is rarely translated into positive action except in the newer companies or multinationals.

The accuracy of detecting training needs from performance appraisals is often doubtful. Some companies feel that the real needs are not identified and that there is frequently little relationship between training dominated and the individual's objectives or his strengths and weaknesses. Some companies try to avoid courses being recommended, suggesting instead such activities as counselling, communicating, delegating to develop subordinates.

Organisation Development

The main function of OD is to solve operating problems using the team of managers whose problem it is. In typical cases, working teams examine problems, produce plans and implement solutions under the direction of their manager working with an OD specialist. The group moves on from examining work problems to examining working relationships within the group and the group's relationships with other departments. The benefits of OD are that the groups who work together are all involved in training at the same time, looking at problems highly relevant to the group's work and providing results which are measurable. Furthermore, training is integrated into the lifeblood of the operation rather than being an outside activity.

(IV) MEASURING RESULTS

Measuring the effectiveness of training is difficult and often impossible. Mostly the best that can be achieved is to test participants' reactions to the programme. The whole qualitative and quantitative side of measurement is still in its infancy.

The main problem is that a trainer has little control over participants after the course has finished. The participant himself and his manager are responsible for achieving change on-the-job, but change is mostly subordinated to dozens of other work pressures to which a subordinate is subjected on return after a course. In the absence of accurate systems of measurement, companies put considerable effort into accurate diagnosing of needs so that programmes are relevant to manager's jobs.

Within the variety of ways of measuring results, three basic ways are the most frequently used:

(i) *Course evaluation forms*: To measure participants' reaction to the course.

(ii) *Demand*: The amount of repeat business is considered to be a measure of success.

(iii) *Subjective evaluation*: Training staff discuss the effectiveness with managers both during and after courses.

In addition, a variety of ways are used to test how well training is performing:

- The interest by chairman and directors and their willing involvement as faculty on courses and as evening visitors is a measurement of training effectiveness, albeit subjective.
- Training staff interview both participants and their bosses before and after each course. The Critical Incident Method is used. Managers are asked to support their judgement of subordinates

by itemising critical incidents, changes and differences in subordinate behaviour after courses.

- Every two years the training manager interviews a sample of managers who have been on recent courses, to task what they think a year or so after the course.
- Participants meet for one day, three or four months after the course. The purpose is partly to build on learning, partly to find out what participants have done and partly to find out the barrier to progress. In this way, trainers can examine the effectiveness of the programme in terms of improvement in job performance.

The question of measurement poses certain difficult questions. Should measurement stop at the achievement of learning objectives?

Not all managers agree that transfer of knowledge to the job is a training manager's problem. A strong case has been made that this is clearly the responsibility of the participant and his manager. The training function's responsibility stops at achieving learning objectives during the course. The training function should be concerned with education and not with a participant's behaviour. Participants and their managers should be made absolutely clear on this point and accept that it is their responsibility to make training work on-the-job. The training function cannot hope to influence what goes on outside the training room and should stop thinking that it can.

One great advantage of Organisation Development projects is that the problems addressed by the management groups are work problems, so there is no question of needing a separate transfer stage. Action on-the-job are an integral part of the OD programme.

(V) MAJOR PROBLEMS

Most problems are special to the company although three are common, recruiting high calibre training staff; gaining management acceptance of training; and moving training away from courses towards OD.

Other problems vary depending on the character of the company. For instance:

(a) Separating job-related training from conceptual training. Most training is job-related concerned with the here and now. There is not enough concentration on thinking ahead and planning ahead.

(b) To be one step ahead of the business. To relate training to business changes and business planning so that managers are coping with the future rather than dealing with the present.

(c) To decide what managers need when the company has not clearly decided its general direction and policy. As a result, training is concerned in dealing with present problems and has no idea of what it should be training for in the future.

(VI) PREFERRED TRAINERS

Generally speaking, managers or functional specialists are the preferred trainers because they are the people with the specialist job knowledge—not the training staff. The need to use managers and specialists as trainers has increased as job-related problem-solving training has increased. Obviously, training in business planning can best be conducted by business planners, rather than by members of the training department.

Managers are the preferred trainers for another reason. Companies are beginning to accept that the best training is for a person to work for a competent manager who delegates, counsels, and gives subordinates challenging worthwhile work. No amount of formal training can beat this type of development. Some companies are working towards the acceptance of this philosophy. In short, training should be an activity which everybody does continuously on-the-job, rather than solely a separate function conducting courses.

SUMMING UP

The above points are summarised below:

(i) Training for change is the fastest growing training need. Almost any business change creates a training need somewhere—Changes in organisation, systems, methods, rules, policies, markets, facilities, equipment—all cause things to be done differently. Somewhere, someone needs instructing.

(ii) Adults learn better by doing and by experience than by intellectual examination and discussion. Hence, training should exclude passive learning and concentrate on the examination of real live business situations, case studies, syndicate discussions, individual exercises, pre-reading—any activity in which the participant explores for himself either singly or in groups. This is more acceptable to managers and more valuable to the company. It is also proving to be a better learning method.

(iii) Managers who work together should train together. In this way the head of the group is involved and the chances of improvement on-the-job being implemented are increased enormously. Also, teamwork is developed and individual relationships worked at.

(iv) Organisation Development is being neglected. Where it is applied, it has very positive effects. It projects trainers into the mainstream of the business and solves gritty business problems with everyone involved. It has the advantage over training courses in that it includes all the managers at the same time, there are no problems of transferring knowledge to the job, the results are measurable and managers find it personally useful and relevant.

(v) Measuring training effectiveness in terms of improved job performance is generally not possible. There are too many other influence on the participant over which the trainer has no control. Measurement should stop at the achievement of learning objectives. Trainers should stop worrying so much about formal measurement of effectiveness and have faith in their own judgement.

(vi) Managers and staff specialists are the best instructors. They are the people with the specialist knowledge and skill, not the training staff. Their use as instructors frees trainers to widen their roles away from conducting courses.

(vii) The job of the trainer is changing. He is no longer solely an instructor in a training centre (although this is still an important part of his job). In the future, he will need to be a business analyst, a facilitator of change, an internal consultant and a salesman for his function. His tasks will widen into team development and organisation development, into following-up participants on-the-job and into career counselling and developmental projects.

(viii) Management training in the future will use a wider variety of methods. It will be conducted as much on-the-job as off-the-job. Greater use will be made of performance appraisals counselling, career planning, temporary assignments, membership of working parties, developmental projects, self-awareness, behaviour analysis, interpersonal competence and team training. Off-the-job training (courses) will involve managers as instructors and directors in presenting case studies of actual business problems.

(ix) More training in advanced technology will occur so that managers and companies do not become technically obsolete.

(x) Management training will be integrated with management development. Succession planning and career planning will be more practised than at present. Managers will be moved between functions.

Reference

S.K. Bhatia, Principles and Techniques of Personnel Management/HRM, Deep & Deep Publications Pvt. Ltd., New Delhi.

UNIT VI

HRM AND HRD

CHAPTER

35

Uniqueness of Human Resource

1. UNIQUENESS OF HUMAN RESOURCE

Unique aspects of human resource are explained below for proper appreciation:

(a) Human resource is a *critical* resource, a *key* resource for organisation performance. Man is active resource. It *mobilizes* other resources. Other resources are passive resources as mentioned in Fig. 35.1.

FIG. 35.1

Active and Passive Resources

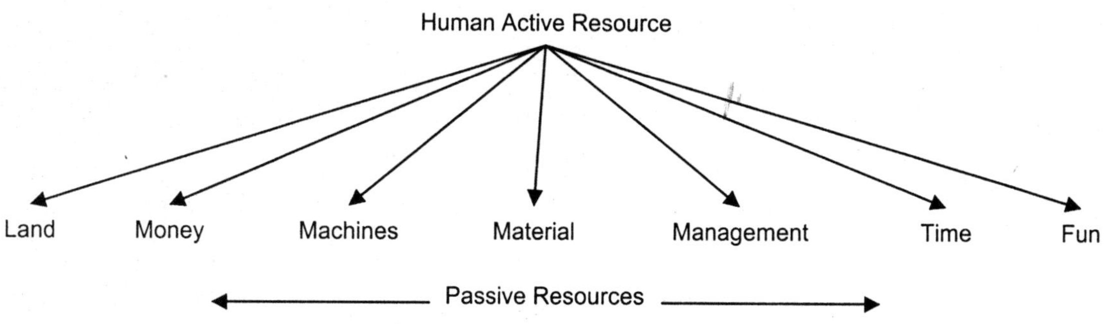

(b) Another uniqueness is that human resource *appreciates* while other resources *depreciate*.

(c) Man has *potential to develop and grow*: Man is dynamic in nature. Man has unique abilities.

(d) Human resource is *renewable*. It is *animate* and living resource.

(e) Men are dynamic and hetrogenous. Men have unique personalities and behave differently.

(f) People are resource, *opportunities*, assets and strengths (not liabilities or problems) in the organisation.

Thus *viability and effectiveness* of an organisation depends upon the people. Man is the ultimate resource. In fact, man management is *oldest management*.

2. IMPORTANCE OF HUMAN RESOURCE

We cite here views of professionals and management thinkers about the importance of human resource:

- "Of all the tasks of management, managing human components is the central and most important task because all else depends on how well it is done."—*(Rensis Likert)* This truism underscores the vital role of personnel management in the corporate sector.
- "Business is a human organisation, made or broken by its people."—*(Peter Drucker)*
- "People are key to corporate excellence."
- *Bill Gates* once said, "take our 20 best people and virtually overnight we become a mediocre company."
- In response, *Alfred Sloan* of GM Corporation, USA had gone one step further and said, "take my physical assets, leave my people, and in five years I will have it all back."

The above messages suggest HRM is crucial in an organisation. The greater the effectiveness and productivity of personnel, the more will be effective functioning of an organisation. It is the people in the organisation who make difference.

Eventually, everything boils down to *people*. How to manage them, retain and train them in order to score competitive advantage over rivals.

Positioning HR to create value is a central concern of every manager in any organisation. This coordination depends on effective human resource management (HRM).

HRM focuses on effective management of people. It is a *value-based* system which aims to achieve corporate goals by optimally allocating the HR's (crucial resource) for maximising the productivity and satisfaction of members.

The *focus now has shifted to involving* (utilising) the human resource rather than using them as a tool for production. The concepts of employee involvement such as quality circles, participative forums, team work, autonomous groups, etc. are now being used. The focus is on *human dignity*.

HRM may be *referred* as a set of policies and practices and programmes designed to maximise both personal and organisation goals. HRM provides *knowledge* (what to do theoretical and practice) to aid process (how to do it) of making decision.

3. HRM: A CENTRAL SUB-SYSTEM IN ORGANISATION SYSTEM

HRM is the *central sub-system* of an organisation. As the central sub-system, HRM interacts closely and continuously with all other sub-systems of an organisation. This is explained in Fig. 35.2.

FIG. 35.2

Organisation Systems, Human Resource as Central Sub-system in an Organisation

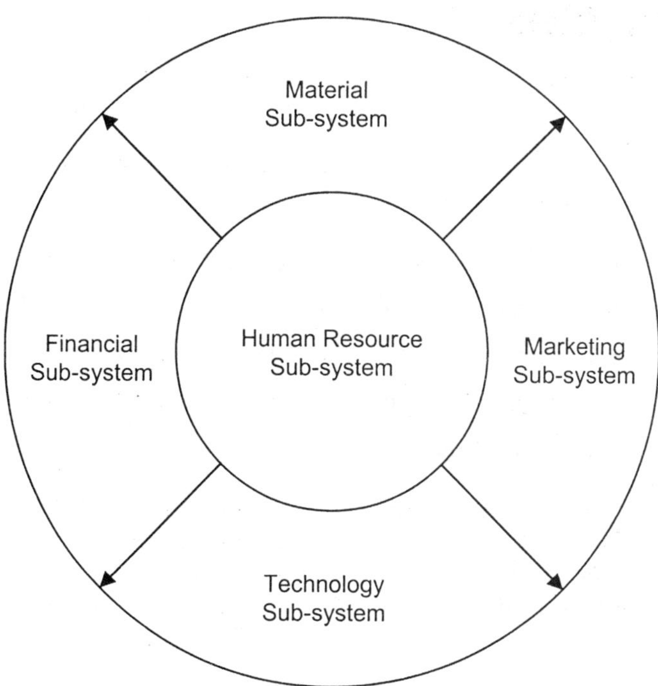

HRM is concerned with most effective use of people to achieve organisational and individual goals. It is way of managing people at work, so that they give their best to the organisation. (Glueck)

CHAPTER

36

Organising Training for HRM Competencies

In this chapter, an attempt has been made to share following aspects in human resource management (HRM):

(a) Roles of HR in building a competitive organisation;

(b) Human resource competencies for meeting the challenges;

(c) Some important issues related to HR success;

(d) Prioritising human resource competencies; and

(e) Organising HR competencies training seminar.

Dave Ulrich, ("Human Resource Champions", Harvard Business School Press), states that as management of human resource is key to future success, HR professional's mentality can shift from—"What I can Do" to "What I Deliver" and identifies in distinct roles that human resources staff must assume in order to make the transition:

(i) becoming a strategic partner,

(ii) becoming an administrative expert,

(iii) becoming an employee champion, and

(iv) becoming a change agent.

(A) ROLES OF HR IN BUILDING A COMPETITIVE ORGANISATION

Peterson, V.P. (HR), Hewlett Packard, USA has experimented with HR roles in building a competitive organisation. For this he has tried with what he calls "Pete Peterson's Multiple Role HR Model".

Under this he "created the environment for the HP", by providing high quality services for employees and utilising human resources more effectively. He states that for today's HR professionals to deliver value to a firm, they must fulfil *multiple roles*.

They must specify outcomes to the firm from each of their roles, and act to accomplish the results pertaining to their roles.

They have to be accountable for their results while building the shared commitment needed to achieve those results. HR roles in building a competitive organisation is presented in Fig. 36.1.

FIG. 36.1

HR Roles in Building a Competitive Organisation

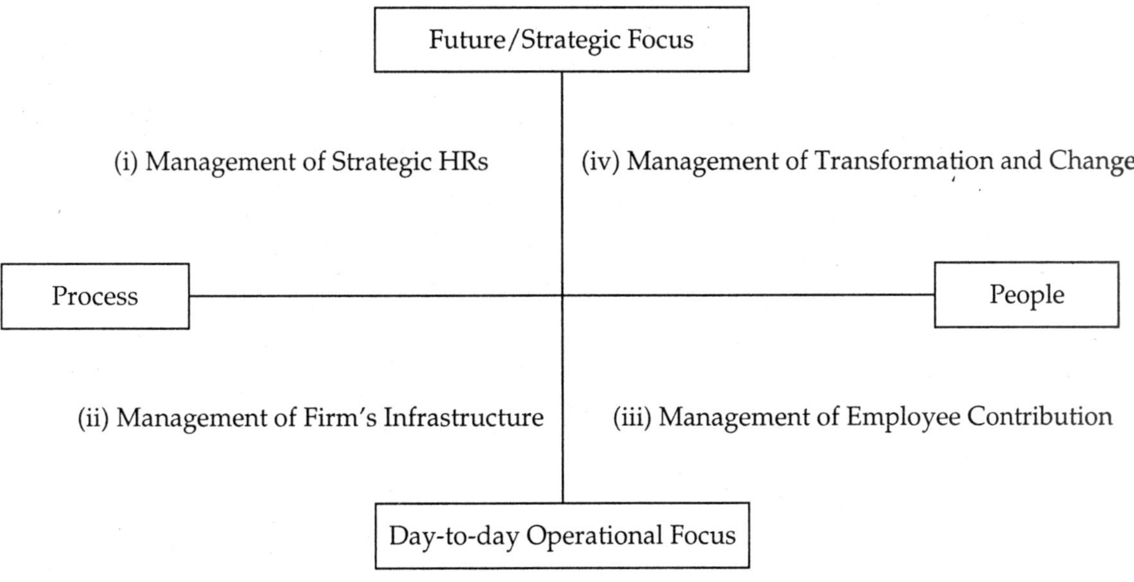

Source: Case Study of Application of the Multiple and Role Model at Hewlett-Packard by Peterson, V.P. (HR), *Who made Dramatic Changes in HP.*

These four roles are explained as under:

(i) Management of Strategic HRs

- The strategic HR role focuses on *aligning* HR strategies and practices with business strategy in playing this role.
- HR professional works to be a *strategic partner*.
- Helping to *ensure the success* of business strategies.
- In fulfilling this role, HR professional has to increase *the capacity of business* to execute its strategy.

(ii) Management of Firm Infrastructure

HR as an administrative expert to provide professional services by hiring, training and rewarding managers.

(iii) Management of Employee Contribution

By increasing employee commitment and competence, HR to pay attention to employee needs (listening and responding to employees and train them) to plead the cause of employees to higher management.

(iv) Management of Transformation and Change

For creating renewed organisation transformation entails to bring fundamental cultural change within the firm, by being change agent. His HR team can do by identifying problems, building relationships, solving problems and fulfilling action plans.

HR professionals, who are change agents help make change happen; they understand critical process for change, build commitment to those processes and ensure that change occurs as intended.

(B) HUMAN RESOURCE COMPETENCIES FOR MEETING THE CHALLENGES

Dave Ulrich ("HR Champions", Harvard Business School Press, 2001) has presented a model for future HR competencies. The competencies/capacities of HR professionals are explained in Fig. 36.2.

I. Business Mastery

Financial capability and strategic capability.

Fig. 36.2

Model for Future HR Competencies

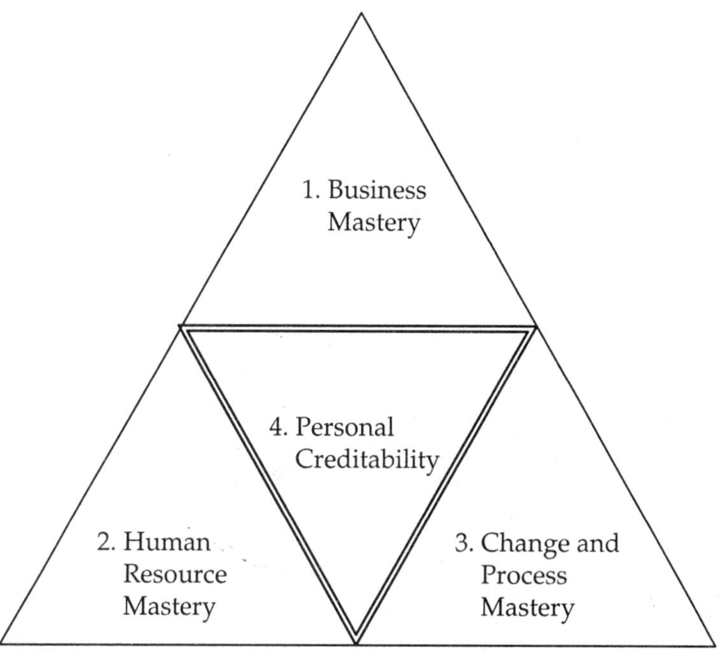

2. Human Resource Mastery

Staffing, development, performance appraisal, rewards, organisation planning, communication.

3. Change and Process Mastery

- Diagnosis of organisation.
- Building relationships with clients.
- Articulate vision.
- Leader change agent.
- Solve problems (proactive).
- Implement goals.

4. Personal Creditability

- Accuracy in HR work.
- Consistency.

- Meeting commitment.
- Good comfortable with peers, subordinates and superiors.
- Confronting—willing to disagree and challenge at appropriate setting and manner.
- Integrity—behaving ethically.
- Thinking outside the box.
- Find out alternative solutions.
- Listening to focusing on problems.

(C) SOME IMPORTANT ISSUES RELATED TO HR SUCCESS

Experience shows that successful companies follow a combination of policies of growth, i.e. those related to *efficiency, productivity* and *HR development*. Some human resource issues in achieving corporate success are:

1. Aligning *business strategy* with *HR strategy*.
2. *Knowledge* management and creating *learning* organisation.
3. Developing moral excellence through *ethics* audit and creating a *value-based* culture.
4. Competency mapping and *skill development* through assessment centre.
5. *Re-organisation of work* through job enlargement and enrichment.
6. Development of mutual trust and synergy among *work teams*.
7. Managing *change* through people.
8. Restructuring and *transformation in organisation* to add value to the business.
9. Bringing about *rationalisation of workforce* through internal transfers and resorting to employee reduction (as a last choice).
10. Hold *opinion surveys* to get the perceptions of employees and apply mid-course corrections, if necessary.
11. Linking the organisation's mission and objectives to individual performance objectives. This can contribute to organisation growth and culture.
12. Recruitment and selection processes can contribute to competitive strategies.

(D) HUMAN RESOURCE COMPETENCIES

We reproduce here findings of a Michigan University Research Study relating to HR competencies given in importance of rank:

Competency	Details
1. Personal creditability	• Success track record • Has earned trust • Instill confidence in others • Demonstrate integrity • Take appropriate risk • Providing candid observations • Provides alternative insights on business issues • Good relations with key constituents
2. Ability to manage change	• Establish visionary creditability • Take proactive role in bringing about change • Build supportive relationships with others • Encourage others to be creative • Identifies problems relating to business success
3. Ability to manage culture	• Share knowledge across organisation • Champion culture—transformation process • Challenge the status quo • Change behaviour for new culture
4. Delivery human resource practice	• Verbal communication effective • Clear communication to managers and work with them • Design development programmes for change initiative • Facilitate international communication • Attract appropriate employees • Design compensation system • Facilitate sedimentation of customer information
5. Understanding of the business	• Understanding of HR practices • Understanding of organisation structure • Competitor analysis • Finance • Computer IMS • Marketing and sales

(E) ORGANISING HR COMPETENCIES TRAINING SEMINAR

Module I

- Senior HR executive highlights key business challenges and HR vision.

- Emergence of HR as strategic partner and competitive advantage.
- HR roles and deliverables as value creation.
- Competencies for HR professional

Module II

- Strategic HR: Turning HR goals into HR priorities.
- Organisation diagnosis.
- HR best practices—staffing and development.

Module III

- HR best practice—measure performance and rewards.
- HR best practice—organisation design and communication.

Module IV

- Being a change agent—learning and applying a change model.
- Measuring HR effectiveness.

Module V

- Personal leadership—building creditability.
- Action planning for HR function and the individual and making commitment to act.
- Align HR function—HR system—strategic employee behaviour that emphasise implementation of the organisation business strategy.

Reference

Dave Urrich, Human Resource Champions, Harvard Business School Press, 2001, Cambridge, MA, Gratefully Acknowledged.

CHAPTER

37

Upcoming Issues in Human Resource Management

In order to face the challenges of the 21st century and acquire competitive edge, the *human resource management* has to be reformed and reconstructed to make it more *qualitative, informative* and *technologically more acceptable*. Human Resource Management as a vital specialized area can build a strong base where human potentiality can be realized to the fullest possible extent. Human Resource *Planning, development* and *utilization* policy is basically derived from the felt needs of the organisation. It is concerned with quality of human behaviour and relationships because it influences human as well as the organisation's performance significantly.

The organisation have to *take steps to create a positive environment where human resources could be more efficiently utilised*. Keeping the current and anticipated growth pattern of the organisation in the forefront, *various need-based measures* need to be taken to develop the *competencies of human resources*. Following innovative measures could help an organisation to develop its human resources:

I. HUMAN RESOURCE PROFESSIONAL'S ROLE IN BUILDING COMPETITIVE ORGANISATION

HR professionals can collaborate to create an organisation that can change, learn, move and act faster than the competitor. HR role in building a competitive organisation are:

(i) Becoming a *strategic partner* in aligning HR strategies and practices with business strategy.

(ii) Becoming an *expert* to provide professional HR services by developing innovative hiring, training and rewarding policies.

(iii) Increasing employees commitment and competence for enhanced contribution.

(iv) Becoming a *change agent* in renewed organisation transformation by identifying problems, building relationships, solving problems and fulfilling action plans, developing moral excellence and creating learning organisation.

HR professional to acquire adequate competencies in these areas to be successful.

2. ADOPTING 360° PERFORMANCE APPRAISAL SYSTEM AS DEVELOPMENTAL TOOL

To know more about an employee from different angles 360° performance appraisal came into existence. This innovative multi-rating 360° appraisal system involves collecting responses from people through structured questionnaire simultaneously from his bosses, peers, subordinates and by at least a minimum of 15 colleagues, at least two of them being his bosses, four of them peers and six of them subordinates. Immediate supervisors are best people to evaluate performance parameters, peer judgment provides a comparative and even competitive perspective. Evaluation through juniors is crucial because many came to limelight as "applets of the boss." An ideal 360 degree often includes customers and vendors too for better results. Lastly, it presents the findings of the appraisal to assessee in the form of charts and graphs. The 360 degree tool shall be more effective when used from the top down. 360° performance appraisal is a systematic process of collection of data on an individual, obtained from number of persons.

This is used as a *fact finding and self-correction technique*. The technique collects information on parameters like *performance as well as behaviour*—How effectively a manager handles his boss and his juniors, how clearly he communicates, how deftly he delegates, how abrasively he administers—Ethics, values, fairness, balance and courtesy, etc., are also coming under the purview of 360 degree appraisal. 360 degree outshines other forms of appraisal because it reflects the intrinsic qualities which a manager must have in order to lead. It reveals many invisible hidden affairs like — insecurity among managers, unsystematic approach, authoritarianism, etc. Executives shall manage people better after being administered with 360° technique. It heightens *self-awareness* of employees which helps the organisation to compete in a better way. This programme can transform a company into a learning organisation. The leadership rating of the 360 degree assessment can be linked with promotions and increments. Team spirit shall thrive vigorously among peers if assessment by peers is allowed. It is more easily acceptable to organisation with knowledge management and TQM cultural orientation.

3. STRATEGISING RETENTION OF EMPLOYEES

In the new millennium every CEO has lamented the dearth of talent and its shortening life span in the organisation. That is why companies are using different strategies and innovative retention tools to hold on their star performers at any cost. Following retention tools can be utilised for better results:

(i) *Rewards* (Both economic and non-economic)—A highly rated retention tool.

(ii) Too *much job clarity* hinders retention and inhibits out of box thinking.

(iii) Clear *growth path* helps in retaining employees.

(iv) *Two-way communication* improves retention.

(v) Variety through *job rotation* helps in retaining employees.

(vi) Regular *need-based* training helps in retaining employees.

(vii) The *role of family* is important in retaining employees' work and life balance.

(viii) *Internal recruitment* helps retention.

(ix) *Increments attached* with "A feeling of ownership and pride in the company" helps retention.

(x) *Overseas exposure* is a good retention tool.

(xi) *Benefits with lower tax* liability helps in retaining employees.

(xii) *Brand image* of corporation helps in retaining employees.

(xiii) Effectively communicated *vision* enables faster growth and improves retention.

(xiv) Effective *mentors* helps retain fresh talent.

(xv) Provide job challenges and assignments.

(xvi) Respect dignity of individuals.

(xvii) Timely recognition and rewarding of contribution and potential shift focus on support individuals (rather control) in their performance.

(xviii) Provide more autonomy and empowerment to employees to facilitate faster decision-making, flat structure and team working enhances motivation.

4. CONDUCTING EXIT INTERVIEW FOR CORRECTIVE MEASURES

The practice of collecting information from employees who are leaving the organisation is to conduct exit interviews. However, the issue of *trust* is very crucial in case of person conducting the interview. Well trained HR managers used to be the best choice for *extracting quality* information. Formal questionnaire reveals only a part of the picture. It is only through an in-depth and informal interview that one gets the real picture.

5. TRAINING HR PROBLEMS OF MERGERS AND ACQUISITIONS (M&As) WITH SENSITIVITY

One of the major HR problems encountered in case of a merger (during the combination phase) is that the *dominant company adopts* a strategy where it wants to retain its own prevailing management style unless the acquired company possesses a group of critical people. But in case of merger of parties having nearly equal power, the issue poses a very challenging situation which creates lots of adjustment problems specifically for human resources. People tend to view every thing through the filter of merger and this *leads to stress both* at the individual as well as at organisational level. When both the parties meet each other, a critical political dialogue dominates the atmosphere where the revenue sharing is more important to form a new organisation rather than human resource problem.

Important HR Problems of M&As

(a) Problems of *compensation parity.*

(b) The *attraction and retention* of the potential talent.

(c) *Restructuring problems* in M&A.

(d) Problem of *dual organisational* culture.

Strategies to Deal with HR Problems of Mergers and Acquisitions

(i) Generate Awareness in Employees of Benefits of M&A

The primary steps in the merger process deals with comprehending the distinct *psychological foundations* of expected winners and losers in the amalgamation process. The objective behind this psychological analysis is to *generate awareness* among the people of both the organisations about the need, importance and benefits of M&A that is going to occur. The above psychological exercise is a must which can eliminate resultant stress, fear and uncertainty from the mind of the people meaningfully. Study shows that at least four key ingredients like *trust, compatibility, shared purpose,* and *co-operative spirit* are essential to create the right mind set in M&A.

(ii) Positive Attitudes of both CEO's and Encouraging Dialogue on Issues of Concern of Employees

But everything depends on the *positive attitude, commitment* and *dynamism* of both the CEOs who can generate a sense of equality in the new relationship. Result-oriented exercises like business emulation and role reversals can be effectively used to promote the dialogue over issues.

(iii) Align HR Policies

Besides the above, there is an urgent need to *manage individual misapprehension, anxiety and stress* with the helping hand of *HR policies* and interventions. They are prescribed below:

- Taking the help of a management consultant.
- By developing innovative employee communication strategies.
- Developing hiring/severance policy.
- Designing special need-based training programme for the transition.
- Developing a compensation and renewal scheme.

(iv) Provide Development Opportunities in Upcoming Professional Competencies to meet Growing Organisation's Business Expansion

To *recognize* its human resources and provide *opportunities* for their development in the context of changing business scenario and growth of organisation. Employees to keep their skills sharpened, relevant, rather ahead of times to face radical changes. Learning has to be encouraged as a continuous process for value addition in career and life. Competencies will lead to effective performance. This requires developing *professional skill. Managing professionals* is *sine-qua-non* of a growth-oriented organisation. Organised human resource planning, development and utilization creates a strong foundation on which an organisation grows incessantly.

6. BUILDING POSITIVE MINDSET

The foundation of success in mindset, thus the right orientation of attitude is critical factor in success of employees and the organisation. The golden rules for building positive attitude are to focus on *professional values* including quality, integrity, fairness, justice, character achieving realising goals, being visionary, solution and team-oriented, empathetic understanding of others, willingness to change with open mind.

7. DEVELOPING GROSS-CULTURAL SENSITIVITY FOR GLOBAL BUSINESS EFFECTIVENESS

Cultural diversity is one of the major challenges facing global business organisations, as it is important for success and vitality of the organisation. The ways to manage the cultural diversity is necessary for achieving competitive advantage. So awareness and understanding of common characteristics of a country relating to their customs, ethics and etiquettes, body language will enable professionals to relate successfully in international business environment. Cultural adaptability is essential in cross-cultural environment.

8. MAINTAINING MOTIVATION OF KNOWLEDGE WORKFORCE WILL BE CONTINUOUS CHALLENGE

Knowledge management (KM) is the process through which organisations generate value from their intellectual and knowledge-based assets. Knowledge or know-how is contained in people's heads. The objective is to achieve the synergy of information technologies and the creative and innovative capacity of human members. The knowledge workforce will develop overall understanding of the business of their organisations and to deliver results. Knowledge professionals convert ideas into business opportunities, through knowledging network systems. Cross learning is incorporated in the KM network system. This is done by developing strong learning culture. Through networking in the organisation, otherwise KM system becomes static. The motivation of knowledge people is essential to gain significant competitive advantage.

As such, successful handling of above issues and concerns can only facilitate development of the organisation.

References

Ganesh Prasad Das, The Role of HRM in the Present Business Scenario, *Pragyaan*, Vol. 1, July 2003.

Dick Grote, Performance Appraisal Reappraised, HBR, Jan.-Feb. 2000.

C. Balaji, Leading Change through Human Resources Towards a Globally Competitive India, Tata McGraw Hill Publishing Company Ltd., pp. 39-65.

Ansu Tandon, The 360-Degree Technique, HRD Education Towards A Paradigm Shift, p. 129, July, 1999, Academy of Human Resources Development, Hyderabad.

M.P. Srivastava, Human Resource Development to Achieve More, *Yojana*, March 2000.

Rajiv Raghunath, Leap into the Unknown, *The Financial Express*, June 27, 1999, Vol. I, No. 23, p. 14.

CHAPTER

38

Six Sigma Intervention in HR Profession

In this chapter we shall discuss various aspects of SIX sigma intervention in HR profession as under:

1. Making six sigma initiative—the quality mantra
2. Best utilization of people, process and technology ensures high quality HR services
3. Six sigma process approach in HR
4. Process measurement of HR operating systems—gaining control
5. Six sigma is more than cultural change

I. MAKING SIX SIGMA INITIATIVE—THE QUALITY MANTRA

Six Sigma is a way of life. It helps to identify variation, isolate and control the same, and ultimately eliminate that variation. Six Sigma helps in improving any kind of process ... the following steps

- Identity the practical problem,
- Changing it into statistical problem,
- Identifying the statistical solution,
- Changing the solution to practical solution.
- Invented at Motorola, perfected at General Electric (GE), and now practiced by a handful of companies in India. Six Sigma is converting defect prone business into powerhouse of perfection.

Six Sigma is as much as a description of an organisation culture as it is of performance

- Six Sigma is an overall strategy to accelerate improvements in processes, products and services. It is also a measurement of total quality at the company it is in eliminating defects and variations from its processes. It applies to every function in the company, not just the factory floor.
- Six Sigma is fact-based approach to problem-solving. It is a new way of thinking about work and customer value and is a powerful force to create one corporate culture. The difference between Six Sigma and the other quality approaches is that it measures the output — not just the capability for meeting some quality factors.
- Jack Welch, Chairman, GE has said "Six Sigma is the most important initiative we have ever-taken". Companies like GE, Allico Signal have increased their profitability.
- Six Sigma is a proven management philosophy that can dramatically improve productivity by improving the effectiveness and efficiency of any organisation. It attempts to improve customer satisfaction to near perfection. It is for managing the balance between cultural and technical change. There are three components of six sigma:

  (a) The strategic,

  (b) Technical, and

  (c) Cultural.

  Quality of your technical and strategic activities (multiplied) by acceptance leads to excellence in our six sigma results. The six areas to improve Six Sigma are:

  (a) Create Awareness for Change

  Create the need for six sigma and make people understand need for change. It involves brain storming and people to visualize what would happen organisation in terms of:

  * Short-term threats * Short-term opportunities

  * Long-term threats * Long-term opportunities

  (b) Shape the Vision for Six Sigma

  This vision enables employees to understand the desired results and new behaviours of six sigma organisation.

  (c) Mobilise commitment to six sigma initiatives and overcome the resistance by identification of support by key stakeholders.

(d) Change your systems and structure to support the new six sigma culture.

(e) Measure six sigma cultural acceptance.

(f) Develop six sigma leadership (commitment, involvement and motivation)

The quality experts under six sigma fall under three different categories

- Green Belts
- Black Belts
- Master Black Belts

2. BEST UTILIZATION OF PEOPLE, PROCESS AND TECHNOLOGY ENSURES HIGH QUALITY HR SERVICES

Greatest challenge of HR professionals is meeting their customers expectations and add value to business bottom line in very dynamic business environment. Human Resources professionals have been focusing on HR on transactional level. Success of this function depends on ability to understand the customer expectations and align the people capability and process to achieve these expectations. The best utilization of people, process & technology ensures high quality HR services at lower cost, on time (Speed), thus ensuring high level of customer satisfaction. (Fig. 38.1)

FIG. 38.1

Optimisation of People, Process and Technology

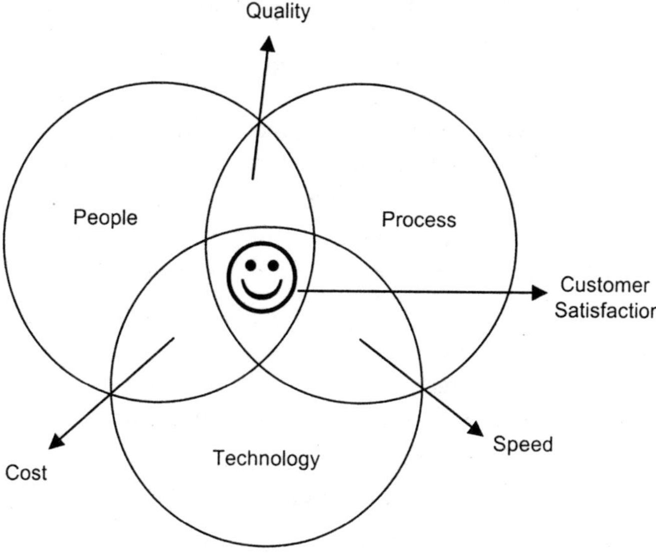

3. SIX SIGMA PROCESS APPROACH IN HR

The philosophy that underlines the Six Sigma process begins with the fundamental assumption that unless we understand a process mathematically, we know little about it. If we know little about it, we are not in a position to control it, then we are at the mercy of chance variation. (Fig. 38.2)

FIGURE 38.2

HR Process Approach

HR Proces	*Supplier*	*Input*	*Process*	*Output*	*Customer*
Hiring	Consultants/ Job Portals/ Employees (Referrrals)	Resumes/ Potential candidates	Selection process	Selected candidates	Hiring managers
Training	Training House/ Training Consultants	Know how/ Manuals	Training need identification delivery evaluation	Improved knowledge and skill	Employees/ managers

In the simplest of terms, Six Sigma is a quality improvement methodology that provides a systematic approach to the elimination of defects that affect something important to the customer. Those aspects of service that are of importance to the customer are termed "Critical To Quality," or CTQs in Six Sigma jargon. The tools associated with Six Sigma are qualitative, statistical and instructional devices for "observing" process variables, "quantifying" their impact on outcomes, as well as "managing" their character. Six Sigma is based upon four simple principles

a) What is important to the customer? A customer is defined as anyone who receives a product, service or information. Therefore, when coupled with the Balanced Scorecard approach . . . internal quality impacts internal customers and external quality impacts external customers.

(b) What is an opportunity ? An opportunity is represented by every chance to get something right . . . or get it wrong.

(c) What defines success? Every result of an opportunity either meets the customer's CTQs and is a success, or fails to meet the customer's CTQs and is a defect. In Six Sigma, an indicator of success or failure is referred to as defects per million opportunities:

Every human activity contains variation. The term "Sigma" is a symbol for standard deviation, a measure of variation. Six Sigma refers to the idea of being able to achieve six standard deviations between the mean performance of the process and the customer determined specification limit. If Six Sigma performance is achieved in a process, then that process will generate less that four defects (occurrences of getting it wrong) per one million opportunities.

(d) The idea of measuring the number of standard deviations that fit between the mean performance of a process and the customer's expectation (translated into specification limits) is referred to as the process Z-Score." The Z-Score allows for comparative analysis of the performance of dissimilar process, based upon the tendencies of each to either satisfy or disappoint their respective customers, the higher the Z-Score the less probability of customer disappointment.

4. GAINING CONTROL

The last and continuing step in this process involves monitoring changes and key metrics. That's the purpose of the scorecard itself—to serve as a tool that assures the achievement of the HR strategy on an ongoing basis. The balanced scorecard should have a top level appearance along with the ability to drill down to the metrics associated with those activities that create the greatest organizational leverage. (Fig. 38.3)

5. SIX SIGMA IS MORE THAN CULTURAL CHANGE AND HAS CHALLENGES

Creating a Six Sigma company is more than a culture change, more than customer focus, more than the manufacture and delivery of quality products and services. It is an environment where all processes are designed to meet customer's requirement an environment held together by the glue of quality tools and techniques. Six Sigma rigor can be used to bring down costs, improve productivity of resources, improve efficiency of a system, reduce the turn around time for producing an item, reduces defects in a product, etc. The consequence of following six sigma would be a better and faster way of performing tasks and increased customer satisfaction. Six Sigma intervention in HR services can ensure high level of customer satisfaction.

However, the challenges confronting HR are complex, and no overnight solution will make the problems disappear. Taking a calibrated approach to performance improvement, however, can help HR systems regain control and realize substantial benefits. The deployment of Six Sigma in HR can be useful for improving HR service quality. Some steps suggested by Vineet Sharma are—define core and support process, create dashboards for lead and lag indicators; constitute an HR FQC for identifying

FIGURE 38.3

Making Process Measurement of HR Operating Systems

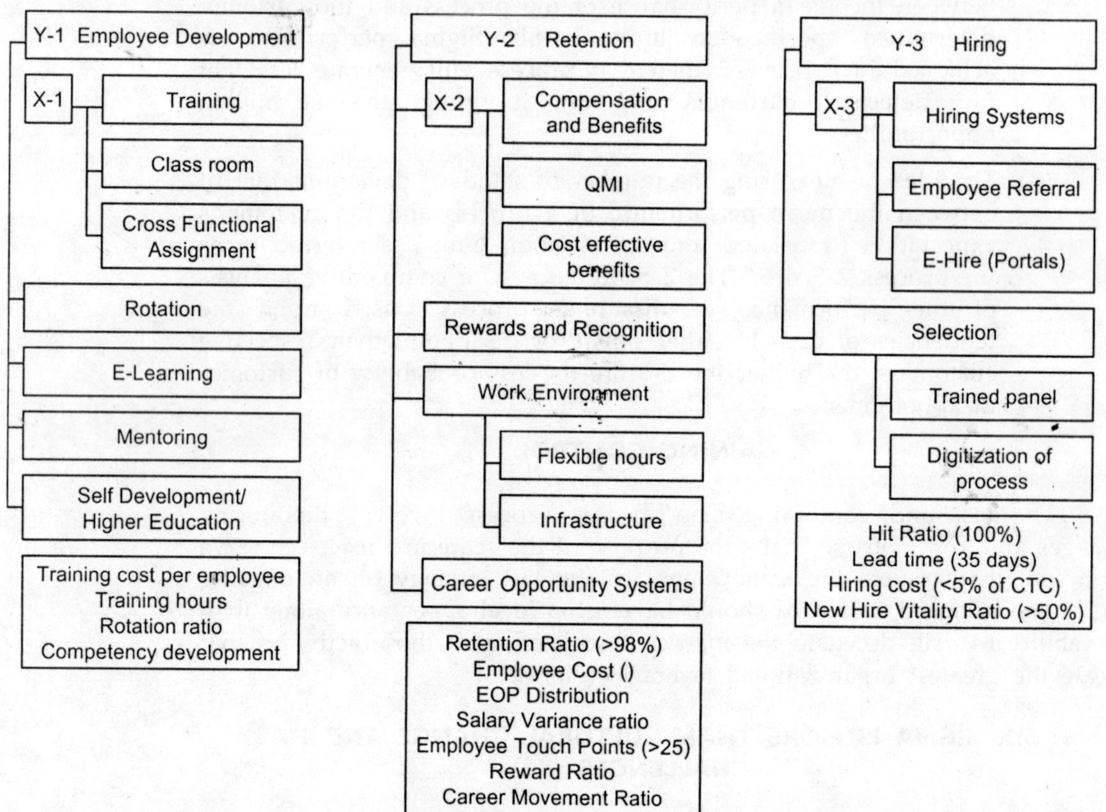

opportunities allocate resources based on complexity. Kill fluff and celebrate success!

REFERENCES

This an abstract of an article by A.K. Sreekanth, Six Sigma—A Tool for HR Professionals, *HRD News Letter*, April 2004.

Vineet Sharma, *HRD News Letter*, April 2004.

S.K. Bhatia, Boost Your Professional Career, Deep & Deep Publications Pvt. Ltd., New Delhi.

CHAPTER

39

Human Resource Development (HRD)

In this introductory chapter on HRD we shall cover following critical aspects of HRD:

- Concept of HRD
- Meaning of HRD
- Need for HRD
- Factors contributing to growth of HRD
- HRD objectives
- Difference in HRD concept of man
- HRD philosophy
- Outcomes of HRD
- HRD at Micro and Macro-levels
- Difference between Personnel Management and HRD

These are explained as:

CONCEPT OF HUMAN RESOURCE DEVELOPMENT (HRD)

Human Resource Development is to *bring the best* in man. HRD is the process of increasing the *capacities* of human resources *through development.*

HRD is a process of *adding value to individuals, teams, organisation* as human system. HRD includes development of people, organisation and society.

HRD concept is concerned *in developing*:

(i) Knowledge—technical, management

(ii) Skills (abilities)

(iii) Attitudes

(iv) Build values/beliefs

More focus on items 3 and 4. HRD is latest innovation in management. HRD is most vital for success of an organisation through well developed and committed people.

MEANING OF HUMAN RESOURCE DEVELOPMENT

HRD is a process to help employees in *planned* and *continuous* way:

(a) Develop *capabilities/competencies* to perform *present and future* roles,

(b) Develop capabilities as *individuals* to exploit potential for own and organisation,

(c) Develop *organisation culture* to build superior subordinate relationships, team work, collaboration among departments promoting a healthy climate.

HRD is a strategy for creatively *matching* the *organsational needs* arising from business strategy and *human aspirations.* HRD involves integration of both individual and organisation needs.

NEED FOR HUMAN RESOURCE DEVELOPMENT

HRD is needed to achieve following basic objectives:

(a) People need competencies to perform their tasks. Quality performance of tasks requires higher degree of skill thus without *continuous development* of *competencies in people*, an organisation is not likely to achieve goals.

(b) So competent and motivated people are essential for growth, survival and *excellence of the organisation.* HRD develops a proper climate for achieving organisation.

(c) HRD systems *motivate* the individual's to develop and utilise their capabilities.

(d) HRD is needed for *improving systems and services,* renewal and most effectiveness.

(e) For becoming *more dynamic* and for playing leadership roles.

FACTORS CONTRIBUTING TO GROWTH OF HRD IN ORGANISATIONS

These factors stem from changing organisation *environment* and organisational *necessities* to adapt and innovate in response to these changes. *Factors* contributing to growth of HRD are:

(i) *Increasing competition*—requires higher efficiencies in people and focus on core competencies.

(ii) *Explanation and growth*—requires managers higher level of competencies to handle complex operations and restructuring of organisations.

(iii) *Rapid technological changes*—demand changes in systems, structures, skills and these changes create conflict, stress and obsolesence and need innovative solutions.

(iv) *Lack of suitable manpower*—requires to train own employees.

(v) *Changing needs of people*—to develop their competencies for achieving organisational objectives and by empowering of employees. HRD interventions can establish new work ethics and values to build greater employee commitment.

HRD OBJECTIVES

Some aims or goals achieved are through HRD as under:

(i) To maximise the *utilisation* of human resources for the achievement of *individual* and organisation goals; HRD involves integration of both individual and organisation needs.

(ii) To provide opportunity for development of human resources for full expression of their talent and potentials.

(iii) To develop *constructive mind* and overall personality of the employees.

(iv) To develop the sense of team work and inter-team collaboration.

(v) To develop organisational health, culture and effectiveness.

(vi) To generate information about HRs.

(vii) HRD is concern of all managers in the organisation.

DIFFERENCE IN HRD CONCEPT OF MAN

How the *concept of HRD differs* from what earlier management theorists have visualised the "Man", his "Motives" and his "Achievements". This is explained below:

Concept	*Man*	*Motives*	*Achievements*
Rational man concept of 'man' (F.W. Taylor)	Economic man	Fulfilling material economic needs	Increase in output
Human relations concept of 'man' (Elton Mayo, Likert)	Social man	Fulfilling social and psychological needs	Job satisfaction
Human resource concept of man (Maslow, A.R. Gyris, Herzberg, McGregor)	Self-actualisation man	Fulfilling ego/ achievement —self-actualising needs	Improved productivity and job satisfaction
HRD concept of man	Developmental man	Enhancing/improving skills	Attainment of organisational and *personal goals*

Man remains central point in all concerns. As the concept of man changes, perceptions about man's motives get changed.

HRD approach, too, is emphatic on productivity, because if productivity is increased, goals (organisation and personal) will take care of. So HRD means safeguarding/maintaining/improving *existing skills* as well as *potential skills* of human resource so as to increase their productivity for ultimate well-being of the organisation and individuals.

HRD PHILOSOPHY

According to P.C. Tripathy, perhaps the most fundamental part of an HRD is HRD philosophy. It represents those basic beliefs, ideals, principles and views which are held by the management with respect to the development and growth of its employees. A well-established HRD philosophy plays two important functions. *First,* it gives rise to what one may call 'style of management'. A manager develops his practices on the basis of his philosophy. *Second,* it makes organisational goals more explicit. For example, in organisations that have unshakable belief in the development of human potential, though profit may still be the most important goal, investment in human resources also becomes a powerful sub-goal.

Following *beliefs* are essential for the success of any HRD programme:

(i) Human beings are the most important assets in the organisation.

(ii) Human beings can be developed to an unlimited extent.

(iii) Employees feel committed to their work and the organisation if the organisation develops a feeling of 'belonging' in them.

(iv) Employees are likely to have a feeling of 'belonging' in them if the organisation adequately cares for the satisfaction of their basic and high-order needs.

(v) Employees' commitment to their work increases when they get opportunity to discover and use their full potential.

(vi) It is every manager's responsibility to ensure the development and utilisation of the capabilities of his subordinates, to create a healthy and motivating work climate, and to set examples for subordinates to follow.

(vii) The higher the level of a manager the more attention he should pay to the HRD function in order to ensure its effectiveness.

(viii) A healthy and motivating climate is one which is characterised by openness enthusiasm, trust, mutuality and collaboration. (P.C. Tripathy)

OUTCOMES OF HRD

HRD assumes significance in view of *fast changing* organisation environments and needs of the organisation to *adopt new techniques in order to respond* to environmental changes.

Organisation has to be *dynamic, growth-oriented* and fast changing should *develop their human resources.*

The *vitality of human resources* to industry depends on the level of its development, quality, competence and dynamism.

The *outcomes of HRD are four-fold,* viz.:

(i) To the organisation,

(ii) To individuals,

(iii) To groups, and

(iv) To society.

1. *Benefits to organisation* by developing employees and making them ready to accept responsibilities, welcome change, adapt to change, enables them implementation of programmes for better quality, improve services, cost reduction maintenance of good human relations, increase in productivity and profitability. Top management becomes more sensitive to needs of employees.

2. *HRD benefits individuals* in achieving their potentials, acquiring competencies, understanding their roles, greater trust and respect for each other. These increase in their performance and fulfils their needs and enhances social status.

3. *Helps groups* to increase overall climate of cooperation.

4. *Helps society* by developing human resources it increases their contribution to society through better products, services, capable citizens. The net result of the above outcomes is that the organisation becomes more effective. It achieves new heights in terms of productivity growth, profits and public image.

HRD serves mutual interest of four parties in win-win results explained in Fig. 39.1.

FIG. 39.1

HRD Serves Mutual Interests Leading to Win-Win Results

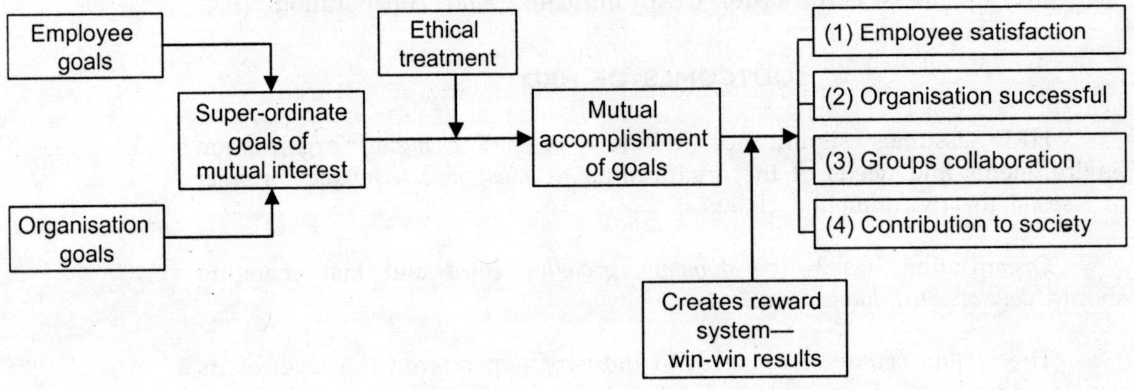

Adapted from: John W. Newstrom and Keith Davis, Organisation Behaviour, Human Behaviour at work.

HRD AT MICRO AND MACRO-LEVELS

The term HRD is being used at both micro and macro-levels.

At macro-level is in the context of improving the quality of human life, i.e. peoples development for nations well-being. It takes wealth, capabilities, skill attitudes of people which are more useful to the *development among them* and *nation's overall* development as well. Ministry of HRD is to mobilize human potential of the country.

At micro or plant level, HRD represents the improvement in the quality of employees so as to achieve higher levels of productivity. The objective is to develop certain new capabilities in people to help them perform present job in a better way and to accept future job challenges.

The optimum utilisation of human resource is possible when HRD is adopted as a *total system* approach within the organisation, the value of openness, trust mutuality, collaboration and enthusiasm within the system should be recognised by every member of the organisation. If implemented properly, *integrated HRD* system can contribute significantly to *positive cultural changes, increased productivity* and *excellence* in the organisation.

Chinese sage Chug Tru said:

If you wish to plan for a year, *sow seeds;*

If you wish to plan for *ten* years, *plant a tree;*

And, if you wish to plan for a *life time, develop men.*

HRD as a concept gives high premium to development aspect of the individual who contributes to organisation growth.

DIFFERENCE BETWEEN PERSONNEL MANAGEMENT AND HRD

1. Personnel management is viewed as independent function whereas HRD viewed as *sub-system* of large system, i.e. organisation design and HRD cannot be considered in isolation. It must take into account its linkages and interface with all other parts of the organisation.

2. While traditional personnel function is mainly a *service function,* responding to the demands of the organisation. HRD is regarded as *proactive function.* The function of HRD is *not merely cope* with the *needs* of the organisation, but to anticipate needs and to act on them on advance.

3. While the traditional personnel function is supposed to be the *exclusive responsibility* of personnel department. HRM/HRD is regarded as the *concern of all managers* in the organisation. In fact HRD aims at developing the *capabilities of all line managers* to carry out various personnel functions themselves. It believes that functions like IR, reward and punishment, performance appraisal, promotions, etc. should increasingly become the responsibility of the line managers.

4. While the traditional personnel function, takes a very *narrow view* of its scope and aims at *developing people only,* HRD takes a much *wider view* of its scope and aims at *developing the total organisation.*

5. The emphasis in traditional personnel function is on *increasing people efficiency.* The emphasis in HRD is on building the *right type of culture* in the organisation. A culture which has such characteristics as mutual trust, collaboration, clarity of goals and risk-taking capacity

6. While the traditional personnel function considers, salary, rewards (economic), job simplification and *job specialisation as important* motivators. HRD emphasises the importance of higher needs in motivating individuals. It considers informal organisation, autonomous work groups, job enrichment, *job challenge and creativity* as the main motivating forces.

7. While the traditional personnel function (with human relations orientation) considers *improved satisfaction* and morale as the cause of improved performance. HRD considers other way round. It considers *improved performance* (due to better utilisation of human resources) as the *cause of satisfaction* and morale as its results.

CHAPTER

40

Mechanism and Focus of Human Resource Development

In this chapter following aspects of HRD are discussed:

- Mechanisms of HRD
- Focus of HRD
  - o Developing human sub-systems in the organisation
  - o Developing HRD climate
  - o Developing HRD processes
- HRD practices
- Trend in HRD practices (sub-systems) in organisation

MECHANISM OF HUMAN RESOURCE DEVELOPMENT

Some mostly used methods or techniques or sub-systems of HRD for developing the competencies and motivation of individuals in an organisation and building the organisation's climate are explained in the Fig. 40.1.

Fig. 40.1

Mechanism of Human Resource Development

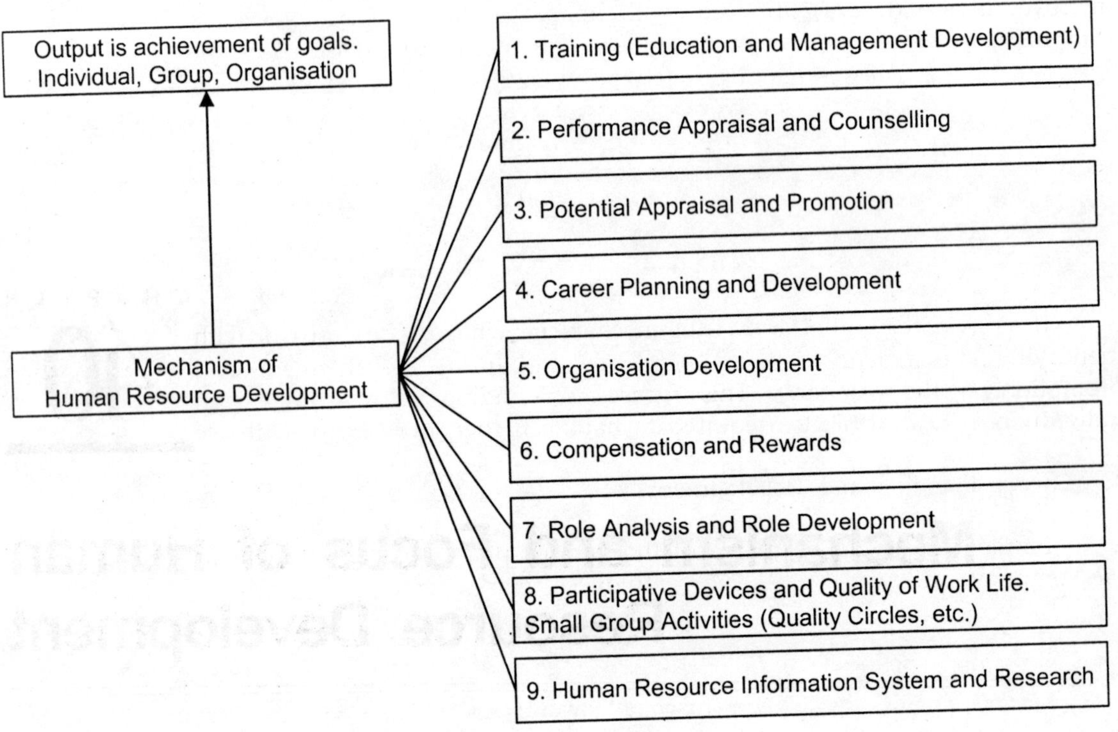

I. Training, Education and Development

Three different HRD mechanism with different focus and purpose as shown in the following figure are used:

Activity	*Focus*	*Purpose*
Training	Learning of present job	Improved performance on the present job of the employee
Education	Learning of other related jobs	Prepartion of the employee for related jobs is not too distant a future
Development	Learning not related to any specific present or future job	General growth of the employee

Three broad areas in which training may be imparted are technical, behavioural and conceptual.

2. Performance Appraisal and Feedback

It is very critical HRD mechanism under which the performance of an employee is periodically appraised by the employee himself in collaboration with his boss. They jointly set the goals. The mechanism emphasises the development of the employees (by indentifying their growth needs) rather than their evaluation. Open, objective and participative appraisal and feedback develop better superior-subordinate relations. During the appraisal interview the superior shares the concerns of the subordinate and even guides him to achieve his targets.

3. Potential Appraisal and Promotion

It is another important HRD mechanism which is concerned with identifying the potential of an employee for future development and promotion in the company. This focuses on finding to which a given individuals critical attributes required to handle higher level responsibilities.

4. Career Planning and Development

Employees should be aware of the various phases of development in the company, and plan with senior employees their specific career path.

5. OD (Organisation Development)

Many organisations make use of several OD techniques for the development of their human resource. These include team-building to learn how to work in collaboration with each other. Certain interventions are designed to improve the relationships between groups and increase the inter-group effectiveness. Similarly, for improving inter-personal relationships and leadership styles are used.

6. Compensation and Reward

They should be clearly related to the performance and behaviour of employees. These serve as positive reinforcement.

7. Role Analysis and Role Development

This is an extremely important technique of HRD. Under it the job of an individual in the organisation is analysed and enriched in terms of his role and not in terms at his job. He, his immediate superior and subordinates sit together to discuss their *expectations* about the job from each other. They then arrive at a consensus about the individual's role and prepare his role description. It is always ensured that a role is sufficiently challenging for the individual, provides him adequate autonomy for taking initiative and is linked with other organisational roles to avoid a feeling of isolation.

8. Participative Devices and Quality of Work Life

For overall development of employees they need good physical conditions and motivating work. Work is redesigned for better quality of work life through quality circles, information sharing and participative forums.

9. Human Resource Information System and Research

This also is a very important HRD mechanism to maintain systematic information about every employee so that this may be used for counselling, career planning, training, promotion, etc. Moreover, this information also serves as a base for research on employee problems.

FOCUS OF HUMAN RESOURCE DEVELOPMENT

HRD's basic emphasis is on three areas as under:

(i) Developing human sub-systems in the organisation.
(ii) Developing HRD climate.
(iii) Developing HRD processes.

(i) Developing Human Sub-systems in the Organisation

(a) Individual—as person and his role in organisation.
(b) Superior-subordinate relationship.
(c) Work groups (team work).
(d) OD techniques for relationships in the organisation.

(ii) Developing HRD Climate

A healthy organisation climate is required for *utilising, enhancing* employee *competencies* and to develop *motivation* and *satisfaction*.

The extent to which the following values are promoted and valued in the organisation the better HRD climate—*dynamism and competence of employees*. (Fig. 40.2)

HRD *climate can be developed* if top management has:

(a) Strong *belief in the capabilities* of people,
(b) HRD policies show *high concern for employees,*
(c) HRD staff has a supportive role and line managers are committed.

	OCTAPACE	*Culture*
O	Openness	• Open *v.* closed oganisation • Expression of opinion • Risk taking • Experimenting ideas and suggestions
C	Confrontation	• Recognise problems explore and solve problems • Face and not avoid problems • Diagnose problems
T	Trust	• Trust each other and rely upon • In company systems, e.g. PA, Promotion policy
A	Authenticity	• Acknowledge feelings
P	Pro-active	• Anticipate • Creativity in solutions
A	Autonomy	• To self and others in job
C	Collaboration	• Working for common cause • Team strength • Cooperation in departments
E	Experimenting	• Problems, mistakes and difficulties are handled with learning orientation • Innovative ways of solving problems

(d) Good HRD—sub-systems for increasing effectiveness.

HRD aims at developing such a climate through periodic diagnosis and appropriate interventions. Such values develop pride and a sense of belonging.

(iii) Developing HRD Processes

U. Pareek identifies nine human processes for efficient working for behavioural change better interaction and for sound organisation environment.

(i) *Existential processes* in the person to meet needs for existing. These processes help in integeration of the individual with the organisation and his quality of work. These practices are—feedback, counselling, job enrichment, etc.

(ii) *Empathic process* between two persons help in inter-personal relations. These processes are communication, cooperation, etc.

(iii) *Role coping process.* Individual has to play various roles and individual has to be aware of the competencies required for them such as role analysis.

(iv) *Group building process* such as team-building helps to contribute to the goals of the organisation.

(v) *Inter-group collaborative process* can be improved by creating a climate of trust, openness, etc.

(vi) *Organisation growth and decision-making process* which involve issues relating to organisation climate, self-renewal and change.

(vii) *Process of social awareness* in the community such as corruption, castism violence, unemployment, etc.

(viii) *Influence processes* at organisational environment interface such as individual influencing honesty.

(ix) *Value shaping processes* in society (beliefs in society).

Thus, focus of HRD is on various *human sub-systems* along with development of *organisation* as well as with its *environment.*

HRD PRACTICES

In nutshell HRD practices can be summarised as under:

- Open communication.
- Participative involvement processes.
- Performance appraisal system based on mutual goal setting, feedback, potential areas of improvement, development relationship building.
- Top management involvement and commitment as a change agent for renewal of organisation effectiveness.
- Training and development thrust on:
  - o Team working
  - o Organisation values
  - o TQM/Quality
  - o New role and empowerment
- Developing HRD climate

Thus, focus in HRD practices helps the organisation as under:

(i) In attainment of the objectives

(ii) Provides *opportunities to people* for fuller expression of their potential

(iii) Provide maximum *job satisfaction*

(IV) TREND IN HRD PRACTICES (SUB-SYSTEMS) IN VARIOUS ORGANISATIONS

HRD is relatively new phenomenon in Indian context. HRD practices have played a significant role in building *positive* climate and growth of organisation.

We share here trend of some HRD practices/approaches implemented by some organisations in 1990-2000.

1. New innovations in HRD have shown high degree of *top management's involvement and commitment.*
2. Some organisations are laying focus on *HRD climate* to ensure effectiveness, (e.g. L&T, Voltas, BHEL, Eicher Good Earth).
3. Wider use of following HRD mechanisms:
   (a) *Performance appraisal* as potential instrument to bring about change in organisation culture and utilisation of people (e.g. L&T, Voltas, BHEL, BEML, Jyoti Ltd., Eicher Good Earth, MUL).
   (b) *Organisation development*/HRD approach as a turn around of a company and building management employee relations (e.g. BHEL, Jyoti Ltd., Eicher Good Earth, BEML).
   (c) Role analysis (IOC).
   (d) New open communication systems (BHEL, BEML, Eicher Good Earth).
   (e) Training function upgraded as HRD department.
   (f) External consultant associated with high level internal task force for long-term HRD.

CHAPTER

41

Role of HRD Manager and Facilitator

In this chapter, we have highlighted following aspects of HRD:

(i) Role of HRD managers in new environment

(ii) Values of HRD professionals

(iii) Role of HRD facilitator

(I) ROLE OF HRD MANAGERS IN NEW ENVIRONMENT

The *new environment* has thrown many challenges and opportunities. These challenges include:

- To be customer-oriented
- Cost effective
- Quickly responding
- Technology adoptive
- Quality-oriented
- Service centred and Organisation

All these challenges require employees at all levels to change. It is *people who can make difference* in the organisation.

HRD staff have key role to play in this direction:

1. First and foremost role is *continuous education of employee about the changes and challenges facing country*. Its share and standing in global business where we have lacked and others Taiwan, Korea, Singaproe, Malaysia, China have progressed.

2. Task is in terms of *educating employees about the company*. In respect to sale progress, balance sheet, share price, financial parameters, productivity, plans, etc.

3. To assess and keep *assessing the core competencies* required at different levels and groups function-wise:

   Strategies for developing these competencies to be evolved such as quality orientation, cost consciousness entrepreneurship, team work, attitudes may be for all employees.

4. Fourth task is to plan and implement strategy *to develop new competencies* at all levels, group work, appraisal system feedback, etc.

5. Fifth task is to *review, rewamp the existing people management systems,* e.g. reward systems, incentive schemes, organisation structure, promotion policies, training policies, etc. HRD manager can play important role. All personnel policies *have motivation* implications and motivation development is one of the key concerns of HRD manager.

Thus, *five roles* of HRD managers are critical in new environment.

HRD manager to closely maintain *link with head of the organisation*/unit and also keep them abreast with HRD philosophy. To be successful HRD manager, he should develop in-depth *knowledge of various departments* functions as well as linking HRD with organisation mission, goals and strategies, i.e. organisation building, inspire line managers to develop HRD manager also to develop *HRD for unions/workmen/women* employees by explaining concepts of TQM, ISO 9000, HRD, Performance Management, etc.

HRD manager to design and experiment with new methods to build the right type of HRD climate and achieve organisation goals.

To conclude by quoting Peter Drucker—"I am asked what objectives, I would set for *business. Every organisation* need to *think its own objectives.* There is no general prescription. But there is one prescription for all organisations. *Five years from now,* you should be able to *do twice the amount* of work you are doing, without adding a single person. *Ten years from now,* you should be able to have double *the productivity* of human resource. And you do this mainly by working on the development of people and by working on their assignments."

(II) VALUES OF HRD PROFESSIONALS

Basically HRD is to prepare people to meet business challenges. Some values of HRD facilitators are as under:

1. *Deep concern for people,* their employees and customers. Respect for individuals, to have complete understanding of persons and commitment that subordinates grow and contribute. Faith in the capacity of people to change and develop at any stage of their life. Free from bias, with patience, good listener and interacting with employees.
2. HRD professionals to *change according to business* and social needs. Constant improvement through innovation, i.e. open mind and flexibility.
3. Should take deep interest in *self-introspection* and *self-development.*
4. Enthusiasm to take new assignments and *develop achievement spirit.*
5. *Strong faith in values and ethics.* Practice and persuade others to practice.
6. *Informal authority and empathy.* Change approach from being "overpowering" to "empowering".
7. *Constructive confrontation* is questioning "off-the-track" behaviour and reform.
8. Create *non-threatening psychological climate* through being warmth, caring, helpful, understanding and openness.
9. To *have professional knowledge* of the various HRD sub-systems, how they are designed, introduced and implemented.

(III) ROLE OF HRD FACILITATOR

To act as HRD facilitator, the main emphasis needs to be on *HRD approach and philosophy* whether practised by line managers or HRD managers. Basically HRD is joint responsibility of line managers and HRD personnel, while the HRD manager can design and provide mechanisms for use by line managers to develop their employees.

HRD facilitators should integrate following *four planks of HRD approach or processes* into their roles:

(i) Development of Identity of Individual Employee for Integration with the Organisation

Some steps in *identity formulation* are:

- Develop employee's *role* so that he is proud of it.
- Development of *concern for excellence and self-actualisation* would contribute to the development of individual identity.
- *Career planning* to help the process of identity formation.
- Development of key performance areas (KPAs) as part of performance appraisal system to contribute to development of identity of a role.
- An organisation gets its identity by development a *distinct culture*—values and norms (rituals) leading to traditions by which organisation is known. Persons joining organisation get socialised with such values and develop pride and a sense of belonging.

(ii) Management of Power Effectively

It means processes:

(i) of *empowerment*,

(ii) of *sharing power* with others, and

(iii) power based on *persuasive*.

These come through expertise, modelling, rewarding and development of others. This has greater influence on others and motivates them.

Counselling and mentoring are HRD practices of empowerment. Mentoring empowers young persons through their close association with senior managers.

HRD facilitators should pay attention to *empowerment of teams* also by providing autonomy and accountability, through participation in decisions on team tasks.

(iii) Developing Synergy

Developing synergy in organisation so that teams work effectively for organisation goals.

Added attention is needed on collaboration and team work. In some organisations two items are included for assessment in performance appraisal:

(i) Functioning as team player, and

(ii) Developing teams of employees.

This may be considered when promoting employees. Team-building has been the main emphasis of OD. All OD work from diagnosis to evaluation is done through teams. Where team work is weak, interventions for team development are used.

If top management team is weak and not cohesive, it will be difficult to develop teams down the line. OD, therefore, starts with development of the top management team.

(iv) Promoting Equity and Justice

One of the roles of HRD is to ensure that people are rewarded according to their contributions.

Linking of performance appraisal results with rewards develops a sense of equity amongst individuals.

The *essential test of success of HRD in an organisation* is the extent to which *four main HRD processes are used. HRD facilitators to integrate these HRD processes in their own roles.* Line managers' role will *include* developing individuals and teams (identity formation) empowering human units, promoting synergy, optimising equity and then they function as HRD facilitators.

Training in competency development is important for faciliators, such as process competencies (communication, motivation, decision-making, problem-solving, conflict management, etc.) can be developed through training programmes. Training in facilitating change, intervention designing and OD may be useful.

CHAPTER

42

Application of HRD Approach in Industrial Relations

The pivotal factor that distinguishes the Japanese from rest of the world is their unique emphasis on the human factor, work ethics and work culture. In this context HRD has become the key factor in India in handling industrial relations to usher new industrial era.

Managing men at work has been a most complex problem for management scientists. Some studies are:

- Scientific Management—1910.
- Time and Motion Studies—1910.
- Human Relations Approach—1920.
- Behaviour Science Movement—1950.
- Human Resource Development (HRD) Movement—1980.

As a result of these studies coupled with emergence of strong trade union movement and labour legislation, man management has gone evolutionary change. Inspite of this evolution of management thought, it is still a dilemma as to which approach is best in handling industrial relations. The two extreme trends are:

I. At One Extreme

1. Trade Unions have become 'second-line' management. Managerial prerogatives are eroded.
2. New generation of workers is more conscious of rights and privileges rather than duties and obligations towards the organisation.
3. Trade unions remain silent about workers' obligations towards organisation, forth-right leaders, if talk, they are dubbed as "management stooges".
4. Trade unions succeed in getting more through pressures and violence than by reasoning.
5. Collective bargaining has become a pressure game. Unions are exploiting the emotions of workers.
6. Only fear and force can restore discipline.
7. Trade unions should be dealt with a heavy hand. (Authoritarian or hard approach)

II. At the Other Extreme

1. Human beings are considered as assets not liabilities.
2. Employees should be cared for, persuaded and motivated.
3. It is felt forced discipline is not enduring.
4. Trade union's though a pain-in-neck, are a reality. They have role to play.
5. Conflict and confrontation to be avoided. Win-lose strategy does not work for long.
6. Manager's should not spend much time on trade union wrangles but on preventive and proactive approaches and actions. Environment in the organisation is creation of the management. An environment of conflict can be converted into cooperation and collaboration. (Humane and soft approach)

III. Human Resource Development (HRD) Approach

Balanced approach lies somewhere in between two approaches mentioned above:

- ❑ Human Resource Development (HRD) generally covers some sub-systems, e.g. training and development, counselling, performance appraisal, career planning, etc. But HRD can be extended to industrial relations (IR).

- HRD is new concept. It is a renaissance of traditional ways of man management.

HRD concerns are:

(a) It looks human beings with more insight, with increased sensitivity. It advocates core values like—human dignity, openness, positiveness, flexibility and family feelings as against hatred, suspicion and animosity.

(b) HRD approach is *proactive,* not reactive. It does not wait for things to happen. It anticipates things and prompts managers to take preventive action. It envisages evolving of systems and processes, to care of areas of frustration and grievances/ indiscipline, which add to industrial relations problems.

(c) *HRD systems* and process which *concern the individual* are:

- Formal and informal grievance handling,
- Suggestion schemes,
- Recognition of merit,
- Work place communication,
- Counselling,
- Emphasis on constructive and remedial disciplinary procedure, etc.

(d) *HRD systems* and processes which concern *the organisation* are:

- Mission and objectives,
- Healthy interaction with trade unions,
- Goal-setting through mutual discussions,
- Participative forums,
- Effective communication processes and team working.

(e) HRD approach believes in *reduction of levels* and elimination of red-tapism.

(f) HRD does not believe in great divide between workers and executives. Hence, HRD recommends many *uniform benefits,* perks and working conditions for both.

(g) Focus of HRD is on *developing the individual* as a whole and not merely his job-related skills. Another focus area of HRD is to build organisation culture which involves better relationship between boss and employees and between departments in the organisation.

(h) Total emphasis is laid on *concept of trust* as a major lubricant to worker and manager relationship.

In Nutshell HRD Approach Basically Envisages

1. Continuous training and development for all including workers, especially attitudinal and multi-skilled. Prof. M.B. Athreya has suggested industrial harmony triangle as under:

About 80 per cent of the employees of an enterprise in the organised sector are in the unionised category. HRD for executives has potential benefits which may not be realized if industrial relations are poor. Even if they are good, the benefits will only be direct. It is only in an atmosphere of industrial harmony that total HRD can take place, covering all the human resources of the enterprise.

We can be guided in this process by the industrial harmony triangle shown in Fig.. The main features are:

- Historically, much time and energy have been infructuously spent by overemphasis on union relations.
- The recognised union needs to maintain its representative character by improving member relations.
- Every executive needs to know his men well and maintain good employee relations. The triangle can enhance of climate for HRD. The sub-systems and skills will flourish in such a climate.

2. Performance planning and objective appraisal.

3. Emergence of self-managing groups with less supervision.

4. Constructive discipline preceding punitive discipline.

5. Enriched job contents.

6. Meaningful participation of workers in management.

7. Creation of a will to work.

8. Creation of "we-feeling" by putting collective values above personal considerations.

9. A culture through dialogue and not through directives.

10. Unions and workers to appreciate the importance of customer satisfaction, quality of product and low price to remain competitive.

Thus, HRD approach should not be mistaken as an approach to compromise or appeasements. It envisages proper planning and strategies for healthy long-term and enduring industrial harmony.

Even a conflict situation helps and forces the group to bring out issues of differences into the open. It then becomes easier to solve. For example, a conflict situation was created in Visakhapatnam Steel Plant (VSP) after the recognised union (CITU) submitted charter of demands and threatened with strike. VSP management could have faced strike situation or compromised on vital issues. Instead, VSP went into prolonged (more than 200 hours) negotiation and dialogue with firmness and sincerity and signed an agreement hoping to convert the environment of conflict and mistrust to mutual appreciation and understanding of each other. Occasional conflict situation could be an investment in future good relations. Business like approach can promote team work.

TO CONCLUDE

An organisation has to believe in HRD as its declared philosophy and display that in day-to-day working. The process is time-consuming and painstaking. It may take time to bring results. It requires management's sincerity attention and commitment. It requires lot of education and training for all—managers, workers, trade union activists, to understand the process and its usefulness.

In absence of HRD approach, an *ad hoc* and traditional approach based on suspicion and hatred will continue. The outcome will be constant struggle or compromise—both of which are undesirable. Conflicts when end in win-lose situations, the organisation is the ultimate casualty.

To avoid such situations and achieve healthy industrial relations peace, HRD approach in industrial relations may be an appropriate answer.

UNIT VII

TRAINING DESIGNS FOR SPECIFIC AREAS

CHAPTER

43

Training and Development of Expatriates for Global Assignments

1. As companies go global, there arises the need for training employees for international assignments. As is well-known, habits and practices relating to work motivation, profit motivation, negotiating skills, gift giving customs, eating and dressing, body gestures, holidayings, interpretation of colour and numbers vary across countries. It is essential that the employees are trained to handle these nuances before being posted overseas.

Fallout to train results in poor performance of the expatriates. These failures are costly with respect to goodwill, reputation and finances of the company. Despite its importance, training employees for overseas assignments has not received much attention. Some countries, such as Japan, are more committed to the importance of training for international assignments.

Few companies *provide preparatory training* on foreign assignments, despite the fact that expatriates fail and knowing the fact that it increases chances of success.

In order to develop and design effective preparatory training, companies must implement a *systematic approach* which includes analysis of *training needs* of target population, establishing training goals, and a careful training design.

Following Fig. 43.1 gives *systematic training cycle* four stages.

FIG. 43.1

Systematic Training Cycle

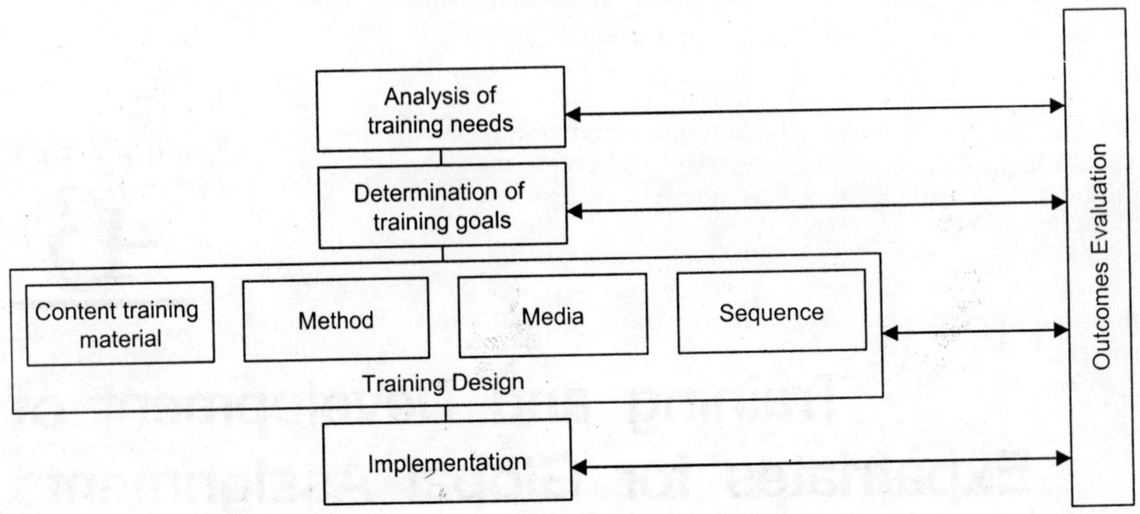

Profiles in terms of competencies needed for success on international assignments may form an important basis for development of effective training for international staff, continuous research required.

An "ideal people" which summarises the competencies needed for international success can be drawn, on the basis training needs of specific assignee can be determined by adding or deleting.

The six competencies that were perceived, in one study, as being most important for success of international managers (in descending order of importance) are:

(a) Leadership skills

(b) Initiative

(c) Emotional stability

(d) Motivation

(e) Ability to handle responsibility

(f) Cultural sensitivity

(g) To handle stress

(h) Flexibility

4. Training and development of international staff should be approached *as a process and not as a one-time event* just prior to departure.

Many of the competencies needed for international success lie in the area of *abilities and attitudes* and therefore require development and strengthening over an extended period of time. The recommended approach is to begin preparing managers for global assignments early in their careers by means of a phased, cumulative approach.

5. *The goals of cross-cultural training*: The next step is translation of training needs into training goals and objectives. A *goal* is fairly general *statement of intent*. Whereas *objectives* are very specific statements what candidate should be *able to do* at the end of learning session.

The goal of cross-cultural training should be to equip the trainees with knowledge, skills and attitudes which enable them achieve the following three adjustments and effectiveness which are indicators of international success:

(a) *Personally* adjusted, i.e. he feels happy and satisfied with situation abroad.

(b) *Professionally* effective if he performs his tasks, duties and responsibilities on the job competently.

(c) *Inter-personally* adjusted and effective if he takes interest in interacting with locals capably.

6. *Methods of cross-cultural training*: Once the training needs are identified and translated into specific objectives, we know 'what', we want to achieve with training. Different methods of cross-cultural training are as under: (Fig. 43.2)

FIG. 43.2

Different Methods of Cross-Cultural Training

Instructional strategies	*Specific methods*
Simulations	• Role playing • Case studies • Instructional games
Programmed instruction	• Cultural assimilator (computer focuses on key differences in critical incidents. Trainee is asked to make choice among alternatives and is then given feedback) on negotiation skills, etc. • Lectures (Area briefing) • Tutorials • Reading Assignments • Audio/Visual presentations
Sensitivity training	• Training group for self-awareness communicatino styles, empathy, listening skills.

Behaviour modification methods	• Drill and practice (practice and feedback) • Modelling (learners' observe models perform desired behaviours)
Field experiences	• Field trips (viist to organisation/country) • Assignments to micro-cultures (trainees are placed in situation and are forced to interact with people with different values, customs, beliefs, behaviour) • Meetings with experienced international staff understanding social skills, codes of conduct, reward systems in the host country, languages, etc.
On-the-job training	• Coaching by managers on company operation and institutions • Job rotation in different positions and business areas

Cross-cultural training thus usually combines both *informational* and *experiential* approaches.

Choice of training methods depends upon the training goals and that these goals on training needs.

Not all competencies can be acquired through the same training methods.

The required level of rigour of the training method depends upon the situational factor of the assignment.

7. *Cross-cultural training is seen* as short duration one-shot remedy. However, to increase its effectiveness of development, it should not be seen as an event, but *as a process.*

Many of the competencies lie in the area of attitudes, abilities and even personality traits: leadership, initiative, motivation, emotional, stability, cultural sensitivity, etc. Such competencies cannot be acquired on a short-term basis. They need to become strong and develop and cannot be done in short duration. So *phased approach* is required to develop competencies.

First phase: of training and development soon after selection and joining company with international prospects.

Focus on *strengthening abilities* needed for an international career and motivation to work abroad.

Second phase: after selection for international career focus on fulfilment of an international assignment.

Third phase: training is for specific skills needed for his assignment and knowledge of *specific cultural issues* in host country, *logistical information and business practices* and procedures is imparted. They are exposed to workshop on pros and cons of expatriate life. Training expatriates in negotiation and conflict resolution skills is necessary to enable them cope with, and resolve, the unexpected issues and problems.

8. *Inclusion of the partner of host country in cross-cultural training* is vital as inability of the partner to adapt to different environment is cause for failure of international assignments. So partner has to be given support while deciding for or against a life abroad. Partners are exposed to pros and cons of international life. Partner must be well equipped for international life.

9. *Inclusion of HCNs (Host Country Nationals)* in cross-cultural training as ultimate success of an expatriate assignment depends not only on the expatriate himself but also *upon the local people with whom he has to work*. So training and development of this (HCNs) group of employee is very important. Content of training *must focus* on development of *technical and managerial skills* and parent corporate culture and the cultural background of the parent country.

We conclude that in addition to training of expatriates, their families, companies should take care to train host country nationals (HCNs). Special attention should be to international training. Personnel as to overseas posting must learn the host country's language, customs and practices. Even the wives of the employees must be involved in such a training programme.

In fact, training represents a long-term investment in both the individuals and in the organisation.

10. *Design of training for international staff* Training and development of international staff must be viewed in the light of the complete *deployment cycle,* and will be more effective when linked to career planning development plans. (Fig. 43.3)

- Here we lay emphasis upon: (i) *Prepatory training for* foreign assignments, (ii) during the *assignment itself,* and (iii) training during the *re-entry* phase.
- The ideal deployment cycle can then be depicted as under:
  - (i) The employee is in a position in the home country organisation. That offers him international prospects.
  - (ii) Once he has shown that he posseses the basic abilities and motivation needed for international career. He is selected and receives further training.
  - (iii) After selection for a *specific assignment,* country specific *preparation follows,* both for the future expatriate and his partner.
  - (iv) *On the assignment* he (and his partner) receive onsite

FIG. 43.3

Deployment Cycle for International Assignments

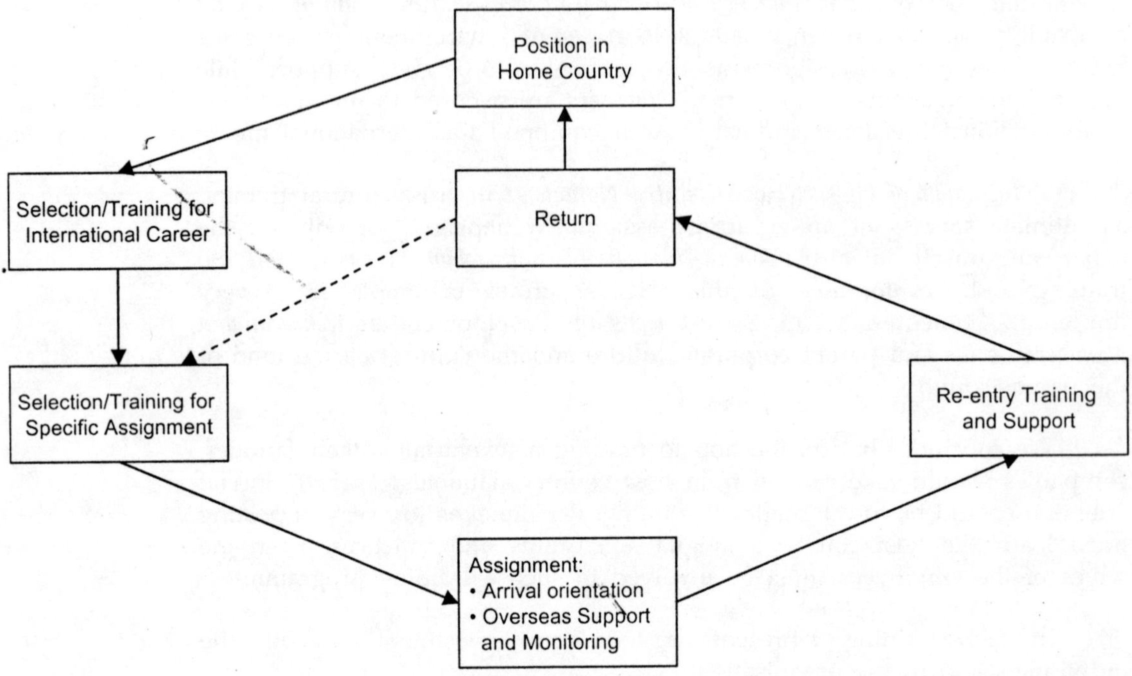

orientation and briefing, as well as support and monitoring from home organisation.

(v) *Upon completion* of the assignment, he is given support during the re-entry process and finally *resume a position* in the home organisation.

- It should be clear that this 'ideal cycle' can only take place if the home organisation is committed to supporting its expatriates in all phases of deployment. These training and support activities fit well into broad *Career development plan.* These assignments should not be just *ad-hoc* staffing purposes.

Design of Training

Levels of training which organisations particularly MNCs are to ensure for success of overseas assignments can be summarised as under:

1. In-level training to focus on learning about *host country's* culture, language, politics, business, geography, religious values and history. Through seminars, videos, meetings with citizens of the country before assignment begins.

2. Second level training deals about *assignment itself*. Requirements of the position and technical, managerial knowledge needed company officials can do that before leaving.

3. Third level training deals with preparing him for *new job* at *new location* to be done by whom he is replacing.

4. Fourth level training—how *he adjusts and adapts* to new environments, by providing assistance.

5. Fifth level training addresses *re-entry* back home and contact with people at home and visit home during vacation.

Training and development of international staff must be viewed in the light of complete deployment cycle, and the same will be most effective when linked to systematic career development plans.

CHAPTER

44

Training for Cultural Diversity

As managing diversity in organisations has gained more importance, the diversity training is equally becoming vital in recent years. The objective is to change behaviour of employees how they would behave in circumstances involving racism, ageism or sexism, etc. in working with diversity. (Prof. David Asbton)

IMPORTANCE OF DIVERSITY TRAINING

Diversity training is done due to basically following reasons:

(a) *Legislative Compliance,* e.g. Equal opportunity and against race discrimination, disability discrimination. Diversity policies frequently cover gender, ethnic status and disability covered in various laws of the country. Sometimes diversity laws cover age and sexual harassment.

(b) Diversity training provides organisation with a *competitive advantage* with diversity training employees utilise increased heterogeneity of their markets, customers.

(c) Diversity training provides opportunity to bring together mix of people where differences are valued. An environment is provided where people grow with innovative ideas and these help in improving productivity and solving problems of the organisation.

COMPONENTS OF DIVERSITY TRAINING

David Asbton has highlighted the elements of learning can be as identified in the Aske Model (Frame, 2001) and which can be effective. These four elements relate to: attitudes, skills, knowledge and emotions as explained below:

ASKE Model: Learning elements	*Examples of the components of diversity training*
Attitudes	• Understanding your own attitudes • Understanding different attitudes • Openness to cultural difference
Skills	• Interpersonal communication • Cross-cultural communication • Problem-solving • Teamwork • Leadership • Conflict resolution
Knowledge	• Legislation • Company policy and procedures • Professional standards
Emotions	• Recognizing emotions • Managing emotions productively

TO CONCLUDE

More efforts are needed to make diversity a significant part of business practice particularly in global and multinational corporations. In this way, training becomes essential in the implementation of diversity policies and building open culture.

The diversity training is to be provided, in addition to managerial personnel, also to non-managerial staff as diversity implementation is to be practiced by the whole organisation.

References

David Asbton, "Training for Cultural Diversity", *Human Capital*, January 2004.

S.K. Bhatia and Poonam Choudhary, Managing in Cultural Diversity in Globalisation, Deep & Deep Publications Pvt. Ltd., New Delhi.

CHAPTER

45

Web-based Training for Call Centers

The IT enabled services industry is emerging as one of the largest employers in the country. The demand for skilled professionals is tremendous and so are the stakes. The challenge to retain employees is enormous, since skilled staff is known to change jobs even for paltry jump in salary. Interestingly, companies are now using focused training as a valuable tool to improve performance and reduce attrition rates.

PLAYING FIELD . . . VAST IS THE NAME

Basic skills required in a call center include *listening* and *speaking skills*. In other words, the agent must have effective communication skills. This usually comprises of written communication, vocabulary, accent and voice modulation. A good training programme focuses on teaching agents to listen effectively so that they can ask good questions. There are even training programmes to help the agent cope with disgruntled clients. Call center agents usually operate under stress, leading to burnout and job change. Stress is also caused by not knowing what the next customer contact will bring. And the very fact that agent positions are generally entry-level jobs, is stressful for some workers who want to move up the ladder

Training in call centers is basically divided into three major categories. *Induction training* usually lasts for a day or two. Here the basic content is the business overview, functioning of call centers, expectations and role of new employees. The HR department of the organisation usually imparts this training. *Pre-process training* covers a major part of training. The course duration ranges from 80 hours to 140 hours. The basic content covered here is *communication, customer service* and *accent training*. Trainers specializing in accent and soft skills deliver this course to call center associates. The final category is the *process training*. This training is highly client specific and is used only in transaction processing industries. For example, a BPO unit working with a client in the insurance sector would typically require training in claims processing, compliance training, etc. The duration of process training typically depends on the client's processes.

There is an extensive use of audio and video. Audio used extensively by playing English songs and singing along with them. This helps in improving the accent they would like to achieve. In the same way, accent listening and comprehension skills are illustrated using American movies. Games are also used extensively so as to keep high levels of interactivity in the training session. A tried and tested methodology of training is the role-play and the simulation done in the training room. The concept of taking 'mock calls' in the training room has been proved very effective and has been used frequently to enhance the process of learning.

E-LEARNING . . . OPTIONS UNLIMITED

In India, e-Learning is still a relatively new concept and call centers have been hesitant and cautious in investing in online training solutions for the agents. Comparing this to the call centers abroad, e-Learning has been readily accepted as an integral part of training. Most call centers in India do have e-Learning but it is mostly reduced to one or two CD-ROM's, which have a basic course on customer service. There is no means of assessment techniques using these CD-ROMs. More mature call centers in India, have tested e-Learning and are finding them highly cost effective. Repetitive courses, which hardly need any human interaction, can be made online and deployed on the corporate intranet. For example, selling skills can be made into a highly interactive web-based training module with both pre- and post-assessment, where the grades go into a central database for easy administration of the agents performance. As time permits, more courses could be made online and deployed on the intranet. Wouldn't it be a relief for the HR manager to click a few buttons and get the complete grades and performance sheet of the whole batch?

Web-based training has been of particular benefit to call centers especially in the US and England. Call centers usually has a high turnover, which implies that the induction process operates at a high volume. A call center with an annual employee turnover of 40%, with 500 full-time equivalent operators and all persons working half time, would need some 35 persons per month to be hired and retrained. Web-based training can have specific applications for a call center.

Evaluating Candidates

Using the testing function, it is possible to test if a candidate is able to summarize what a caller says. The candidate hears a recording and he or she types into a field and the instructor reviews the response. In addition, a whole range of multiple choice, true and false and fill in the blank questions has been asked; all of which are evaluated automatically by the software. Open-ended questions can also be asked and evaluated by an instructor.

Client Training

Client training is highly client specific and is more in the transaction-based call centers. Clients usually have a different process for their back-end work. So studying each process and training the agents is a lot of work. These processes can also be put on a custom-built e-Learning programme and effectively train the agents on the processes. For example, a client in the insurance sector would like the agents know the laws and regulations of the country in which they are operating. A module on compliance training can be built into the system, which can be taken by the agents at their own time. It could also be a source of reference, if it is made accessible always on the corporate intranet. So if an agent wants to look up something regarding a particular law, he could search the training programme and get the required material. Wouldn't everyone like to have a constant reference material of courses online and on demand?

Making e-Learning Work for Call Centres

Start the process starts right from the time of evaluating candidates...

1. During the hiring phase, test candidates for ability to comprehend, summarize, and respond to caller.
2. Use automated multiple choice questionnaire to assess candidate on client handling.
3. Deploy online psychometric tools for personality profiling.
4. Give English grammar tests through web-enabled technology.

Make use of various tools of e-Learning to impart right skills to new call centre agents...

1. Use e-learning for training on soft skills and communication skills.
2. Employ online modules for fine tuning customer interaction skills.
3. Enhance learning with interactive CD-ROM-based training on taking calls, cold calling and handling angry callers.

Equip employees to handle clients interactions better...

1. Customize client training for your business using e-Learning programmes.
2. Build web modules on compliance training that can accessed from the desktop at any time.

CHALLENGES . . . AND ISSUES

There are a few mindsets that the training department of a call center needs to overcome before implementing e-Learning. To begin with, one needs to gain understanding about pros and cons of using e-Learning to make an informed decision. e-Learning is a viable solution to some training problems but certainly not all. Large groups of 300 to 500 participants warrant e-Learning implementation. Another issue is the initial expense of installing such a system in the network. If e-Learning is to be used on an intranet, it calls for infrastructure like a dedicated server, a software license, and training for an IT person in maintenance of the programme. Trainers need to become familiar with the delivery platform. Programmes like Macromedia Dream Weaver, Flash and Fireworks are useful for sophisticated training programmes. However, training costs per person are low. Once the system has been set-up, the investment can be recovered quickly.

Web-based learning promises a host of benefits. Well-designed modules allow learners to track their personal progress and repeat modules that they find more challenging. It also allows new recruits to practice unfamiliar tasks in a safe, unthreatening environment. Many call center managers are using e-Learning for staff orientation and refresher training. And the flexible nature of web-based training means that when call volumes are low, agents can quickly catch up on training modules. But training for training's sake just doesn't cut it in the world of call centers. Training effectiveness must be measured. Although web-based training tools allow supervisors to monitor a learner's progress, the behavioural results must also be tabulated. There always is the old debate of how effective is e-Learning compared with instructor-led training.

A better approach would be to opt for a *blend of online learning* and *instructor-led training*. Online learning can be an ideal complement to classroom learning. e-Learning today is more of a cultural change than a technology change. As Albert Einstein said, "I never teach my pupils; I only attempt to provide the conditions in which they can learn."

Reference

Extract from an article by Ajit Premkumar, Learning Solutions Group, Peopleone Consulting (I) Pvt. Ltd., Bangalore, in *Human Capital*, July 2002, Gratefully acknowledged.

CHAPTER

46

Training for Team-building

Team process encourages high motivation and consequent achievement. It meets member's social need to affiliate. Members also exert social pressure for achievement of goals. Level of commitment of members to team decision/goals is much high and it has collaborative strength. Team members have clear focus on "mission and vision" of the organisation.

STRATEGIES FOR TEAM-BUILDING

Crucial task is how to build teams. Some interventions are directed toward four main areas:

- Diagnosis,
- Task accomplishments,
- Team relationships, and
- Team and organisation processes.

WORK TEAM-BUILDING ACTIVITIES

A. Diagnostic Meetings:

- ❑ Unfreeze the members to be ready.
- ❑ Joint data collection.
- ❑ Feedback data and discuss problem areas of the group.

B. Team-building Focused on:

- ❑ Task accomplishment, including problem-solving, decision-making, role clarification, goal-setting.
- ❑ Building and maintaining effective inter-personal relationships, including boss-subordinate and peer relationships, communication and conflict-solving.
- ❑ Understanding and managing group process and culture, identifying barriers and seek collaboration.
- ❑ Role negotiation techniques.

CHARACTERISTICS OF EFFECTIVE WORK TEAM

(i) *Clear purpose to all*—Members in the team know their goals' mission, vision as they are shared by all.

(ii) *Participation*—All members are listened and there is effective interaction.

(iii) *Consensus decision-making*—When problems arise, the situation is diagnosed by joint discussion. The problems are solved through cooperation and supportive relationship.

(iv) As needs of *leadership* arise, anyone, feels free to volunteer. Leader's role is supportive and informal.

(v) Members in team's *trust and respect* one another.

(vi) *Clear roles and work assignments.* Group is also flexible in resources and seeks new and better ways of growing.

(vii) Teams are collectively creative and possess task skills.

(viii) Members have *close sense of identification* with the group. They have high degree of group loyalty, group solidarity or cohesiveness.

(ix) *Positive synergy* through coordinated effort. Team effort results in a level of performance that is greater than the sum of those individual inputs.

(x) *Self-assessment.* Members carry out periodic examination, how well the team is functioning?

(xi) *High performance teams.* Smith says have all above characteristics plus following:

- ❑ Strong personal commitment to each other.
- ❑ More ambitious performance goals.
- ❑ Fuller mutual accountability.

- ❑ Members are inter-changeable as well as have complementary skills.

SKILLS OF LEADER FOR TEAM WORK

Most important factor for quality of team-work is role of the leader. He may build or destroy the team and may not use the team. Some skills of the leader to be successful are:

1. He *listens* before deciding.
2. He is *available and responsive* to peoples' problems.
3. Keeps team members *up-to-date* on regular basis. Open and honest communication.
4. Develops a *balanced* team. Develops his men and has optimism of his men.
5. He *allocates* work based on their *capabilities*, i.e. balancing task and relation roles.
6. He encourages *respect, understanding* and *trust* among members.
7. He empowers and delegates work to his team members.
8. He *sets an example* and only agrees for high *quality standards* with the team.
9. Leader sets *achievable targets* for team but always presses them for improved performance.
10. He *involves* members in *problem-solving* of key issues.
11. He *represents* team members.

ENHANCING EMOTIONAL INTELLIGENCE IN TEAMS FOR IMPROVING THEIR OVERALL PERFORMANCE

Much of the important work in organisations is now done in teams. Most effective teams can attain emotional intelligence. Daniel Goleman (Working with Emotional Intelligence, 2000, Bantam Books) explains, that the ability to manage one's feelings, interact effectively with others, and communicate are more than twice as important as IQ or job skills in determining team success. Teams can thus develop greater emotional intelligence and can boost their overall performance.

Emotional intelligence means exploring, embracing, and ultimately relying on emotion in work, that is, deeply human. It is behaving in ways that build relationships and that strengthen the team's ability to face challenges.

Building Emotional Intelligence in Teams

To build a foundation for emotional intelligence, a team must be aware of and constructively regulate the emotions of:

(a) individual team members,

(b) the whole group, and

(c) other key groups with whom it interacts.

Groups are most creative when their members collaborate unreservedly. People stop holding back when there is mutual trust, rooted in emotionally intelligent interactions.

CHAPTER

47

Training for Interim Staff

Manpower outsourcing or contract employment or interim staffing—call it by any name—it is here to stay.

OUTSOURCING HR FUNCTIONS

HR outsourcing is not an unfamiliar concept for corporate India . . . although we now recognize it by a new brand name. Functions like recruitment and training have been outsourced since decades. But its nothing like plain old wine in brand new bottles. Current favourites include a host of functions like payroll, benefits administration and contract staffing. Interest is leasing out HR activities is growing by leaps and bounds. A survey by an HR association showed that 72% of Indian companies have outsourced at least one HR activity and 50% of these are operational in nature. Another crucial development: India's HR outsourcing market has long been monopolized by the unorganized sector. The arrival of professional global players like India. Life Hewitt and Exult has added a new glow to the complexion of the business. And as the mad rush to join the bandwagon continues, BPO vendors of all sizes are adding HR services to their product portfolio.

REASONS FOR OUTSOURCING HR

Now it is gaining popularity with large and medium sized Indian companies too, specially those with seasonal products, those seeking to restrict their overheads, and those who are proactive and open to change. HR outsourcing is on a high because every company is thinking lean, acting smart and concentrating on core competencies.

"Today, every organization is aiming at achieving productivity by enhancing return on investments and achieving the economies of scale. In this context, it makes business sense to focus only on the organization's core competencies and outsource non-critical business activities."

Three most important drivers leading companies to outsource: financial gains, lesser administrative hassle and focus on core areas, though not necessarily in that order.

(a) For instance, workforce intense industries outsource due to the *sheer volumes*, and the smaller companies to keep themselves lean, also global companies.

(b) The *employment boom in the Indian service* sector is also responsible. In the service sector, key differentiators are service quality and price, and both are largely influenced by the quality of HR in the company. Why HR outsourcing will succeed is precisely of this that both price and quality can be determined through an outsourced arrangement *versus* in-house operations.

(c) Another major factor that is fuelling interest in outsourcing is the *evolving-HR function* itself.

(d) Now there is a realization that 80 percent of valuable HR time that expended in managing critical *yet non-core tactical and transaction-oriented operations* can be saved by outsourcing these operations.

(e) HR is now making a clear transition from backroom to boardroom to concentrate more on productivity enhancement. HR functionaries recognize that they need to align with business objective of the organisation and *play a key role in delivering results and focus on core* people functions. Outsourcing leaders unanimously foresee increased opportunities to outsource in the future.

(f) Thus, experts outline five top benefits of outsourcing: the opportunity for HR to focus on strategy and core competencies, substantial reduction in operational and transactional costs, sharing of risks and increase in mobility, access to world-class services and the option to convert fixed cost to variable cost. All these benefits are linked to *direct cost savings and indirect savings.*

(g) Mr. Surendra believes that "the interim mode of staffing provides *flexibility to the organisations to scale up its manpower*, so as to take advantage or business opportunities, while at the same time allowing it to scale down in a short span of time and avoid the financial and emotional costs associated with a large benched workforce when business is down," he ventures. "Such an arrangement also enables client companies through their new hires on contract to establish new benchmarks for skills and competencies in use, set new norms for superior pay commensurate with performance without upsetting the apple cart, and align themselves to the dynamic and highly competitive environment. Through interim staffing the organisation can bring on board the required skills at the most optimal cost."

(h) HR too wanted to follow with a rationalisation of its transactional services to one site with a consolidated HR system portfolio. If this transformation could be brought into the mainstream, HR services delivery would be consistent.

(i) Today most of the transactional operations are outsourced. This has brought in centralization of most of the HR processes and enabled consistent HR services delivery.

(j) Financial implications are just one side of the story. The payoffs can be many more. Outsourcing transfers various risks involved in compliance, financial, technology, legislative and corporate restructuring issues to the vendor. Further, companies need not invest capital to maintain and upgrade high-quality, prohibitively expensive HR systems and infrastructure. Third party outsourcing agencies can offer leading-edge technology, highly developed programmes and software to manage employee data, along with specialized expertise, minus the accompanying costs of hiring and retaining the best HR professionals. The best of both worlds! Is it really easier said than done?

ARE CONTRACT EMPLOYEES COMMITTED?

How do contract employees feel about working on temporary jobs? Does it affect commitment levels? Not really. "HR outsourcing grew at a time when permanent workforces were being sent out by corporate through voluntary, compulsory or early retirement schemes. Today the security in a job is considered a myth. Ambitious professionals look for jobs that could give satisfaction and good pay. Wherever they are they know that *performance is the key* and that if they are good they will definitely have a career path for themselves. So *employees give their best during their tenure regardless* of the job being temporary or permanent".

DIFFERENT NAME FOR OUTSOURCING HR

Manpower outsourcing, interim staffing or contract employment . . . call it by any name . . . its here to stay. But employee leasing is just one slice of the pie. Think payroll and benefits administration, and you've grabbed a 22% share of global HR outsourcing.

WHEN TO USE INTERIM STAFFING

- Businesses that have seasonal of time based shifts
- Businesses where flexibility is required
- Businesses needing speedy adjustment
- Bringing flexibility in structure
- Fixed cost projects
- All non-core areas of business
- Competitive environments calling for constant increments in quality
- Post-downsizing, when recruiting permanent staff may be awkward
- To establish new benchmarks for skills and competencies in use
- To establish new norms for superior pay commensurate with performance

(Based on inputs by M.R. Surendra, Head, Lobo Interim Staffing.)

HR FUNCTION INTERNAL DEPARTMENT WILL CONTINUE

Handling over the reins of responsibility to an external service provider does not absolve HR of its accountability. "Outsourcing will never lead to the complete elimination of the internal HR function. Instead, HR will play a lead role in terms of supervising, implementing and successfully carrying out the process of outsourcing." In other words, the scope and definition of the HR function will transform considerably. "The HR function is a business need and it would continue to perform all core activities. The functions that will get outsourced would be largely transactional and administrative in nature." The size of the HR team could reduce due to outsourcing in the process.

"Internal HR sees the large picture and has to constantly work towards employee retention especially at key levels, succession planning, fine-tuning available human resources, ensuring people to productivity ratio and such strategic functions. HR *outsourcing cannot be a substitute for the HR department.*

Implementation of HR outsourcing could initially face resistance from employees, "Once internal customers understand the advantages, this congestion gives away to active participation. In most cases, HR outsourcing brings 60% increase in the productivity, 30% reduction in costs and eradicates labour union problems to a great extent."

Some of the basic reasons hampering the growth of HR outsourcing in

India are confidentiality and cost factors. "The fear of losing jobs, losing control over confidential data, ethics and quality of outsourcing vendors, security breaches and overall confidence in the vendor deters many organisations," which naturally makes the service provider has to be evaluated and review on various aspects of confidentiality and the agreement should capture all the evaluation aspects, penalties not leaving it open ended at any point of time." To tackle this issue head on, many outsourcing service providers ensure that the client data is accessible to only the team working on the account, and that team does not work for a competitor.

FUTURE SCENARIO

"The case for HR outsourcing is strong since the processes are well defined, the players have now consolidated across services and geographies and people have begun to see the value addition in terms of expertise in administration and superior experience in query resolution." Quality will be the focal point in defining parameters of success, when it comes to leasing out HR services. Training and self-development will play important role as individual has to keep himself competitive. It is not important to be the best, but also to keep evolving to stay the best. Individual has to form this the basis of his future individual's are masters of their destiny in competitive era. Individual has to assume responsibility and has to make conscious efforts to exploit his strengths. Individual's are valued for their unique competencies, contributions, attitudes and values which enhance value to the organisation. One has to stay life-long learner. Companies proposing to transfer administrative burdens to an outsourcer also need to do a reality check on their expectations from the outsourcing arrangement. Finally, only those ready to embrace a transformation will find that outsourcing will bring access to world-class processes, competitive advantage and increased shareholder value.

References

Human Capital, Jan. 2004, New Delhi.

Source: www.humancapitalonline.com

CHAPTER

48

Apprenticeship Training

The intake, regulation and control of apprentices in the organisations is governed by the Apprentices Act, 1961. Apprenticeship training is intended to provide on-the-job training and to increase availability of trained technical manpower for the industry.

The Apprentices Act, 1961 makes it obligatory on the part of all employers in the specified industries to place apprentices in the designated trades in terms of a standard laid down. The training involves basic training accompanied by on-the-job training with related instruction embracing the entire period of training. During the training, each apprentice is given minimum stipends as laid down. The Act specifies 217 industries and designates 134 trades for the apprenticeship training programme.

It may be noted that the Government of India has received the assistance of United Nations Development Programme (UNDP) under the India-87 Project for the development of the programme. An all-India apprentices competition is organised every year to encourage a healthy competition among the apprentices as well as their employers.

The Directorate General of Employment and Training (DGET) lays down the general policies for training programmes, formulates standards, prepares syllabi, imparts training to instructors, and industrial supervisors, conducts examinations and issues the appropriate certificates. However, the actual administration of the Industrial Training Institutes and the Apprenticeship Training Programme is the responsibility of the respective state governments. The Government of India has established two advisory bodies including the National Council for Training in Vocational Trades (constituted in 1957) and the Central Apprenticeship Council for the Apprenticeship Scheme under the Apprentices Act, 1961. These bodies advise the Government in formulating training policies, training standards, standardisation of tools and equipment and allied issues. Explicitly, they are tripartite in nature consisting of representatives of central and state governments, industry and labour. The Union Minister for Labour is the chairman of these councils.

The DGET conducts the training of craftsmen in the Industrial Training Institutes involving 38 engineering and 26 non-engineering trades. This training is accomplished in 1,447 Industrial Training Institutes with an overall training capacity of 2.64 lakhs. The duration of training in these trades ranges from six months to two years. The educational qualifications for admission purposes for certain trades is eighth class while for others it is a matriculate. After the successful completion of training, the trainees are awarded National Trade Certificates which form a recognised qualification for recruitment to the subordinate positions in organisations under the Government of India. There are stipends and several other facilities for the trainees. Obviously, the training is imparted free of charge. Besides 64 trades, the state governments and union territories have introduced such craftsmen training in additional trades to meet the requirements of the new industries established in their areas. Four Model Industrial Training Institutes were established during 1981-82 to supplement craft training with a modular training.

Some important provisions of the Apprentices Act, 1961 are given below:

Objectives

- To supplement the programme of institutional training by on-the-job training and increase availability of trained technical personnel for the industry.
- Regulate and control the training of apprentices in designated trades.
- It also covers graduate engineers and diploma holders for giving them practical training under factory conditions for improving their employment potential as per amendment of the Act in 1973.

Scope and Administration

- The Act applies to industries specified by the government.
- The Act is administered by the Central and State Governments.
- The State and Central Governments have to appoint the following

authorities for administering the Act.

(a) The National State Councils for training in vocational trades;

(b) Apprenticeship Councils;

(c) All India and State Councils of Technical Education;

(d) Regional Boards of Apprenticeship Training at Chennai, Mumbai, Kolkata and Kanpur; and

(e) The Central and State Apprenticeship Advisors.

Obligations of Employers

1. Engagement of Apprentices

A person can undergo apprenticeship training in any designated trade only if,

(a) he is not less than 14 years of age,

(b) he satisfies the prescribed standard of education and physical fitness, and

(c) has entered into a contract of apprenticeship with the employer.

2. Registration of Contract of Apprenticeship

The employer to submit the contract of apprenticeship within three months to the apprenticeship advisor for its registration.

3. Make Arrangements for Practical Training

- The employer should make arrangements for imparting practical training for the period specified in the contract of apprenticeship. The duration of training varies from six months to 4 years depending on the requirements of the trades.
- The employer who has more than 500 workers has to bear the cost of basic and practical training and payment of stipends to the apprentices.
- In case of graduates and technical apprentices the cost of stipends may be equally shared the Government upto prescribed limit.
- In case of establishments employing less than 500 workers, basic training is to be imparted in industrial training institutes set-up by the Government.
- Syllabus and other facilities for practical and basic training are approved by the Government.

4. Working Hours, Leave and Holidays

- The employer should not require the apprentice to work overtime, in excess of the weekly hours prescribed under the rules and on any day between 10 p.m. to 6 a.m.
- The apprentices should be allowed casual leave, medical leave and extra-ordinary leave, as prescribed under the rules. Holidays will be as are observed in the establishment.

5. Payment of Compensation in Accident Injury

In case of personal injury, an apprentice is entitled to compensation payable under the Workmen's Compensation Act and the Schedule Appended to this Act.

6. Status of Apprentice

An apprentice is only to be trainee and not a worker, and provision of any labour law are not applicable to him.

7. Record of Progress and Submission of Returns

- Employer has to maintain records of progress of training of each apprentice in the prescribed form. He is to furnish returns to authorities.
- On completion of training and passing the test conducted by the National Council, the apprentices are granted a proficiency certificate in the trade by the council.

8. Employment of Apprentices after Training

There is no obligation to provide a job to the apprentice. Similarly, an apprentice is not bound to accept the employment under an employer. If there is any such condition in the contract of apprenticeship, the employer will have to offer a suitable employment to the apprentice after completion of training. However, there is a practice of giving reference to apprentices for regular appointment.

9. Compensation for Termination of Apprenticeship

- The contract of apprenticeship terminates on the completion of training.
- It can, however, be terminated earlier by the apprentice or employer, on payment of prescribed compensation, i.e. three months' stipend.

Offences and Penalties

Any employer who:

(a) fails his obligations under the contract;

(b) does not engage the required number of apprentices;

(c) refuses to furnish any information or return;

(d) obstructs any inspection, examination or inquiry; and

(e) requires an apprentice to work overtime or to do any work not connected with his training;

shall be punishable with imprisonment upto 6 months or with fine or with both.

CHAPTER

49

Transforming Anger

In this era of competition, success or failure, we are caught by a phenomenon called anger. Anger is a very basic human emotion that plays an important role in the way we communicate with others. Anger is a feeling that occurs regularly in life of every person.

REASONS FOR ANGER

Following are basic reasons for anger:

(i) Anger occurs when we are *not getting something*, we want. Your personal rights are violated. Desires make us angry. Frustration is a type of anger. If you cannot do anything about your anger, you get frustrated and depressed. Anger is a power, if it is sustained over a long time without expression or sublimation, it leads to hatred.

(ii) Anger has in it a sense of *righteousness*. We feel right in certain situations and when someone differs, we feel angry.

(iii) Anger is usually a *defence* against something you value.

(iv) Another reason for anger is when we want to *change other people*. But nothing will change. Thus, there comes disillusionment and anger. The way the world it is, let us not try to change others. Let us try to clear our muck and change ourselves.

(v) Anger is a *demonstration of power* you want the world to know that you are angry. If other person is shouting and you speak calmly, it will cool down the other person.

MANIFESTATIONS OF ANGER

- Anger is the first enemy of man. Anger is to show a false sense of strength.
- When anger delusions we lose intelligence. Anger reduces us to animals and obstructs differentiation from right to the wrong.
- We blame some one for our anger.
- Anger if not expressed, but if directed inward, causes illness such as—blood pressure, headache, ulcers, asthma, etc. The result is teeth grinding, loud voice, frowning, tight muscles, stress, etc. like pressure cooker, which releases extra steam, we also need to release pent up feelings to avoid self-harm.
- What we normally see is displacement of anger feelings. If your boss gets angry in office, you show anger on your attendant when attendant goes home he finds something in food, he shows anger on his wife. In turn wife displaces anger on little child. Finally, when child is helpless, he kicks the puppy in front. Often, we do not know how to manage our feelings and we express this inappropriately.

It may be mentioned that basically, feelings are positive. Without feeling we are "dead bodies". Feelings make us human and sensitive towards others. It is natural to have feelings. Since, we do not know how to express them, we turn them negative. Then we suffer and become cause of suffering for others.

HOW TO TRANSFORM ANGER?

Anger is double edged weapon. Anger can be a constructive force and can also be destructive towards one's own self and others. It is like nuclear energy which can be harnessed for constructive or destructive purpose, and it depends upon the scientist.

(i) Negative Expression

Being angry can be an unpleasant experience. We make other person resentful and hostile. Create troubles in relationships. We hurt others and humiliate them. In this process we develop enemies.

(ii) Positive Expression

(a) Anger provides energy and increases vigour to act. Anger helps us to move *toward specific action*.

(b) Anger rings out *problems on surface* and helps to identify them. It leads to *problem-solving* and *decision-making*.

(c) Anger helps us to maintain *a sense of virtue and righteousness* in face of opposition. It helps to *maintain a belief* that we value and is justified.

(d) We accept our feelings and give them direction and express anger appropriately.

We should *not attack the personality* of the person, but should *describe the behaviour*. Using the 'I responses' instead of using 'you responses'.

For example: Negative expression of anger—You make me angry. You are clumsy. You do not know how to keep the room clean.

Positive expression of anger—I am angry *the way* this room has been kept. Thus, when we attack the personality of a person, we threaten other person and *communication* link with him is affected.

Infact, we need not suppress anger, but *release* appropriately to be *effective in our relationship*. We should have *direct communication* with whom we are angry. We should go with the intention of reconciliation, forgiveness and work out mutual understanding the way we would like to interact and express feelings in future. So do not *hold on* the anger, or hurt others. Anger steals your energy and keeps you away from love and relationship.

Transforming anger into positive force. It is appropriate to quote an example given by Swami Nikhilananda. If I can understand anger and use its force in an intelligent way can transform it and use it to my advantage. Mahatma Gandhi was thrown out of the train in South Africa. Just imagine being thrown out like that, it would make you feel insulted and angry. What would I do? I'll be angry with the person and want to beat him and throw stones at him. If that doesn't work, I'll throw stones at the train. Then I'll go home and beat my wife. Once my frustration is expressed, I would feel relaxed.

Mahatma Gandhi did something wonderful. He got angry, no doubt, but not with the person. He directed his anger at the system, which made the man behave the way he did. He directed the anger at apartheid and decided to work for freedom. That was his revenge. He converted anger into a positive strength. To fight for freedom of any country, strength and energy is required. Anger is an energy. If you express it at every little thing, you are wasting it. Therefore, some thinking is needed to transform an anger.

Kroodh (anger) is like fire, and water helps to calm it down. Drinking cold water when you're angry will quell the fire raging inside you. Similarly, taking a cold shower when you are all steamed up emotionally helps.

It is wrong to say we should not get angry. Selfish anger is bad, but anger for the welfare of the world is not. If your anger creates a power in you to change what is wrong, it is positive. So petty anger is bad and destroys you. So it is necessary to understand how to deal with anger. Man is as big or as small as he thinks. So make man a magnanimous human.

FEELINGS OF JOY—HAPPINESS

Joy is wonderful feeling. It gives a sense of satisfaction and peace within oneself. But *some are hesitant to express* joy as we have a belief what others will think about us. This is due some sort of guilt or shame which we develop.

It is natural to *express our joy*. If *we are smiling, others will smile too*. Let us *share our joy* with others when we experience this feeling. We need to express our feeling appropriately and communicate. So that relationship is built. Particularly, *if we are depressed*, angry and worried, we should *experience joy in our lives.*

Reference

Swami Nikhilananda, "Transforming Anger", *Hindustan Times*, New Delhi, April 25, 2003.

CHAPTER

50

Learning to Build Self-Esteem

People differ in the degree to which they like or dislike themselves. This trait is called self-esteem.

When you look in a mirror, what do you see? Well, of course, you see yourself, but if you were to be asked to describe yourself, what would you say? The whole point about this is that if you do not respect and feel good and positive about yourself, how, as a manager, will you be able to respect and feel good about others?

CHARACTERISTICS OF PEOPLE WITH SELF-IMAGE

The *characteristics of people* who have a healthy self-image, and are far more able to adopt a positive attitude to the range of management skills they have. People with healthy self-image:

- ❑ usually have *strongly held* views, and are willing to stick to them, but at the same time have the capacity to listen to and respect the views of others;
- ❑ have a *willingness to change*, if they are shown to be wrong; have open mind, do not fight change;
- ❑ have *confidence in their decisions* and are not prone to feeling guilty or regretful about making them;
- ❑ *accept mistakes* as part of a learning process and determine to find out what went wrong with a view to improvement;
- ❑ *feel equal* to others, regardless of their skills or qualifications, and

can accept their achievements with good grace;

- are able to *accept positive feedback;*
- think that *other human beings are important* and tend to look for the best in them;
- are *not shy about being* emotional and don't see this as a weakness;
- are *not dominated* by other people;
- are satisfied in job; and
- have fun. Future is more exciting.

People with a healthy self-image make managers with a good, positive attitude! People with high self-esteem feel unique, competent, secure, empowered and connected to the people around them.

REBUILDING SELF-ESTEEM

To rebuilding of your self-esteem, here are some practical tips to get you started:

- Self-awareness through self-analysis. Make an inventory of all your good attributes, first those that you like about yourself and then those that others like about you. Are you caring, attractive, intelligent, community minded, etc. Just make sure you focus on the positive aspects. Label your areas of talent. A persons great opportunities for improvement lie in his talents, not his weaknesses. Build these talents up into strengths. They will enable you to excel. So focus on your talents and nurture your attitude.
- Consciously reject those aspects of yourself about which you are unhappy. Say to yourself that they are not important to you and that's all that matters. If there are problem areas which you can't ignore but can do something about, make a plan to get yourself to where you want to be. Take care of yourself and becoming responsible to yourself. Do not dwell upon depressing thoughts. Replace them at once by healthy optimistic beliefs.
- Learn go control situations which you find difficult, or avoid them.
- Only set realistic targets and you will achieve them.
- Learn always to say something good about yourself and your achievements.
- Have self-confidence. By acquiring competence, courage, trust others, care for other people. Treat others the way you want to be

treated. Believe in yourself. You are unique to this world so are your talents.

- ❑ Self-esteem is increase by playing on success in the past.
- ❑ Self-love. Nurture and care yourself. Forgive yourself of past guilt feeling and come out of shame feeling.
- ❑ Develop your self-worth by having a purpose and meaning in life. Feelings of sadness are blocks.

Don't ignore your emotions. You need to learn to feel comfortable with yourself, the way you look and your skills inventory, and feeling comfortable has an emotional dimension. Basic energy comes from how I am communicating myself—self-image.

CHAPTER

51

Identifying Training Needs of Small Scale Enterprises

According to PHDCCI, it is unfortunate that no systematic effort has been made to evaluate the training needs of the Indian small-scale enterprises, despite their dominant contribution to the national economy

With the objective of identifying the training needs of employees in small-scale enterprises, a field survey was conducted, especially with reference to the fast changing competitive business environment. Based on the findings of the study the ultimate objective was to initiate a more systematic technique and methodology to improve the capacities of small-scale enterprises through a dynamic training system.

SAMPLE CHARACTERISTICS

A close-ended questionnaire was administered to the small-scale enterprises spread across north Indian states of Delhi, Madhya Pradesh, Uttar Pradesh, Haryana, Punjab, Rajasthan and Himachal Pradesh.

The selected enterprises represented a cross-section of industrial segments such as light engineering, etc. as well as types of businesses such as exporters, service providers *et al.*

The survey threw some interesting insights, some of which are listed below:

- 41.0 per cent of the enterprises were of the view that small-scale industries generally prefer to maintain their traditional identities.
- 72.3 per cent of the respondents felt that gaining training and knowledge is important for enhancing profitability.
- 56.9 per cent of the respondents preferred Marketing as their first choice for training programmes, while 54.9 per cent preferred Quality Management. 43.6 per cent showed their preference for Exports/Trade-related programmes.

RECOMMENDATIONS

In the light of the data above, some recommendations are:

- Small units can be given capsules of training programmes on to how to benefit from the Cluster Approach.
- The programmes should create awareness among them with doses of knowledge in new products, business practices, technology market development, quality standards, trends in packaging, changing customer preferences, etc.
- Future training programmes should be relevant to the changing needs of the customers of participating enterprises.
- A "Centre of Excellence for Training of Small Entrepreneurs" may be established for the purposes of meeting the training needs of small-scale enterprises.

Reference

Secretary General, PHDCCI, *HT Careers*, 15.01.2004, Delhi.

CHAPTER

52

Techniques for Trainers to Improve Voice

We use every means at communication to deliver talks effectively and a key tool at our disposal is our voice. If people like the sound of what they hear it will help them 'buy in' to what we are saying and help to maintain interest. Sonal Batra states: Research shows that an audience picks up five times as much from the voice compared to the actual words you are saying, so expanding your range of tone, volume and pitch for example, can be powerful for any communicator.

We give here some techniques mentioned by Sonal Batra in her article in *Training and Management*.

So knowing a few techniques on how to care for your voice can be invaluable and applicable to anyone who is working in an occupation that carries a high voice load—including lecturers, professional speakers, aerobic instructors and yes, definitely trainers.

HEALTHY VOCAL HABITS FOR QUALITY OF VOICE

Most of the time, we assume that our voices just 'work' by themselves and don't need any special care. Here are seven areas that impact on the quality of your voice and how you can stay fit with some looking after that voice of yours.

Breathing

One should always try to breathe long and deep—it's an instant way to calm down.

Posture

Your posture affects the quality of your voice. When standing, balance your weight evenly; keep your feet a width apart and pointing forwards. *Avoid leaning forwards and straining with your neck or chin. An imbalance in posture can set-up tensions in the body.*

Warm-ups

A tired, husky sound or painful throat often indicates we have over-used our voices. Make vocal workouts part of your working routine at the start of each day to keep your voice tuned and healthy. Finding time to do *some gentle warm-ups pays-off dramatically in the long-run.*

Pitch

Use your natural pitch. Talk using a pitch that is comfortable for you and naturally fits your own vocal instrument.

Stress

A common cause of voice strain is stress and relax your jaw often we don't even realise it. The jaw is a very strong hinge that gets used thousands of times each day.

Your Environment

Smoky, noisy environments can be very damaging to the voice. Extreme temperature changes can also occasionally cause voice strain.

Drinking Habits

It's a good idea to have a large glass of water to hand. It is impossible to speak clearly with a dry throat and it could cause strain and damage if you try. You need to take extra care when these you act cold or a sore throat.

EXERCISES TO TAKE CARE OF VOICES

- An instant remedy to stress is to drop the jaw. It relaxes all the facial muscles and gives everything a moment to recover.
- Taking time to go through breathing and relaxation exercises will sort out most cases of tense jaw.
- Stretching the neck and shoulders will promote good breathing and posture habits and relieve tension.
- Go through all the vowels and 'sing' them as you breathe out.

Try saying tongue twisters as well.

- Next, imagine that you've just put the most enormous sticky toffee in your mouth and chew it very hard.
- Make really exaggerated chewing movements, including getting it stuck on the roof of your mouth and in your teeth!
- To increase breath control, begin by breathing in for three counts and out for six counts.
- Establish this as a breathing pattern and try to do ten repeats.
- When this is comfortable, breathe in for four counts and out for eight. Gradually add sounds to the outward breath—for example, counting, speaking your name and address, or a line from a poem or story.
- Drinks as many as ten to 12 glasses of fluid each day. Juices and herb teas are fine. However, avoid iced water. You should also avoid drinks that include caffeine such as tea, coffee and coke because these are diuretic (water-expelling). They dehydrate instead of rehydrate. If you have to drink caffeine to get you going, then re-fill your mug afterwards with water and drink it all.

SPEAKING TO LARGE GROUPS

To make your voices louder combination of working on more breath, more energy and slightly lowering your pitch that will result in good voice control and help to fine tune volume. Train yourself to be sensitive to each situation so you are aware of when you need to turn it up volume, turn it down or turn it off. Be absolutely sure to begin and end on a strong note.

Four techniques on how to make your voice seem louder

- Use your mouth energetically to produce more sound without shouting.
- Aim your voice forward.
- A fuller voice produces more volume than a thin, ready one. Using as much breath as you can behind each phrase will help to strengthen and fill out the voice.
- Finally, pay special attention to sentence endings. This is when many people find their voice tails off. Make a point of finishing on a strong note.

REFERENCE

Sonal Batra, Article on Vocal Awareness for Trainers, from *Training and Management*, New Delhi, Nov. 2002, Gratefully acknowledged.

UNIT VIII

TRAINING INSTRUMENTS/TESTS

CHAPTER

53

Psychometric Tests

Tests are used for various purposes such as: to supplement in the selection process, for career counselling, for creating awareness to the training and development process, to evaluate the effectiveness of training programmes, etc. Thus, there are various types of tests which serve specific purpose. We mention different types of tests:

TESTS

Skill Tests

Shorthand, computing, driving, Fig. work, map-reading, etc.

Aptitude Tests

There are six major aptitude tests:

- Clerical
- Spatial
- Manual dexterity
- Verbal
- Mechanical
- Numerical

Intelligence Tests

There are quiz books, such as what is next in this sequence?

A, B, D, G, ?

Insert one word that completes the words either side:

PEND (. . .) HILL

Some are little diagrams or pictures in a sequence. You have draw the next one or find the odd one out.

Psychometric Tests

Examine aspects of personality. These look at traits. They examine a whole range of personality traits to checkout whether you are:

- Reserved
- Mentally active
- Shy
- Trusting
- Conservative
- Relaxed
- Stable
- Confident
- Reflective
- Impulsive
- Obsessive
- Outgoing
- Humourous
- Venturesome
- Suspicious
- Happy
- Risk-taking
- Expressive
- Susceptible to guilt

Test of this type usually involve answering a lot of questions in a short time. They are usually multiple choice.

You do not have much time to think. Some tests 'lie' questions, which show whether you are trying to make you look better. Also, they tend to ask the same question in several different ways to check the consistency of your answers. It pays to be honest because interviewer will know, the type of person need to do the job and whether you fit the job. Some psychometric tests to look at some aspect of personality can be of following types:

(a) Team Role Tests

One of favourite tests in this category is the building team role questionnaire, which tests the type of role we take in a team. It shows, for example, whether we are good in fine detail, are the sort of person who comes up with bright ideas, are good at making other people feel good, or are a good leader. Some times creativity tests are given. One test can be to see how well they can juggle with three balls.

(b) Graphology Tests

Graphology tests look at aspects of your personality through an examination of your handwriting. If you see in an advertisement or job application form that you should apply in your own handwriting, this may be because the forms are being sent to a graphologist.

As with the personality tests, it is difficult to cheat at this. A skilled graphologist would probably know if you were trying to disguise your writing. You could get someone else to complete the form or write the letter for you, but what advantage would this be? Unless you know a lot about graphology yourself, you wouldn't know who to ask, even if you knew exactly what the graphologist had been asked to look for. They are certainly not just looking for neat handwriting.

(c) In-tray Tests

These are occasionally used to test the candidate's sense of priorities, logic and time management. They vary, but will usually include a list of items requiring attention. You to decide in which order to deal with them. Here is one use can be with people on a time-management course to test their skills in prioritising.

You arrive in your office early Tuesday afternoon, having been away from the office for the morning. The following greets you when you walk into your room. Place the items in order of priority.

(i) A rep from ABC Ltd. is waiting outside to see you about the order you placed for some new equipment. (Time needed for task 10 mins)

(ii) The head of department wishes to see you as soon as possible. (Time unknown)

(iii) The phone is ringing. (Time unknown)

(iv) You haven't eaten yet. (30 mins)

(v) You have an urgent message on your desk telling you that there is a flood in the basement. You are requested to give advice immediately. (15 mins)

(vi) A piece of machinery has broken down. You are the only person in the office who knows how to fix it. Three people can't get on with their work until it is mended. (15 mins)

(vii) Your secretary has a problem with some mail from yesterday. (5 mins)

(viii) An attractive person of the opposite sex is sitting outside your door—you don't know who it is. (Time unknown)

(ix) The accounts manager wishes to see you in connection with the end-of-year accounts. (1 hour)

(x) One of your staff is in the staff room, requesting permission to go home sick. (5 mins)

Tip: If you are asked to do this type of test, think about what is urgent and what is important. It makes the decision-making easier.

There is no 'right' answer to this type of test because you must make some assumptions. In this test, for example, you may be able to assume that you have a secretary to whom work can be delegated.

A suggested order for the test above might be:

(i) Ask the secretary to tell the rep to come back in a couple of hours or to make another appointment.

(ii) Ask her to phone the head of department to say you will be with him as soon as possible.

(iii) You'll never be able to concentrate while the phone is ringing. But refuse to get into conversation, say you'll call back. Now the phone is free for you to attend to other matters.

(iv) Ask her also to get you a sandwich.

(v) Return the call about the flood in the basement and give advice over the phone. If necessary arrange to go down there.

(vi) Fix the machinery, three people are being prevented from working while it's out of order.

(vii) See to the mail from yesterday with your secretary.

(viii) Ask her to find out what the attractive person outside the door wants and make a decision based on the answer.

(ix) Arrange to see the accounts manager at 4 pm.

(x) Phone your secretary and ask her to tell the sick person to go home. This took 30 seconds instead of five minutes by not going to see the person.

Feedback from Tests

Many organisations now offer feedback after they have tested you and this can be extremely helpful. If you are not offered feedback, you could ask for it. Do so politely, don't demand. The feedback you get will help you to get a wider picture of yourself and your abilities. It may also indicate areas where you need to do some more work. Keep the notes on it in your interview file.

CHAPTER

54

Myers Briggs Type Indicator (MBTI)

More and more tests are emerging to measure competencies of employees. Psychometric tests add to reliability and credibility in the selection of candidates. MBTI is such test which is being used for developmental purposes. Trend is towards use of multiple methods, like behavioural combined with ability testing. Professionally developed tests come with manuals for scoring and analysis. But test interpretation calls for specific training.

Trend for personality profiling is very common in the USA and UK for all levels of recruitment and development purposes.

MBTI (Myers Briggs Type Indicator) is recommended more for developmental purposes—competency mapping. This test is developed by Katharine C. Briggs and Isbell Briggs Myers.

This test helps you to know your own *preferences* and learning about other peoples can help you understand what your strengths are. What kinds of work you might enjoy, and how people with different preferences can relate to one another and contribute to society.

MBTI measures a person's preferences, using four basic scales with opposite poles:

Extraversion/interversion,

Sensate/Intuitive,

Thinking/Feeling, and

Judging/Perceiving.

The various combinations of these preferences result in 16 personality types. This recommended more for developmental purposes. The four basic scales are given in Fig. 54.1. 16 personality characteristics frequently associated with each type are elaborated in Fig. 54.2.

FIG. 54.1

Four Basic Scales

Each type, or combination of preferences, tends to be characterized by its own interests, values, and unique gifts. On this page is a brief description of each type. Find your reported type and see whether the description fits you. If not, the person who administered the MBTI to you can help you identify a better-fitting type. Whatever your preferences, you may still use some behaviours that are characteristic of contrasting preferences. For a more complete discussion of the sixteen types and applications such as career choice, relationships, and problem solving, see *Introduction to Type,* Sixth Edition (Myers, I.B., 1998, Pall Alto, CA: Consulting Psychologists Press), or *Gifts Differing* (Myers, I.B., with Myers, P.B., 1995, Palo Alto, CA: Davies-Black Publishing).

E—Extraversion People who prefer Extraversion tend to focus on the outer world of people and things.	**T—Thinking** People who prefer Thinking tend to base their decisions primarily on logic and on objective analysis of cause and effect.
S—Sensing People who prefer Sensing tends to focus on the present and on concrete information gained from their senses.	**F—Feeling** People who prefer Feeling tends to base their decisions primarily on values and on subjective evaluation of person-centered concerns.
I—Introversion People who prefer Introversion tend to focus on the inner world of ideas and impressions.	**J—Judging** People who prefer Judging tend to like a planned and organized approach to tile and prefer to have things settled.
N—Intuition People who prefer Intuition tend to focus on the future, with a view toward patterns and possibilities.	**P—Perceiving** People who prefer Perceiving tend to like a flexible and spontaneous approach to life and prefer to keep their options open.

FIG. 54.2

Characteristics Frequently Associated with Each Type

ISTJ Quiet, serious, earn success by thoroughness and dependability. Practical, matter-of-fact, realistic, and responsible. Decide logically what should be done and work toward it steadily, regardless of distractions. Take pleasure in making everything orderly and organized their work, their home, their life. Value traditions and loyally.	**ISFJ** Quiet, friendly, responsible, and conscientious. Committed and steady in meeting their obligations. Thorough, painstaking, and accurate. Loyal, considerate, notice and remember specifics about people who are important to them, concerned with how others feel. Strive to create an orderly and harmonious environment at work and at home.	**INFJ** Seek meaning and connection in ideas, relationships, and material possessions. Want to understand what motivates people and are insightful about others. Conscientious and committed to their firm values. Develop a clear vision about how best to serve the common good. Organized and decisive in implementing their vision.	**INTJ** Have original minds and great drive for implementing their ideas and achieving their goals. Quickly see patterns in external events and develop long-range explanatory perspectives. When committed, organize a job and carry in through: Skeptical and independent, have high standards of competence and performance—for themselves and others.
ISTP Tolerant and flexible, quiet observers until a problem appears, then act quickly to find workable solutions. Analyze what makes things work and readily get through large amounts of data to isolate the core of practical problems. Interested in cause and effect, organize facts using logical principles, value efficiency.	**ISFP** Quiet, friendly, sensitive, and kind. Enjoy the present moment, what's going on around them. Like to have their own space and to work within their own time frame. Loyal and committed to their values and to people who are important to them. Dislike disagreements and conflicts, do not force their opinions or values on others.	**INFP** Idealistic, loyal to their values and to people who are important to them. Want an external life that is congruent with their values. Curious, quick to see possibilities, can be catalysts for implementing ideas. Seek to understand people and to help them fulfil their potential. Adaptable, flexible, and accepting unless a value is threatened	**INTP** Seek to develop logical explanations for everything that interests them. Theoretical and abstract, interested more in ideas than in social interaction. Quiet, contained, flexible, and adaptable. Have unusual ability to focus in depth to solve problems in their area of interest. Skeptical, sometimes critical, always analytical.
ESTP Flexible and tolerant, they take a pragmatic approach focused on immediate results. Theories and conceptual explantations bore them—they want to act energetically to solve the problem. Focus on the here-and-how, spontaneous, enjoy each moment that they can be active with others. Enjoy material comforts and style. Learn best through doing.	**ESFP** Outgoing, friendly, and accepting. Exuberant lovers of life, people and material comforts. Enjoy working with others to make things happen. Bring common sense and a realistic approach to their work, and make work fun. Flexible and spontaneous, adapt readily to new people and environments. Learn best by trying a new skill with other people.	**ENFP** Warmly enthusiastic and imaginative. See life as full of possibilities. Make connections between events and information very quickly, and confidently proceed based on the patterns they see. Want a lot of affirmation from others, and readily give appreciation and support. Spontaneous and flexible, often rely on their ability to improvise and their verbal fluency.	**ENTP** Quick, ingenious, stimulating, alert, and outspoken. Resourceful in solving new and challenging problems. Adept at generating conceptual possibilities and then analyzing them strategically. Good at reading other people. Bored by routine, will seldom do the same thing the same way, apt to turn to one new interest after another.
ESTJ Practical, realistic, matter-of-fact. Decisive, quickly move to implement decisions. Organize projects and people to get things done, focus on getting results in the most efficient way possible. Take care of routine details. Have a clear set of logical standards, systematically follow them and want others to also. Forceful in implementing their plans.	**ESFJ** Warmhearted, conscientious, and cooperative. Want harmony in their environment, work with determination to establish it. Like to work with others to complete tasks accurately and on time. Loyal, follow through even in small matters. Notice what others need in their day-by-day lives and try to provide it. Want to be appreciated for who they are and for what they contribute.	**ENFJ** Warm, empathetic, responsive, and responsible. Highly attuned to the emotions, needs, and motivations of others. Find potential in everyone, want to help others fulfil their potential. May act as catalysts for individual and group growth. Loyal, responsive no praise and criticism. Sociable, facilitate others in a group, and provide inspiring readership.	**ENTJ** Frank, decisive, assume leadership readily. Quickly see illogical and inefficient procedures and policies, develop and implement comprehensive systems to solve organizational problems. Enjoy long-term planning and goal setting. Usually well informed, well read, enjoy expanding their knowledge and passing it on to others. Forceful in presenting their ideas.

Introverts

Extraverts

CHAPTER

55

Test for Selection and Training (TST)

Fluid Intelligence is different from the measure of a person's Intelligence Quotient (IQ). IQ makes sense only in the case of children, Where it indicates the relationship between the child's chronological and intellectual age. An IQ of 110, for instance indicates that the child is intellectually just a year ahead of his chronological age, just as an IQ of 90 indicate that he could be a year behind his peer group. But for all adult the IQ concept has no meaning, although we continue to use it as short hand to simplify communications.

For adults an equivalent concept of IQ would be that of *fluid intelligence.* Behaviourist believe that fluid in intelligence is fully developed by the age of 16-18 and does not change till a person has crossed the age of 50. But after that it gradually begins to decline with age.

One psychometric tool that purports to measure a person's fluid intelligence is called Tests for Selection and Training (TST), developed by the British Government's Civil Services and Royal Forces division, now licensed to an India-based company called Thomas International. The score that a person (or an employee) obtains on a TST instrument reflects his or her ability to respond to various training programmes.

Because continuous training has gained so much currency in the knowledge economy, the popularity of TST instruments has risen in India, with all corporate big-wigs subscribing to them, either for competency mapping, recruitment or job profiling purposes.

"Some are using TST in conjunction with other psychometric tools, mainly to help us understand an employee's core strengths or predict future areas of improvement."

"Some are also using it for general recruitment purposes and are quite satisfied with the results."

The top advantage with TST is that anyone who knows English, can relate upper and lower case letters, count up to 30, add or subtract single and double digit numbers, recognise shapes can take these tests, which may appear deceptively simple but are far from being so.

WHAT ARE TST INSTRUMENTS?

These are normative psychometric tests used to compare individuals in the same norm group, say the same department in a company. "They have low entry level, but are capable of measuring the highest levels of ability."

"TST does not measure an employee's knowledge or experience but his overall mental flexibility or the speed and accuracy that he brings to his work."

In the sense, TST are 'ability' tests as opposed to 'intelligence' tests, the scores reflecting an employee's 'General Training Quotient' rather than his 'Intelligence Quotient.'

In predicting whether an employee would be fit for a particular training programme, the TST tests him in the five areas: feature detection, reasoning, numerical speed and accuracy, working memory and orientation. The questions that the instrument tries to answer are: Can this person *think on his feet*? Can take 'X' amount of information and reach some logical conclusion? Is this person comfortable with *numbers*? Does he have a high level of *mental agility*? Can he learn *complex tasks* and procedures? Is he suited to technical and mechanical skills?

TST instruments exposes the true competence level of each employee, after which the HR Manager can easily decide whether to promote him to the next position or not, or whether to invest in his training anymore (if yes, in what kind of training) or whether to assign him a particular role or not!

Reference

HT Career, 11.11.2003.

CHAPTER

56

Passive, Aggressive and Assertiveness (PAA)

IMPORTANCE OF INTERPERSONAL SKILLS

Today at work, it is not enough just to possess the technical abilities to do the job. Most of us work as part of a team and depend on each other to produce results. It is essential therefore to know how to work well with people in a clear and fair way. To be successful at work one needs to build in oneself, the flexibility to deal with a variety of people and situations. Developing your interpersonal ability will help you to achieve this.

Behaving assertively in work situations is an important interpersonal skill. It is important not only for dealing with people but also for getting them to perform. In most interpersonal situations involving conflict, most of us would react by rebelling in anger, or by withdrawing from the situation by remaining silent and keeping our feelings to ourselves. Neither is productive. Few of us would be skillful in expressing what we think and feel in a calm and relaxed manner to achieve what we want. Unfortunately, we are not taught in professional/technical courses how to act assertively or listen actively even though these are valuable work-related skills.

MEANING OF ASSERTIVENESS

Webster defines "assert" is "to state positively with great confidence". It is the extent of forcefulness a person (or leader) uses with a view to express himself. Assertiveness is a term meant to describe the extent of control, the leader tries to exercise over both the followers as well as the situation. It means expressing what you think or feel without endangering the ego of others. It is saying what you mean and having self-respect and respect for others. Assertiveness is a skill you can acquire—not a personality trait. It is an essential skill for a leader.

ASSERTIVENESS

An assertive individual expresses his views and opinions and *convinces* other on data, facts:

His approach *to persuade* is based on *self-respect*, otherwise he will be aggressive or submissive.

He *asserts his rights* and is not submissive. He stands up for his rights. He does not allow his rights to be trampled on. He is not aggressive trampling on other rights also. However, the focus is on the individual exercising his rights in non-aggressive way. It is mutuality principle.

He listens and wants to be listened to. He is straight forward yet sensitive to the needs of others.

How to say what one wants and how to get what one wants. He expresses his *feelings* openly otherwise he is bottling up too much inside himself. They are becoming *weight* and they are going to explode.

WHY BEHAVE ASSERTIVELY?

By using assertiveness skills a manager can give orders appropriately, correct people in a constructive way, get them to perform, handle interpersonal conflicts and difficult employees. Through assertiveness we can learn to express our feelings (both positive and negative) appropriately, request for changes or refuse unreasonable requests.

The ability to express feelings and what you want constructively is important for a manager because it can maximise the chances of getting what he wants out of people and situations.

Expressing what you think or feel to get what you want, has to be done with tact, without sounding rude, at the same time not sounding unsure of yourself.

Assertiveness builds-up our self-esteem and gives us the confidence to go on acting assertively whenever required. So it is important to be assertive not only to get more of what you want but also to feel better about yourself and your behaviour.

FIG. 56.1

Relationship between Assertive Behaviour and Self-Esteem

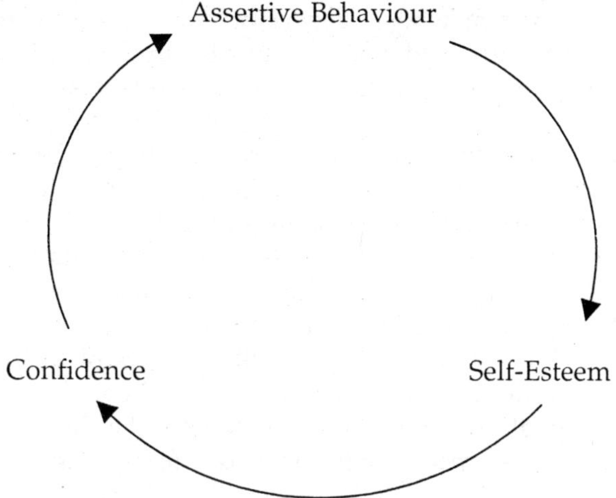

USING ASSERTIVENESS SKILLS TO IMPROVE PERFORMANCE

Let us understand the three types of behaviour—aggressive, assertive and passive when it comes to dealing with people and situations. These three types also refer to degrees of assertiveness.

1. Aggressive Behaviour

Extreme case of "over assertiveness may amount to aggressiveness. Aggressive managers lack sensitivity to the emotional needs of their employees. They express what they think or feel but at the cost of the self-respect of their employees. They may be able to win agreements but this may be by putting a stake on work relationships or employees' morale. They may be able to get things done but more so based on fear or threat. They may often be rude or sarcastic. Aggressive managers are ineffective in handling poor performers and in giving constructive feedback. They tend to overpower their employees. They build relationships based on dominance. Their point of view is "This is what I want done, what you want is of little importance or of no importance at all." With such an attitude they can force some employees into better performance in the short-run but in the long-run overall performance of those working under them may suffer. This is because such managers are not able to inspire others and undermine motivation and morale of their employees. They are self-centred without regard for feelings of others. They believe in I Win-You Lose. I am OK and You are not OK. They are not bothered about relationship building.

2. Submissive Behaviour

Some managers have difficulty in confronting their employees when there is a problem. Submissive behaviour is the very opposite of aggressive behaviour. A person who is generally low in assertiveness is by disposition a quiet person with mild opinions but is supportive in his actions or listens to others. Carried to an extreme it can result in submissive behaviour.

Submissive managers do not express their expectations, feelings, needs and concerns honestly. They may not be comfortable when it comes to pointing out an employee's undesired behaviour or mistake which may actually be necessary in work situations for improving performance. They are poor at expressing their resentment or other negative feelings, thereby making their true expectations unknown to their employees. Such people's self-image is largely based on what others think of them and their behaviour, rather than what they think or feel about themselves. They consciously or unconsciously allow employees to dictate the level and quality of their performance. As a result, they are taken for granted.

ASSERTIVE BEHAVIOUR

Assertive managers manage employees, their performance and their problems without damaging their egos. Most interpersonal situations are handled tactfully. An assertive manager would handle an employee's temper tantrum in a calm and relaxed manner. At the same time, he is able to stand up for what be thinks and feels and expresses the same in a direct and appropriate way.

Assertiveness helps us to meet our needs without violating those of others. Assertive people are firm, yet polite. To be assertive a person has to first learn to control his own emotions. Active listening, empathy, being sensitive to others' needs, use of positive phraseology, self-expression are important aspects of assertiveness training.

To become a competent manager, you must balance your need to get the work done with your need to be a friend to your employees. You can achieve this balance through assertiveness. You will have a more fulfilling relationship with your employees and improve productivity by communicating your needs, expectations and concerns in a way that demonstrates respect for your employees.

HOW TO COMMUNICATE ASSERTIVELY WITH YOUR EMPLOYEES?

Managers may face situations when they have to confront an employee about his performance/work. They may do in three steps:

(i) Non-judgemental Description of Behaviour

The behaviour that is upsetting you, needs to be pointed out in a precise/specific manner without any judgemental overtones. Avoid drawing inferences about the employee's motives, but focus on "what he exactly did", that upset you. Refer to the action/behaviour that is upsetting e.g., "I found the following errors in your report", without making remarks about the person e.g., "How irresponsible of you". The former remark is easier for the subordinate to digest because it is objective.

The following are some examples of non-judgemental behavioural descriptions:

- ❑ When you do not check letters after typing them.
- ❑ When you don't complete your work on time.
- ❑ If you don't take down accurate phone messages.

These examples will be used later to illustrate the other two parts of an assertive message, which are:

(ii) Disclosure of Feelings

While pointing out to an undesired behaviour a senior should also communicate how he feels about it. Expression of feelings you are experiencing by using "I" messages is likely to make the employee feel concerned about it. By saying, "I feel . . . . .", you are helping others to understand what is going on inside you. Feedback about unacceptable behaviour or performance is more likely to be accepted when you express how you feel in a non-threatening way. By contrast "You messages" (e.g., "You always send reports late") may be more difficult to digest even if based on facts because they are too personal and direct, thereby making the receiver feel victimised. Feelings need to be expressed immediately after an inadequate or poor performance but preferably in private.

(iii) Clarification of the Effect of the Behaviour

The objective of any negative feedback or criticism (given in a constructive manner) is three-fold:

(i) To make the employee aware of what is upsetting.

(ii) To prevent repetition of that particular behaviour/action.

(iii) To bring about change/improvement.

The three examples cited earlier can be examined again by incorporating all 3 steps, i.e. non-judgemental description of behaviour, disclosure of feelings and clarification of effects for the same.

- "When you do not check letters after typing them .... I feel annoyed .... because they need to be typed again creating unnecessary work and further delays."
- "When you don't complete your work on time .... I feel disappointed because it reflects poorly on our ability to keep commitments."
- "When you don't take down telephone messages accurately .... I get frustrated as I have trouble getting back to the caller."

Your use of assertive messages can greatly influence your employee's understanding of your concerns and feelings, and the effects of their behaviour.

ART OF GIVING CONSTRUCTIVE CRITICISM

Assertiveness helps us to be more effective in giving negative feedback. Being skilled in the art of giving criticism for example is important for managing employees and their performance. Yet most of the time criticism is given without much tact, leading to hurt and humiliation rather than improvement. The following guidelines will help a senior in giving criticism effectively:

1. Be specific.
2. Be descriptive, not evaluative.
3. Focus on the action/behaviour, not on the person—depersonalise the message.
4. Time it close to the event.
5. Do not take old mistakes but concentrate on issues at hand.
6. Discuss how improvement can be brought about.

ASSERTIVE BEHAVIOUR IS APPROPRIATE BEHAVIOUR

Reddin has said that effective behaviour is that which is appropriate to the needs of the situation.

Learning to be assertive doesn't mean that you must always behave assertively. If someone is about to mug you, it is entirely appropriate to become aggressive. In some situations it helps to keep silent atleast temporarily e.g., while handling a firing. Whilst learning to apply assertiveness skills one should be judicious in ascertaining where and when to apply them.

TO CONCLUDE

Assertiveness training can be of immense benefit as a means of self-development. People with good assertiveness skills will also have enhanced self-awareness, greater confidence and self-esteem, and honest, powerful and effective communication skills. They will have respect for themselves and for others.

Central to all this is positive thinking. Assertive people have a positive self-image; they will use positive language; they will look for positive outcomes to interactions; they will work with the other person to provide positive solutions to problems by which both sides 'win'; they will be positive in their respect for the other person's views and opinions, whether or not they share these views.

References

French, A., *Interpersonal Skills,* Sterling Publishers Pvt. Ltd., New Delhi, 1996.

John Adair, *The Skills of Leadership,* Gower Publishing Co., England, 1984.

Reddin, W., *Effective Management,* Tata McGraw Hill, New Delhi, 1987.

CHAPTER

57

FIRO-B Questionnaire

Write the answer that best applies to you at the left of the statement.

A. Each of the following statements can be answered in any one of these alternatives:

Never	=	0
Rarely	=	1
Occasionally	=	2
Sometimes	=	3
Often	=	4
Usually	=	5

1. I try to be with people.
2. I let other people decide what to do.
3. I join social groups.
4. I try to have close relationship with people.
5. I tend to join social organisations when I have an opportunity.
6. I let other people strongly influence my actions.
7. I try to be included in informal social activities.
8. I try to have close, personal relationships with people.
9. I try to include other people in my actions.
10. I let other people control my actions.
11. I try to have people around me.
12. I try to get close and personal with people.
13. When people are doing things together I tend to join them.
14. I am easily led by people.
15. I try to avoid being alone.
16. I try to participate in group activities.

B. Each of the following statements can be answered in any one of these alternatives:

Nobody	=	0
One or two people	=	1
A few people	=	2
Some people	=	3
Many people	=	4
Most people	=	5

17. I try to be friendly with people.
18. I let other people decide what to do.
19. My personal relations with people are cool and distant.
20. I let other people take charge of things.
21. I try to have close relationships with people.
22. I let other people strongly influence my actions.
23. I try to get close and personal with people.
24. I let other people control my actions.
25. I act cool and distant with people.
26. I am easily led by people.
27. I try to have close, personal relationships with people.
28. I like people to invite me to things.
29. I like people to act close and personal with me.
30. I try to influence strongly other people's actions.
31. I like people to invite me to join in their activities.
32. I like people to act close towards me.
33. I try to take charge of things when I am with people.
34. I like people to include me in their activities.
35. I like people to act cool and distant toward me.
36. I try to have others do things the way I want them done.
37. I like people to ask me to participate in their discussions.
38. I like people to act friendly toward me.
39. I like people to invite me to participate in their activities.
40. I like people to act distant toward me.

C. Each of the following statements can be answered in any one of these alternatives:

Never	=	0
Rarely	=	1
Occasionally	=	2
Sometimes	=	3
Often	=	4
Usually	=	5

41. I try to dominate people when I am with people.
42. I like people to invite me to things.
43. I like people to act close toward me.
44. I try to have other people do things the way I want them done.
45. I like people to invite me to join in their activities.
46. I like people to act cool and distant toward me.
47. I try to influence strongly other people's actions.
48. I like people to include me in their activities.
49. I like people to act close and personal with me.
50. I try to take charge of things when I'm with people.
51. I like people to invite me to participate in their activities.
52. I like people to act distant toward me.
53. I take charge of things when I am with people.

KEY

A respondent's scores for different kinds of needs can be calculated with the help of the following key:

Need for Inclusion

Expressed (See answers to statements 1, 3, 5, 7, 9, 11, 13, 15 and 16).

Wanted (See answers to statements 28, 31, 34, 37, 39, 42, 45, 48 and 51).

Need for Control

Expressed (See answers to statements 30, 33, 36, 41, 44, 47, 50 and 53).

Wanted (See answers to statements 2, 6, 10, 14, 18, 20, 22, 24 and 26).

Need for Affection

Expressed (See answers to statements 4, 8, 12, 17, 19, 21, 23, 25 and 27).

Wanted (See answers to statements 29, 32, 35, 38, 40, 43, 46, 49 and 52).

Reference

Schütz, W.C., 1958, FIRO—A Three Dimensional Theory of Interpersonal Behaviour, New York, Holt, Rinehart and Winston.

CHAPTER

58

Audio-Visual Aids for Training

Audio-visual aids can enhance and reinforce learning.

People remember 20% of what they *hear*.

People remember 30% of what they *see*.

People remember 50% of what they *see and hear*.

Audio-visual aids help in also capturing *attention* in addition to facilitating listening and remembering. Visuals are an aid to instruct and can reinforce the verbal information.

AVAILABLE DEVICES

I. Black Board

Oldest, inexpensive one. Some guidelines for using black board are:

- One should write only important points,
- Erase old material,
- Avoid talking to board to talk when facing group,
- Do not stand in front of board while using board, and
- Write legibly and quickly.

2. Flip Chart

Flip chart consists of sheets of paper and clamped to an easel or whiteboard:

- It can replace black board.
- Difficulty in storing these charts.

3. Magnetic Boards

Mostly used for showing prepared visuals. Can also be used as black board. Magnets are used as pins and also called pin-up boards. It is particularly useful in describing mechanical applications, where movement is critical.

4. Flannel Board

Flannel Board is covered with felt cloth. For pinning charts. However, one needs black board to explain.

5. Overhead Projector (OHP)

Most widely used. Acetate transparencies are prepared with pens, or photo copy process or on computer.

Advantages: Trainer always face audience and retain eye contact and can make talk more effective. For participation different colours can be used in the transparencies to emphasise points. OHP enables students to take notes.

6. Slide Projector

35 mm film slide projector and it is controlled by the trainer with remote control.

7. Film

Film is an effective training media. It stimulates interest and a person can absorb more through viewing.

Film to be followed up by *group discussion* rather than lecture. A film is visual aid to memorisng the core features of a session and should not be tooling.

8. Epidiascopes

Projects objects, models, ages of books, diagrams on to screen. It does not need transparent film in order to illustrate. It is particularly useful for preparing enlargements from an original.

9. Televisual Aids

Video cameras will produce colour pictures and in conjunction with the video cassette recorder (VCR) permanent recordings can be made on video cassettes. The scope of such a system is obviously enormous. The ability to give almost instant feedback for fault correction and checking is very important and on the recording there is no subjective argument. It is also extremely useful in social skills training where role play can be recorded and trainees use the VCR for self-criticism and analysis. The videotape recording is invaluable for communications skills at all levels of the company, for selection interviewing provided the playback is conducted by an experienced trainer with empathy.

10. Models

These are often next best to the real thing, especially if they exist to scale. Models have the undoubted major advantage of being three-dimensional. An investment in a model is a permanent and can be used over and over again.

Thus, visual aids are tools in the hands of the trainer. It is important to choose the correct aid for the job.

CHAPTER

59

Room Arrangement: Creating an Optimum Learning Environment

Arrangements of Low Interaction

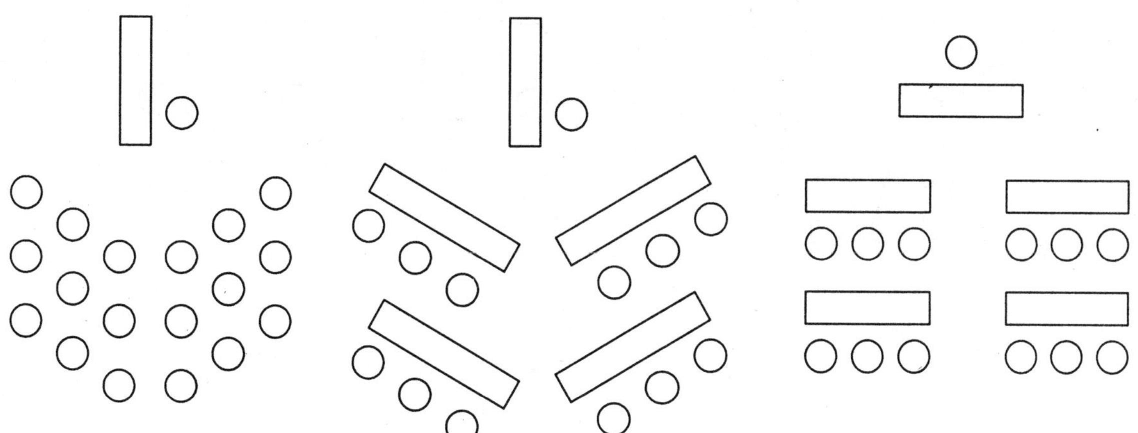

Arrangements of Moderate Interaction

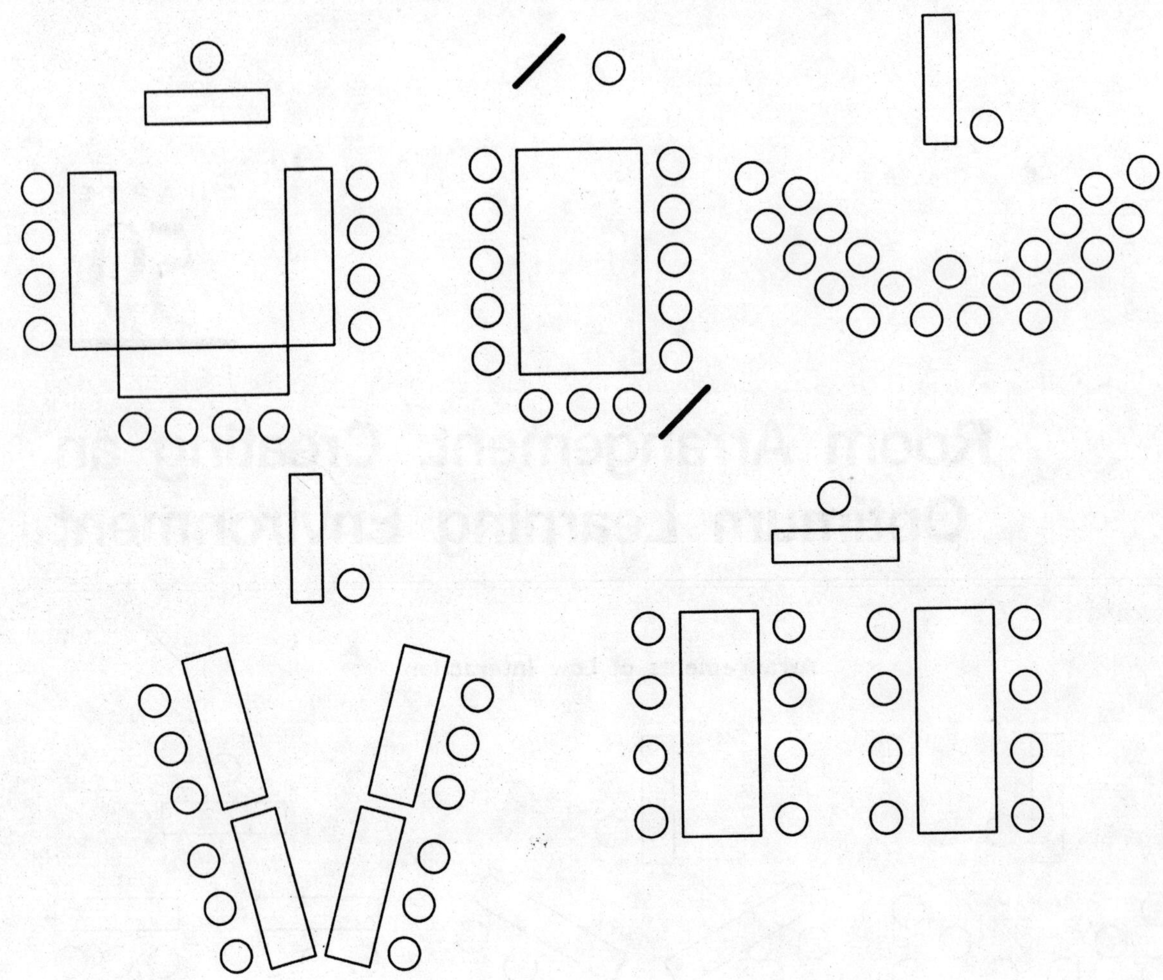

Arrangements of High Interaction

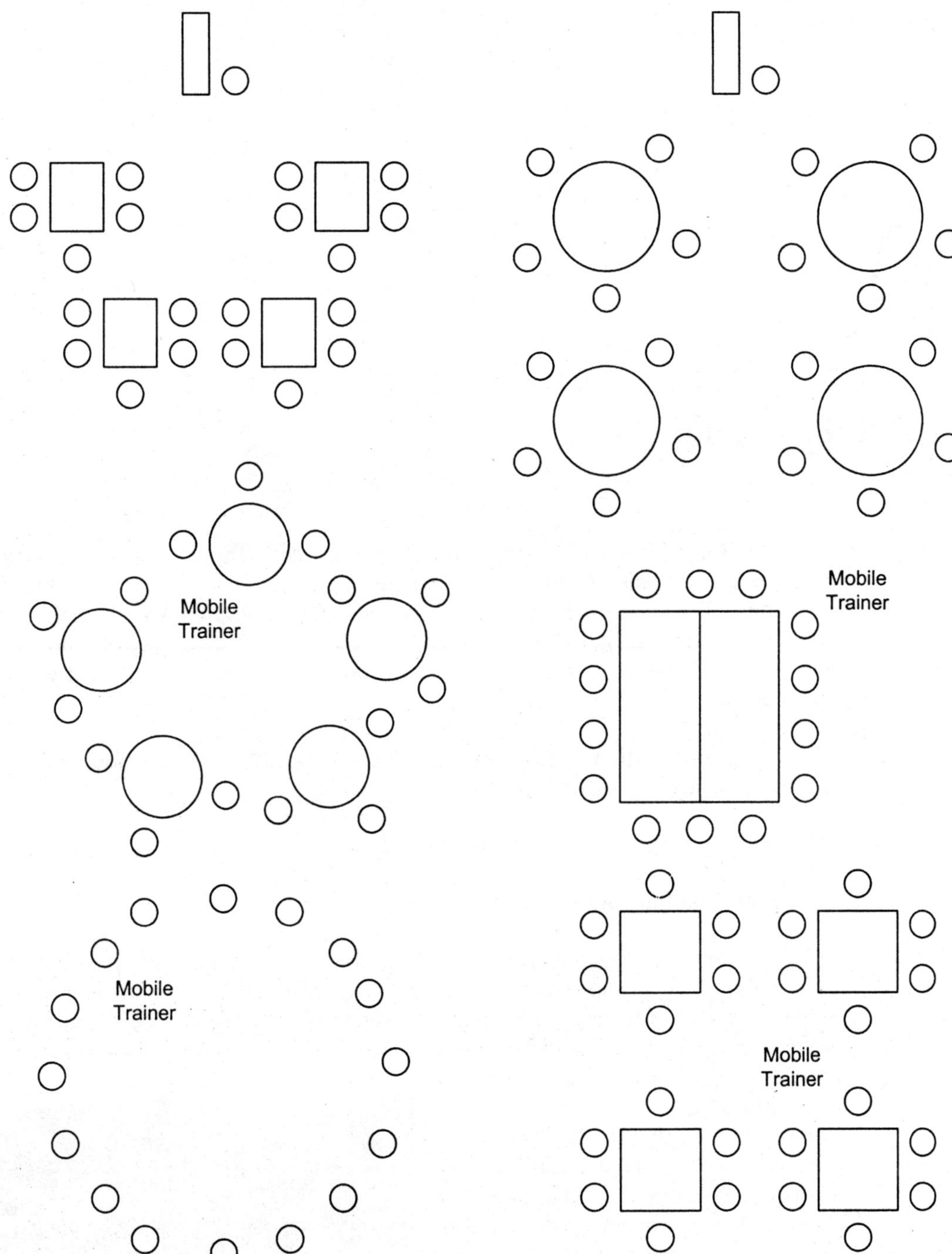

Reference: Trainer's Reference Handbook.

CHAPTER

60

Training Tools

Training tools make a qualitative difference in the conduct of training programmes. Tools provide assessment and answer a leader's eternal questions. These tools have been invented and designed by specialists in order to let leaders get clear insights into the potential of people who work with them. These instruments enhance corporate productivity go up by leaps and bounds.

Exercises with the use of these tools facilitate learning and are very useful for teaching certain concepts.

Some of these tools are mentioned below:

(i) Tower Building Set

Tower building set consists of 50 blocks of wood or plastic. This exercise provides various facets of individual styles of behaviour. Basically it helps to understand one's approach to effective task performance and sound decision-making. It differentiate between guidance, encouragement and building confidence. It also helps to understand significance of goal-setting and expectation in task performance. Whether the guidance being given is extremely directive or permissive guidance. Whether

guidance creates more dependency. The focus in this exercise is to help and to ensure growth of independence and initiative in the person being helped. Does it encourage empowerment in functioning.

(ii) Ring Toss Set

It is for training operations in goal setting and evoking the spirit of intra-preneurship. Ring toss set has a pole and a pole base of wood, four wooden rings. This exercise is used to understand one's approach to risk-taking and attitude towards success and failure. It also highlights the influence exerted by group and social factors by one's behaviour. It brings out the performer's behaviour some aspects such as goal-setting, risk-taking, learning from feedback of the group.

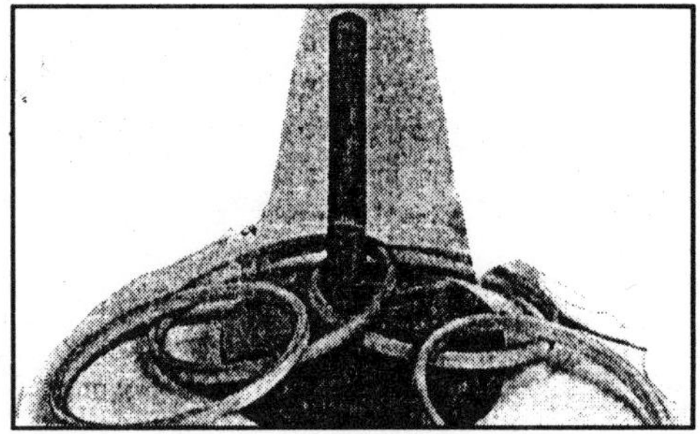

RING TOSS SET

(iii) Manuals for Building Effective Teams

Simulation activities are designed to introduce work teams, the concepts of consensus and synergy in decision-making and to provide immediate feedback to group members on how well they perform as a team. Each activity involves making decisions crucial to surviving a particular situation first as an individual and then as teams.

- Comparing individual and team decisions
- Consensus decision-making
- General problem-solving decisions
- Synergistic decision-making
- Group behaviour
- Team work

(a) Lost in the wilderness

(b) Egyptian odyssey

(c) Space sojourn

(d) Prehistoric problems

REFERENCE

editor@trainingnmanagement.org.

UNIT IX

MISCELLANEOUS

ANNEXURE I

FORMAT TO EVALUATE A TRAINING PROGRAMME

A. Please circle your most appropriate response in the 5-point scale on the right hand side.

	1	2	3	4	5
1. The extent to which you were aware of the objectives of the programme at the time of your nomination for this programme					
2. The extent to which programme objectives were explained at the commencement of the programme					
3. The extent to which the programme objectives were fulfilled					
4. The extent to which the objective of the programme was in line with your need.					
5. The extent to which your need was satisfied					
6. The participant mix for the programme was	1 Very bad	2 Bad	3 Good	4 Very Good	5 Ideal
7. The duration of the programme was	1 Too Less	2 Less	3 Just right	4 Much	5 Too Much
8. Do you agree that the programme would have been more beneficial if some more background material would have been sent in advance?	1 Strongly agree	2 Agree	3 Difficult to say	4 Little	5 Not at all
9. The relative coverage of various topics was	1 Highly Inadequate	2 Inade-quate	3 Average	4 Sufficient	5 Ideal
10. How well was the programme organised?	1 Very badly	2 Badly	3 Well	4 Very well	5 Excep-tionally well

11. Usefulness of the programme in direct work situation	1	2	3	4	5
12. Usefulness of the programme in indirect work situation	1	2	3	4	5
13. Usefulness of the programme in off-the-work situation	1	2	3	4	5
14. Usefulness of the programme in developing others	1	2	3	4	5
15. Usefulness of the programme in long-term	1	2	3	4	5
16. Usefulness of the programme in personal growth and development	1	2	3	4	5

Evaluation of Content and Process

16.1. A duration of the session	1 Too Much	2 Much	3 Just Right	4 Less	5 Too Less
16.2. Level of Inputs	1 Too Advance	2 Advance	3 Just Right	4 Element-ary	5 Too Element-ary
16.3. Relevance and usefulness	1 Very Little	2 Little	3 Just relevant	4 Very relevant	5 Extremely relevant
16.4. Logical Order	1 Very Poor	2 Poor	3 Good	4 Very Good	5 Out-standing
16.5. Training Methodology used	1 Very Poor	2 Poor	3 Good	4 Very Good	5 Out-standing
16.6. Communication	1 Very Poor	2 Poor	3 Good	4 Very Good	5 Out-standing
16.7. Quantity of training material	1 Too Much	2 Much	3 Just Right	4 Less	5 Too Less
16.8. Quality of training material	1 Very Poor	2 Poor	3 Good	4 Very Good	5 Out-standing
16.9. Trainee involvement and participation	1 Very Poor	2 Poor	3 Good	4 Very Good	5 Out-standing
16.10. Level of gains (or net contribution of session)	1 Very Poor	2 Poor	3 Good	4 Very Good	5 Out-standing

Source: P.C. Tripathy, HRD.

ANNEXURE II

QUESTIONNAIRE ON HRD CLIMATE (DEVELOPED AT THE XLRI)

Sl. No.	*Question*	*5*	*4*	*3*	*2*	*1*
1.	The top management of this organisation goes out of its way to make sure that employees enjoy their work.					
2.	The top management believes that human resources are extremely important resources and that they have to be treated more humanely.					
3.	Development of the subordinates is seen as an important part of their job by the managers/officers here.					
4.	The personal policies in this organisation facilitate employee development.					
5.	The top management is willing to invest a considerable part of its time and other resources to ensure the development of employees.					
6.	Senior officers/executives in this organisation take active interest in their juniors and help them learn their job.					
7.	People lacking competence in doing their jobs are helped to acquire competence rather than being left unattended.					
8.	Managers in this organisation believe that employee's behaviour can be changed and people can be developed at any stage of their life					
9.	People in this organisation are helpful to each other.					
10.	Employees in this organisation are very informal and do not hesitate to discuss					

their personal problems with their supervisors.

11. The psychological climate in this organisation is very conducive for any employee interested in developing himself by acquiring new knowledge and skills.

12. Seniors guide their juniors and prepare them for future responsibilities/roles they are likely to take up.

13. The top management of this organisation makes efforts to identify and utilise the potential of the employees.

14. Promotion decisions are based on the suitability of the promotee rather than on favouritism.

15. There are mechanisms in this organisation to reward any good work done or any contribution made by employees.

16. When an employee does good work his supervising officers take special care to appreciate it.

17. Performance appraisal reports in this organisation are based on objective assessment and adequate information and not on favouritism.

18. People in this organisation do not have any fixed mental impressions about each other.

19. Employees are encouraged to experiment with new methods and try out creative ideas.

20. When an employee makes a mistake his supervisors treat it with understanding

and help him to learn from such mistakes rather than punish him or discourage him.

21. Weaknesses of employees are communicated to them in a non-threatening way.

22. When behaviour feedback is given to employees they take seriously and use it for development.

23. Employees in this organisation take pains to find out their strengths and weaknesses from their supervising officers or colleagues.

24. When employees are sponsored for training, they take it seriously and try to learn from the programmes they attend.

25. Employees returning from training programmes are given opportunities to try out what they have learnt.

26. Employees are sponsored for training programmes on the basis of genuine training needs.

27. People trust each other in this organisation.

28. Employees are not afraid to express or discuss their feelings with their supervisors.

29. Employees are not afraid to express or discuss their feelings with their subordinates.

30. Employees are encouraged to take initiative and do things on their own without having to wait for instructions from supervisors.

31. Delegation of authority to encourage juniors to develop handling higher responsibilities is quite common in this organisation.

32. When seniors delegate authority to juniors the juniors use it as an opportunity for development.

33. Team spirit is of high order in this organisation.

34. When problems arise people discuss them openly and try to solve them rather than keep accusing each other behind their backs.

35. Career opportunities are pointed out to juniors by senior officers in the organisation.

36. The organisation's future plans are made known to the managerial staff to help them develop their juniors and prepare them for the future.

37. This organisation ensures employees' welfare to such an extent that the employees can save a lot of their mental energy for work purposes.

38. Job rotation in this organisation facilitates employee development.

ANNEXURE III

MAJOR FACTORS THAT CAN MAKE TRAINING SESSION SUCCESSFUL

These factors will guide the lecturer to immediately pay attention so that training session is effective:

Beginnings and Endings

Of Course, starting out on a positive note makes things easier for lecturer and learners. This is accomplished when lecturer arrive early, get organized before people arrive, and greet them in a friendly fashion as they enter the room. Ending with a sense of closure and accomplishment adds a feeling of lasting value for everyone, that participants are moved to take action on the information they've learned.

Level of Acquaintance

Training session attendees may or may not know each other. Your hope is that they will get acquainted during the process, but getting classroom participation from learners is much easier to achieve when they feel comfortable with each other and have a shared experience, even if it's just a simple classroom icebreaker.

Comfort

People learn best in an environment that is mentally and physically comfortable. There are numerous ways lecturer can create an atmosphere that promotes learning and an open exchange of ideas. It depends on lecturer attitude and approach. Lecturer to pay particular attention to room arrangement, temperature, noise control, programme structure and format, participation level, and group dynamics.

Educational Level

Unless workplace is unique, lecturer will have learners with extensive education and some with limited abilities. By varying presentation methods (rather than relying on just one approach) lecturer can enhance capacity for reaching every individual in audience which will assist learning at all levels.

Group Dynamics

People behave differently in groups than they do one-on-one. Now that lecturer is in the front of the room, we'll have the opportunity to learn a lot about human behaviour; both learners' and his own. One has to assess the tone and mood of group plus strategies for effectively handling some of the more challenging aspects of group dynamics and getting to know yourself better, too.

Training is working when . . .

People laugh easily

Watch people's actions, expressions, and energy level as they enter the classroom. If, during the first ten minutes of session, they become animated, smile or chuckle a bit, trainer can be sure he is off to good start.

Everyone participates with enthusiasm

Watch how people participate in the activities trainer has planned. Eager participation indicates a self-motivated learner.

People complete evaluation forms with comments

When participants are willing to spend time in giving the supportive and sometimes critical information that they have told trainer that they cared enough about your session.

We now present two checklists to help the trainer:

(i) Checklist one: To monitor the four essential factors in training.

(ii) Checklist two: For keeping trainer target centered.

Checklist One: A Checklist to Monitor the Four Essential Factors in Training

Physical Factors

- The room temperature is within comfort range to signature.
- There is adequate lighting and ventilation.
- The size of the room and seating arrangement fit size of group.
- Comfortable chairs are provided for participants.
- Breaks and format variety are planned to offset fatigue.

Participant Factors

- Group members share some level of acquaintance.
- People know what to expect and what is expected to them.
- They are invited to participate and feel safe to get incurred.
- Participants are positively reinforced for their contributors.

Content Factors

- The material is relevant and designed for the group.
- Material is reinforced through a variety of methods.
- Participants are given adequate time to absorb material participations, make contributions, and get actively involved.

Trainer Factors

- The trainer establishes an immediate 'presence'.
- Expectations are clearly stated ("We will . . .).
- The trainer shares the responsibility for learning.
- The trainer communicates with tact and respect to the learner displaying a positive attitude toward the experience of learner.
- The trainer controls time while balancing content and process.
- The trainer invites and accepts feedback.

Checklist Two: A Checklist for Keeping Trainer Targeted Centred

Before the Programme

- Do I know what I want to cover; my key points?
- Have I selected learning activities to reflect my objectives?
- Am I using all available resources?
- Have I selected appropriate materials and time frames?
- Have all of the physical details been taken care of?

Getting Started

- Do I need a warm-up activity? If so, which one?
- Am I clear on the desired outcome I want to create?
- Is there anything that might hamper my relationship with the group? If so, how can I deal with it so it doesn't stand in our way?
- Have I given a clear picture of what my learners can expect and when?

Staying on Target

- Have I planned physical activity?
- Do I have an activity planned if we meet after lunch?

- Have I provided a clear agenda to keep us on track?
- Do my support materials help keep attention?
- Have I encouraged/allowed enough group involvement?
- Are we where we should be at a specified time?

Staying in Touch with the Group

- Am I closely observing body language?
- Have I used enough repetition, examples, and illustrations?
- Have I elicited enough group input to correctly read their reactions to the programme?
- Has there been enough participation/interaction?
- Have I varied the format enough to control fatigue?
- Have I reinforced major points with support materials?
- Have I asked enough questions to adequately test their comprehension of what we've covered?
- If I have noted fatigue, confusion, frustration, or resistance, have I responded to it?
- Am I moving at a pace appropriate for this group?
- Am I using the most effective approach for this group?
- Am I being responsive to expressed needs or concerns?

Wrapping Things Up

- Have I summarized and answered all last questions?
- Have I checked their comprehension of the material?
- Have I left them with a feeling of closure?
- Have I offered out-of-class options (books, tapes, resources, videos, internet and other learning programmes, etc.) for further study?
- Have I been willing to hear private concerns, one on one?
- Am I the last person to leave when the session is over?

Annexure IV

QUESTIONNAIRE FOR EVALUATION OF PRESENTATION SKILLS

Fill in the questionnaire given below. Your answers will be based on your current ability to make presentations. You can encircle the number which is closet to your present level.

5 = Always, 4 = Frequently, 3 = Sometimes, 2 = Occasionally, 1 = Never

1. My main aim in making a presentation is to get my message across.	5	4	3	2	1
2. I specifically define my objectives before the presentation.	5	4	3	2	1
3. I analyze the needs, the composition and the limitations of my audience.	5	4	3	2	1
4. I brainstorm for ideas in order to build my presentation.	5	4	3	2	1
5. I work on the introduction of my talk to make it catchy, and to give the audience the necessary opening information.	5	4	3	2	1
6. I develop the conclusion and, if needed, incorporate the 'call to action' (follow-up action) statement.	5	4	3	2	1
7. The visual aids I use are simple, legible, carefully prepared and have the desired impact.	5	4	3	2	1
8. I use visual aids to support my verbal message, not to replace it.	5	4	3	2	1
9. I rehearse what I am going to present and do on the final day.	5	4	3	2	1

10. I do not rehearse my speech by learning each word. I remember the main ideas, instead.	5	4	3	2	1
11. My notes highlight just the main/key ideas so that I do not need to read from them directly.	5	4	3	2	1
12. I work systematically on my symptoms of nervousness and take appropriate remedial actions.	5	4	3	2	1
13. I maintain a consistent, healthy eye contact with the audience.	5	4	3	2	1
14. I am enthusiastic while communicating my ideas.	5	4	3	2	1
15. I anticipate questions and prepare accordingly.	5	4	3	2	1
16. In case I do not know the answer to any question, I admit it honestly.	5	4	3	2	1
17. My gestures are natural and help me in getting my message across.	5	4	3	2	1
18. I work on my vocal attributes such as clarity, volume and tone.	5	4	3	2	1
19. I arrange the seating of the audience, if possible, in a manner that best suits my presentation. I also check the set-up of the room and the equipment I shall be using.	5	4	3	2	1
20. I keep in mind the time factor while making my presentation including the time of day and the total time available.	5	4	3	2	1

Scoring—Add your scores for the above questions

80-100 Well done. You have grasped the nuances of making an effective presentation. This book will help you confirm the ideas you believe in.

60-80 You are close to the target of becoming an effective speaker. Go through the book to have your skills further.

40-60 You have to work hard to master the ABCs of a good presentation. It is not tough but it takes practice and patience.

20-40 You have a long way to go. Don't lose heart. It is only a question of increasing your awareness, motivating yourself and utilising the inputs this book provides. You will reach your destination sooner than you think.

20 You may have to go through this book from cover to cover to attune yourself to the art of speaking. You can do it, as have many others before you.

After the evaluation some of you may be delighted with your scores and some disappointed. The latter need to bolster their courage and believe that they too will taste success soon. However, to see tangible improvements in your skill of speaking demands commitment and action.

Glossary of Terms

Action learning

A system of management education, invented by the British guru Reg Revans, in which a group of working managers learn by discussing one another's practical problems.

Adhocracy

The opposite of bureaucracy: a term originally coined by Warren Bennis and subsequently adopted by Alvin Toffler, Henry Mintzberg, and Robert Waterman to describe small, flexible project teams or groups that operate freely across the departmental boundaries of an organization.

Active listening

Active listening requires the listener to stop talking. To remove distractions, to be patient, and to empathize with the talker.

Achievement need

The drive to excel, to strive to succeed.

Alienation

A feeling that work is meaningless and that he is powerless to correct the situation.

Apprenticeship

A time-typically two to five years—when an individual is considered to be training to learn a skill.

Attitude surveys

Attitude surveys are systematic methods of determining what

employees think about their organisation. The surveys are usually done through questionnaires. Attitude survey feedback results when the information collected is reported back to the participants. This process then is usually followed by action planning to identify and resolve specific areas of employee concern.

Attrition

Attrition is the loss of employees who leave the organisation's employment.

Autonomous work groups

Autonomous work groups are teams of workers, without a formal company—appointed leader, who decide among themselves—most decisions traditionally handled by supervisors.

Autonomy

Freedom and independence.

Barriers to change

Barriers to change are factors that instance with employee acceptance and implementation of change.

Barriers to communication

Barriers to communication are interferences that may limit the receiver's understanding.

Brainstorming

Brainstorming is a process by which participants provide their ideas on a stated problem during a freewheeling group session.

Burnout

Burnout is a condition of mental, emotional, and sometime physical exhaustion that results from substantial and prolonged stress.

Career

A career is all the jobs that are held during one's working life.

Career anchor

Term coined by Edgar Schein to denote the perceptions that individuals hold about themselves in their jobs—and which encourage them to stay in those jobs.

Career counseling

Career counselling assists employees in finding appropriate career goals and paths.

Career development

Career development consists of those experiences and personal improvements that one undertakes to achieve a career plan.

Career goals

Career goals are the future positions that one strives to reach. These goals serve as benchmarks along one's career path.

Career path

A career path is the sequential pattern of jobs that form one's career.

Career planning

Career planning is the process by which one selects career goals and paths to those goals.

Career plateau

A career plateau occurs when an employee is in a position that he does well enough not to be demoted or fired but not well enough to be promoted.

Champions

Influential individuals, often in research-based companies, whose backing can ensure that a project or invention gets the chance to prove itself. Peters and Waterman's *In Search of Excellence* found that companies that nurtured champions were more likely to qualify as excellent.

Change agents

Change agents are people who have the role of stimulating and coordinating change within a group.

Cognitive dissonance

Cognitive dissonance results from a gap between what one expects and what one experiences.

Communication

Communication is the transfer of information and understanding from one person to another.

Communication overload

A communication overload occurs when employees receive more communication inputs than they can process or more than they need.

Communication process

A communication process is the method by which a sender reaches a receiver. It requires that an idea be developed, encoded, transmitted, received, decoded and used.

Communication system

A communication system provides formal and informal methods for moving information throughout an organisation so that appropriate decisions are made.

Comparable worth

Comparable worth is the idea that a job should be evaluated as to its value to the organisation and then paid accordingly. Thus, jobs of comparable worth would be paid equally. For example, two people with widely different jobs would both receive the same pay if the two jobs were of equal value to the employer.

Competitive advantage

The factor that enables a company to gain an edge on its rivals in the marketplace, the result of competitive strategy. Harvard's Michael Porter has worked out a sophisticated formula for determining how companies—and countries—can gain competitive advantage.

Cognitive learning

Learning situations in which, without explicit reinforcement, there is a change in the way information is processed as a result of experiences that a person has had.

Comparative evaluation approaches

Comparative evaluation approaches are a collection of different methods that compare one person's performance with that of co-workers.

Compensation

Compensation is what employees receive in exchange for their work.

Content theories of motivation

Content theories of motivation describe the needs or desires within us that initiate behaviour.

Counselling

Counselling is the discussion of an employee problem with the general objective of helping the worker cope with it.

Cases

In-depth descriptions of organisational problems.

Coaching

A development activity where a manager takes an active role in guiding another manager.

Collective bargaining

The negotiation, administration and interpretation of a written agreement between two parties, at least one of which represents a group that is acting collectively, that covers a specific period of time.

Critical incidents

Key behaviours that make the difference between doing a job effectively and doing it ineffectively.

Decentralization

The principle of devolving substantial amounts of managerial power and accountability away from the center of a large and diverse corporation to semi-autonomous divisions or business units.

Delegation

Delegation is the process of getting others to share a manager's work. It requires the manager to assign duties, grant authority, and create a sense of responsibility.

Delphi technique

The Delphi technique solicits predictions from a panel of experts about some specified future development(s). The collective estimates are then reported back to the panel so that the members may adjust their opinions. This process is repeated until a general agreement on future trends emerges.

Demographics

Demographics is the study of population characteristics.

Development

Development represents those activities that prepare an employee for future responsibilities.

Downward communication

Downward communication is information that begins at some point in the organisation and then feeds down hierarchy to inform or influence others in the firm.

Due process

Due process means that established rules and procedures for disciplinary action are followed and that employees have an opportunity to respond to the charges made against them.

Discipline

A condition in the organisation when employees conduct themselves in accordance with the organisation's rules and standards of acceptable behaviour.

Empathy

The ability to put one's self in another's place to understand the other person's views and feelings.

Employee involvement (EI)

Employee involvement consists of a variety of systematic methods that enable employees to participate in the decisions that affect them.

Employment tests

Employment tests are devices that assess the probable match between the applicants and the job requirements.

Empowerment

In organisations it is usually taken to mean increased participation by employees in the enterprise for which they work, with a view to stimulating initiative and entrepreneurism. Rosabeth Moss Kanter is the leading exponent of empowerment as an aid to releasing forces for innovation and change within a corporation.

Ergonomics

Ergonomics is the study of biotechnical relationships between the physical attributes of workers and the physical demands of the job. The object of the study is to reduce physical and mental strain in order to increase productivity and quality of work life.

Expectancy

Expectancy is the strength of a person's belief that an act will lead to a particular outcome.

Expectancy theory

Expectancy theory states that motivation is the result of the outcome one seeks and one's estimate that action will lead to the desired outcome.

Experiential learning

Experiential learning means that participants learn by experiencing in the training environment the kinds of problems they face on the job.

Extrapolation

Extrapolation involves extending past rates of changes into the future.

Effectiveness

Attainment of the goal.

Efficiency

The ratio of inputs consumed to outputs achieved.

Experiential exercise

Short structured learning experiences where individuals learn by doing.

Facilitator

A facilitator is someone who assists quality circles and the quality circle leader in identifying and solving workplace problems.

Feedback

Feedback is information that helps evaluate the success or failure of an action or system.

Flexitime

Flexitime is a scheduling innovation that abolishes rigid starting and ending times for each day's work. Instead, employees are allowed to begin and end the workday at their discretion, usually within a range of hours.

Fringe benefits

Membership-based, non-financial rewards offered to attract and keep employees.

Functional job analysis

The Department of Labours' procedure for describing what a worker does, catalogued into three general functions: data, people and things.

Grapevine communication

Grapevine communication is an informal system that arises spontaneously from the social interaction of people in the organisation.

Grievance procedure

A grievance procedure is a multi-step process that the employer and union jointly use to resolve disputes that arise under the terms of the labour agreement.

Graphic rating scale

A performance appraisal method that lists number of traits and a range of performance for each.

Halo effect

The halo effect is a bias that occurs when a rater allows some information to disproportionately prejudice the final evaluation.

Hierarchy of needs

Motivation model constructed by Abraham Maslow which charts the progression of human needs in the workplace from basic urges of warmth, food, and safety to love, esteem, and personal fulfilment. Maslow teaches that none of the wants is absolute: that, indeed, a satisfied want ceases to be important.

Human resources audit

A human resources audit evaluates the personnel activities used in an organisation.

Human resource forecasts

Human resources forecasts predict the organisation's future demand for employees.

Human resources

Human resources are the people who are ready, willing, and able to contribute to organisation goals.

Hawthorne studies

Conducted in the late 1920s and early 1930s, these studies ushered in a human relations movement. Gave new emphasis to human emotional factors and the influence of the informal group on worker productivity.

Human resource accounting

Computing the value of an organisation's human assets along with its financial assets.

Human resource inventory

Describes the skills that are available within the organisation.

Human resource management (HRM)

A process consisting of the acquisition, development, motivation, and maintenance of human resources.

Human resource planning

The process by which an organisation ensures that it has the right number and kinds of people, at the right places, at the right time, capable of effectively and efficiently completing those tasks that will aid the organisation in achieving its overall objectives.

Incentive systems

Incentive systems link compensation and performance by paying employees for actual results, not for seniority of hours worked.

Job analysis

Job analysis systematically collects, evaluates, and organises information about jobs.

Job analysis schedules

Job analysis schedules are checklists or questionnaires that seek to collect information about jobs in a uniform manner. (They are also called jobs analysis questionnaires).

Job banks

Job banks exist in state employment exchange offices. They are used to match applicants with job openings.

Job code

A job code uses numbers, letters, or both to provide a quick summary of the job and its content.

Job description

A job description is a written statement that explains the duties, working conditions, and other aspects of a specified job.

Job enlargement

Job enlargement means adding more tasks to a job in order to increase the job cycle.

Job enrichment

Job enrichment means adding more responsibilities, autonomy, and control to a job.

Job evaluations

Job families are groups of different jobs that require similar skills.

Job flow

Job flow is a monthly report of frequently listed openings from job banks throughout the country.

Job grading

Job grading is a form of job evaluation that assigns jobs to predetermined classifications according to the job's relative worth to the organisation. This technique is also called the job classification method.

Job information service

The job information service is a feature of state employment security agencies that enables job-seekers to review job bank listings in their efforts to find employment.

Job instruction training

Job induction training is training received directly on the job. It is also called "on-the-job training".

Job performance standards

Job performance standards are the work requirements that are expected from an employee on a particular job.

Job posting programme

Job posting informs employees of unfilled job openings and the qualifications for these jobs.

Job progression ladder

A job progression ladder is a particular career path where some jobs have prerequisites.

Job ranking

Job ranking is one form of job evaluation that subjectively ranks jobs according to their overall worth to the organisation.

Job rotation

Job rotation is the process of moving employees from one job to another in order to allow them more variety in their jobs and the opportunity to learn new skills.

Job satisfaction

Job satisfaction is the favourableness or unfavourableness with which employees view their work.

Job sharing

Job sharing is a scheduling innovation that allows two or more workers to share the same job, usually by each working part-time.

Job specifications

A job specification describes what a job demands of employees who do it and the human skills that are required.

Joint study committees

Joint study committees include representatives from management and the union who meet away from the bargaining table to study some topic of mutual interests in the hope of finding a solution that is mutually satisfactory.

Job characteristics model

Identifies five job factors and their interrelationships, then demonstrates their effect on productivity, motivation, and job satisfaction.

Job design

The way in which job tasks are organised into a unit of work.

Job element

The smallest unit into which work can be divided.

Just-in-time

Revolutionary Japanese low-inventory system for speeding up production, keeping it flexible to customers' requirements, and cutting costs. Suppliers supply what is needed when it is needed, resulting in faster responses to the market.

Key jobs

Key jobs are those that are common in the organisation and in its labour market.

Laboratory training

Laboratory training is a form of group training primarily used to enhance interpersonal skills.

Lateral thinking

Seeking to solve problems by unorthodox or apparently illogical methods.

Learning curve

A learning curve is a visual representation of the rate at which one learns given material through time.

Learning curve change

The learning curve for change is a charted representation of the period of adjustment and adaptation to change required by an organisation.

Learning principles

Learning principles are guidelines to the ways in which people learn most effectively.

Listening

Listening is a receiver's positive effort to understand a message transmitted by sound.

Laissez-faire

The view that government should not interfere in the economic affairs of others.

Learning

A relatively permanent change as a result of experience.

Management

The process of efficiently getting activities completed with and through other people.

Management by objectives (MBO)

MBO requires an employee and superior to jointly establish performance goals for the future. Employees are subsequently evaluated on how well they have obtained these agreed-upon objectives.

Management inventories

Management inventories summarize the skills and abilities of management personnel. (See Skills inventories, which are used for non-management employees.)

Managerial hierarchies

The analysis of bureaucratic administration, with each office subordinate to the one above it and every official's role determined by his office.

Merit-based promotions

Merit-based promotions occur when an employed is promoted because of superior performance in the present job.

Mission statement

The distillation of a company's philosophy and corporate goals and values.

Motivation

Motivation is a person's drive to take action because that person wants to do so.

Motivational theories

Elton Mayo, in his seminal work at Western Electric's Hawthorne plant in Chicago in the early 1930s, was the first to identify psychological elements leading to increased productivity. All have stressed the importance of the peer group in job satisfaction and self-esteem.

Norms

Tells group members what they ought or ought not do in certain circumstances.

Non-verbal communication

Non-verbal communication is action that communicates without spoken words.

Open communication

Open communication exists when people feel free to communicate all relevant messages.

Obsolescence

Obsolescence results when an employee no longer possesses the knowledge or ability to perform successfully.

Open-door policy

An open-door policy encourages employees to go to their manager or even to higher management with any problem that concerns them.

Organisation culture

An organisation's culture is the product of all the organisation's features—such as its people, objectives, technology, size, age, unions, policies, successes, and features—such as its people, objectives, technology, size, age, unions, policies, successes, and failures. It is the organisation's "personality".

Organisation development (OD)

OD is an intervention strategy that uses group processes to focus on the whole organisation in order to bring about planned changes.

Organisation development process

The OD process is complex and difficult to implement. It consists of seven steps: initial diagnosis, data collection, data feedback and confrontation, action planning and problem-solving, team-building, inter-group development and evaluation, and follow-up.

Organisational climate

Organisational climate is the favourableness or unfavourableness of the environment for people in the organisation.

Orientation programmes

Orientation programmes primarily familiarize new employees with their roles, the organisation, its policies, and other employees.

Occupation

A group of similar jobs found across organisations.

Operative employee

A non-supervisory worker.

Orientation

The activities involved in introducing new employees to the organisation and their work units.

Pareto analysis

Pareto analysis is a means of collecting data about the types or causes of production problems in descending order of frequency.

Pension

A fixed payment, other than wages, made regularly to former employees or other surviving dependents.

Performance

Effective and efficient work, which also considers personnel data such as measures of accidents, turnover, absence, and tardiness.

Performance appraisal

Performance appraisal is the process by which organisations evaluate employee performance.

Performance standards

Performance standards are the benchmarks against which performance is measured.

Perquisites

Attractive fringe benefits, over and above a regular salary, granted to executives.

Personnel management

The traditional functional areas responsible for the management of human resources.

Peter Principle

The Peter Principle states that in a hierarchy, people tend to rise to their level of incompetence.

Piecework

Piecework is a type of incentive system that compensates workers for each unit of output.

Placement

Placement is the assignment of an employee to a new or different job.

Point system

The point system is a form of job evaluation that assesses the relative importance of the job's key factors in order to arrive at the relative worth of jobs.

Proactive human resource management

Proactive human resource management exists when decision-makers anticipate problems and take affirmative steps to minimize those problems rather than wait until after a problem occurs before taking action.

Programmed instruction

Material is learned in a highly organised, logical sequence, which requires the individual to respond.

Productivity

Productivity is the ratio of a firm's output (goods and services) divided by its input (people, capital, materials, energy).

Promotion

A promotion occurs when an employee is moved from one job to another that is higher in pay, responsibility and/or organisational level.

Psychological contract

Term coined by Edgar Schein to denote what an employee may expect from his employer—less in material rewards than in the opportunities to realize potential. It applies also to the employer's expectations of those who work for an organization.

Pygmalion effect

The Pygmalion effect occurs when people live up to the highest expectations others hold of them.

Qualifiable worker

A qualifiable worker is one who does not currently possess all the requirements, knowledge, skills, or abilities to do the job, but who will become qualified through additional training and experience.

Qualified handicapped

The qualified handicapped are those mentally or physically handicapped individuals who, with reasonable accommodations, can perform successfully.

Quality circles

Quality circles are small groups of employees who meet regularly with a common leader to identify and solve work-related problems.

Quality management

How production faults can be eliminated by a management-led philosophy of continuous improvement in every process of planning, production, and service. W. Edwards Deming laid down the principle.

Quality of work life

Qualify of work life means having good supervision, good working conditions, good pay and benefits, and an interesting, challenging, and rewarding job.

Rap sessions

Rap sessions are meetings between managers and group of employees to discuss complaints, suggestions, opinions, or questions.

Reactive human resource management

Reactive human resource management exists when decision-makers respond to problems instead of anticipating before they occur. (See Proactive management).

Recruitment

Recruitment is the process of finding and attracting capable applicants for employment.

Reliability

Reliability means that a selection device (usually a test) yields consistent results each time an individual takes it.

Repetition

Repetition facilitates learning through repeated review of the material to be learned.

Resistance to change

Resistance to change arises from employee opposition to change.

Resume

A resume is a brief listing of an applicant's work experience, education, personal data, and other information relevant to the applicant's employment qualifications.

Seven "S" model

The system devised by the then McKinsey team of Richard Pascale, Tom Peters, and Robert Waterman to measure the quality of a company's performance: the seven "S" factors divide into three "hard"—strategy, structure, and systems—and four "soft"—style, shared values, skills, and staff.

Role ambiguity

Role ambiguity results when people are uncertain of what is expected of them in a given job.

Role playing

Role playing is a training technique that requires the trainee to assume different identities in order to learn how others feel under different circumstances.

Selection interviews

Selection interviews are a step in the selection process whereby the applicant and the employer's representative have a face-to-face meeting.

Self-actualisation

See Self-fulfilment needs.

Self-fulfilment needs

Self-fulfilment needs are the needs people have that make them feel they are becoming all that they are capable of becoming. This need also is called self-actualisation.

Seniority-based promotions

Seniority-based promotions results when the most senior employee is promoted into a new position.

Skills inventories

Skills inventories are summaries of each employee's skills and abilities. (Skills inventories usually refer to non-management workers. See Management inventories).

Socialisation

Socialisation is the ongoing process by which an employee adapts to an organisation by understanding and accepting the values, norms, and beliefs held by others in the firm. Orientation programmes—which familiarize primarily new employees with their role, the organisation, its policies, and other employees—speed up the socialisation process.

Sociotechnical systems

Sociotechnical systems are interventions in the work situation that restructure the work, the work groups, and the relationship between the workers and the technology they use to do their jobs.

Strategic plan

A strategic plan identifies a firm's long-range objectives processes, and physical condition.

Structured interviews

Structured interviews use a predetermined checklist of questions that usually are asked of all applicants.

Suggestion systems

Suggestion systems are a formal method for generating, evaluating, and implementing useful employee ideas.

System

A system is two or more parts (or sub-system) working together as an organised whole with identifiable boundaries. An open system is one that is affected by the environment.

Sociometry

A method of mapping social relationships of attraction and rejection among members of a group.

Scientific management

Proposed by Frederick Taylor in the early 1900s, scientific management viewed management as a science. Management's responsibilities were clearly distinct from those of the workers. The former planned and the latter executed.

Sensitivity training

Unstructured group interaction in which participants discuss themselves and their interactive processes.

Simulation

Any artificial environment that attempts to closely mirror an actual condition.

Social security

Retirement, disability, and survivor benefits paid by the government to aged, former members of the labour force, the disabled, or their survivors.

Task identity

Task identity means doing an identifiable piece of work, thus enabling the worker to have a sense of responsibility and pride.

Task significance

Task significance means knowing that the work one does is important to others in the organisation and outside of it.

Training

Training represents activities that teach employees how to perform their present jobs.

Transference

Transference refers to how applicable the training is to actual job situations, as evaluated by how readily the trainee transfers the learning to his or her job.

Turnover

Turnover is the loss of employees by the organisation. It represents those employees who depart for a variety of reasons.

Two-tiered orientation programme

A two-tiered orientation programme exists when both the personnel department and the immediate supervisor provide an orientation for new employees.

Two-way communication

Two-way communication means that a sender and a receiver are exchanging messages so that a regular flow of communication is maintained.

Theory X and Theory Y

Theory X managers assume that employees dislike work, cannot be trusted, and must be closely supervised. Theory Y assumes employees do not dislike work, can accept responsibility, and can impose self-control.

Training within Industry (WI)

Programme during World War II to train supervisors to prepare the unskilled for work in industries.

Transactional analysis (TA)

An approach for defining and analyzing communication interactions between people and a theory of personality.

Thematic Apperception Test (TAT)

A projective technique consisting of pictures about which a person tells stories.

Upward communication

Upward communication is communication that begins at some point in the organisation and then proceeds up the hierarchy to inform or influence others.

Vertical integration

The system favoured by some large corporations for integrating a number of companies down to supplier level to act as an in-house chain of manufacture.

Vestibule training

Vestibule training occurs off the job on equipment or methods that are highly similar to those used on the job. This technique minimises the disruption of operations caused by training activities.

Values

Basic convictions about what is right or wrong, good or bad, desirable or not.

Walk-ins

Walk-ins are jobs-seekers who arrive at the personnel department in search of a job without any prior referrals and not in response to specific advertisement or request.

Work flow

Work flow is the sequence of jobs in an organisation needed to produce the firm's goods or service.

Work measurement techniques

Work measurement techniques are methods for evaluating what a job's performance standards should be.

Work practices

Work practices are the set ways of performing work in an organisation.

Work sampling

Work sampling means using a variety of observations on a particular job to measure the length of time devoted to certain aspects of the job.

Work simplification

Work simplification means simplifying jobs by eliminating unnecessary tasks or reducing the number of tasks by combining them.

Work modules

Work activities broken into two-hour task units.

Index